Make your own
Dress patterns

Make your own Dress patterns

Brenda Redmile

B.T. Batsford Limited
London

My thanks to David Joyce and Ladies Pride Ltd for the photographs used and to the students of Winstanley Community College for their help and co-operation. To Graham, for the help and encouragement he has given.

First published 1977

Printed by The Anchor Press Ltd, Tiptree, Essex
for the publishers
B.T. Batsford Limited
4 Fitzhardinge Street London W1H 0AH

ISBN 0 7134 0389 6

CONTENTS

INTRODUCTION

Any person who has a sound knowledge of dressmaking and making-up techniques will find that being able to make their own patterns is very rewarding. Many people attend classes in craft subjects at adult education centres or colleges of further education, and the art of designing and cutting dress patterns is fast gaining popularity. This book follows a course given by the author at such a class.

The method described in this book is known as flat pattern cutting. This means that the styles are created from a basic flat block, using darts and ease to mould the flat shape around the body. At one time, most styles were created by

Figure 1 *Students attending a pattern cutting class at The Winstanley Community College*

modelling cloth around a tailor's stand, suppressing where necessary with darts or style lines, and gathering or pleating where fullness was required. This method is still used by many of the leading couturiers. However, for the general dress trade, it is most practical to use the flat method, and this is used extensively.

Step-by-step instructions are used to enable the dressmaker who chooses to work alone to progress through the book at his or her own pace. A young person hoping to enter the dress manufacturing trade should practise all the examples given in this book whether or not these are in fashion at the time, because it is the fundamentals that must be learnt. Once the principles of dart manipulation, sleeve and collar construction, etc., have been mastered, students may develop themes of their own. It is more practical to use quarter-scale blocks for practise purposes. A copy of the blocks on pages 16, 17 and 19 may be traced off for this purpose.

Follow the fashion scene, keep up to date with new textiles and have knowledge of their properties. It is also advantageous to be familiar with new sewing aids, thread, trimmings and braids, buttons, etc. All these points aid the success of the finished dress.

The equipment required for pattern making is not necessarily expensive or sophisticated, and any initial outlay is quickly recovered after only a few patterns have been cut. Such suitable equipment would be as follows:-

Plain drafting paper—a few sheets large enough for block construction.
Thin card for making the blocks.
Calico test cloth.
A metre stick.
A set square.
A tracing wheel.
A French curve.
Pencils.
A tape measure—preferably a metric/imperial type.
Scissors—one pair for cutting paper and card, and a second pair for use with cloth.
Pins, and all the usual equipment necessary for making up garments.

Note that for general pattern cutting a cheaper alternative to plain drafting paper is to use wall lining paper, obtainable from most home decorating shops.

TERMINOLOGY

The pattern pieces set out on these pages are labelled with the terms used throughout the book. It is important to become conversant with this terminology so that pattern markings can be readily identified. Special note should be taken of certain symbols and abbreviations. These are as follows:-

] Place to the fold.

↕ Place to the straight grain on the fabric.

>< Balance notches, indicating those pieces that have to be joined together in make-up.

〰 Area of pattern to be gathered.

c/b Centre back.

c/f Centre front.

s/p Shoulder point.

n/p Neck point.

c/h Crown height.

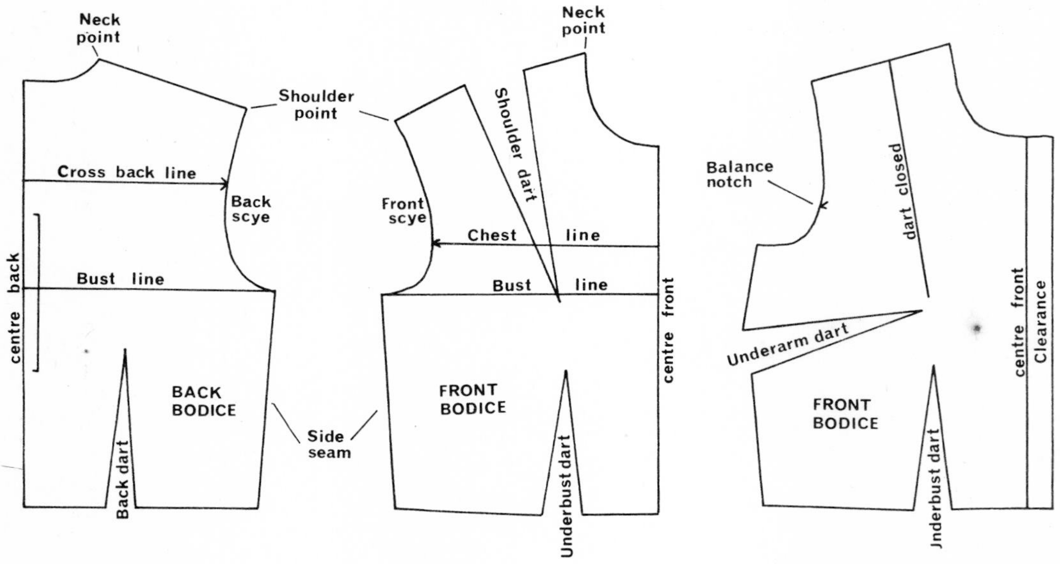

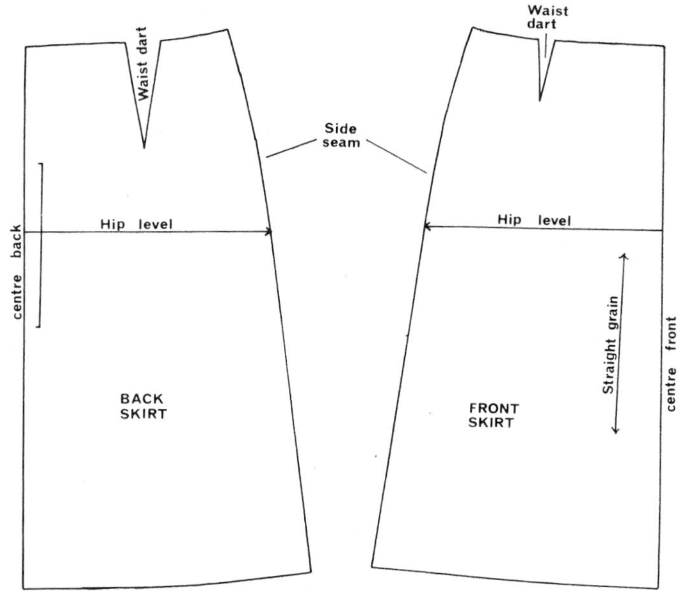
Waist dart
Side seam
Hip level
centre back
BACK SKIRT
Waist dart
Hip level
Straight grain
centre front
FRONT SKIRT

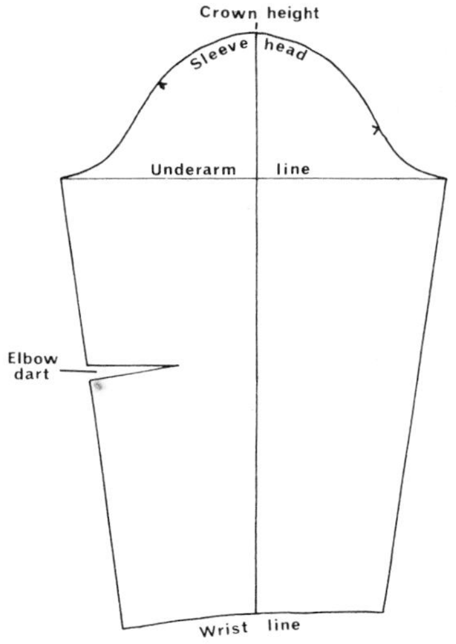
Crown height
Sleeve head
Underarm line
Elbow dart
Wrist line

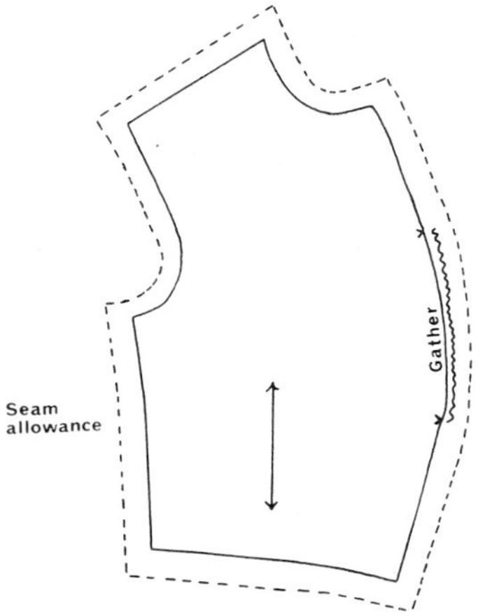
Gather
Seam allowance

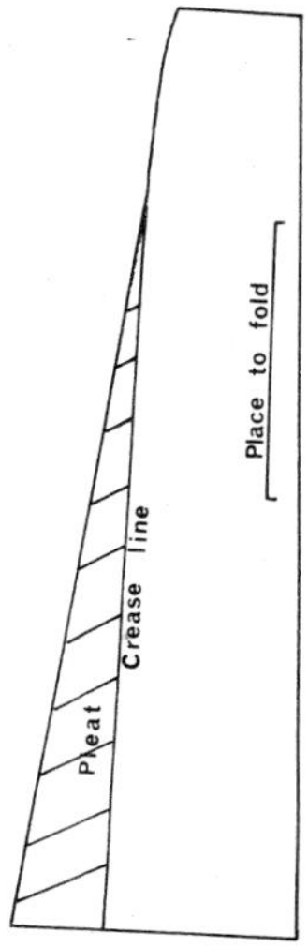
Place to fold
Crease line
Pleat

ONE

Basic blocks and measurements

The basic blocks constitute the foundation patterns and provide the basis for every subsequent pattern. These blocks provide a simple outline shape which, with the aid of darts and ease, are made to fit the body. Although fashion lines are subject to frequent change, the figure generally remains constant. Therefore, details such as shoulder width, scye, cross back and chest are recorded within the bodice block, and when designing more elaborate styles these details usually remain the same. The fashionable shape of a woman does vary from time to time, but this shape is usually confined to waist, bust, etc., and its creation is helped by foundation garments. The shoulder width, scye, cross back and chest are governed by bone structure, and therefore it is virtually impossible to change these.

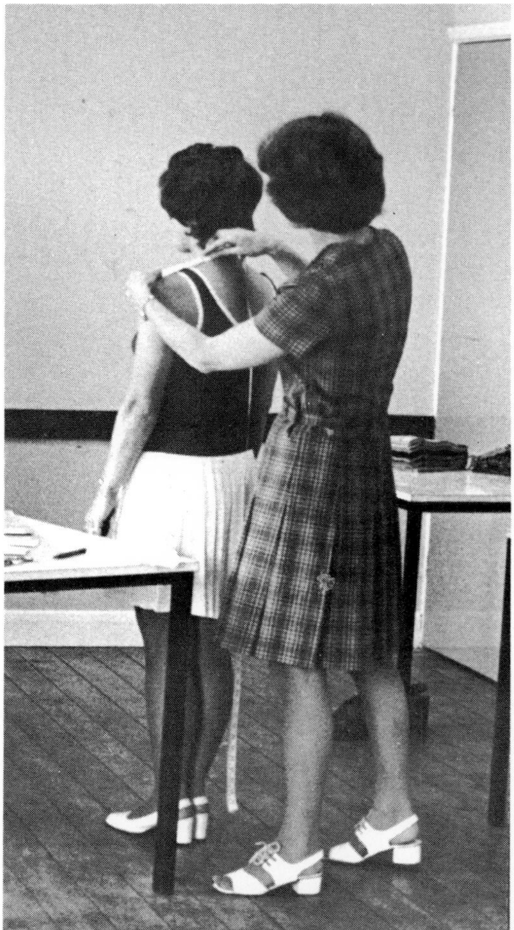

Figure 2 Taking the shoulder width measurement

MEASUREMENTS

The basic blocks described in the book are constructed using metric measurements. Imperial equivalents are best found on a metric/imperial measuring tape.

When constructing the blocks an allowance of 8cm for ease or 'tolerance' is added to the bust and hip measurements. It is therefore advisable to take your measurements wearing only underwear and certainly not over heavy clothing. You will note from the chart that follows that even numbers are used for the main measurements, i.e. bust, waist and hip. It is simpler to work with even numbers, and rounding up your measurements to these will be found helpful. Stand relaxed for measurement taking, and do not pull the tape tight in an effort to reduce the true measurement—you will only deceive yourself and will waste time constructing a useless block. It is a good idea to talk whilst being measured, as it is difficult to pull in one's stomach whilst engaged in conversation.

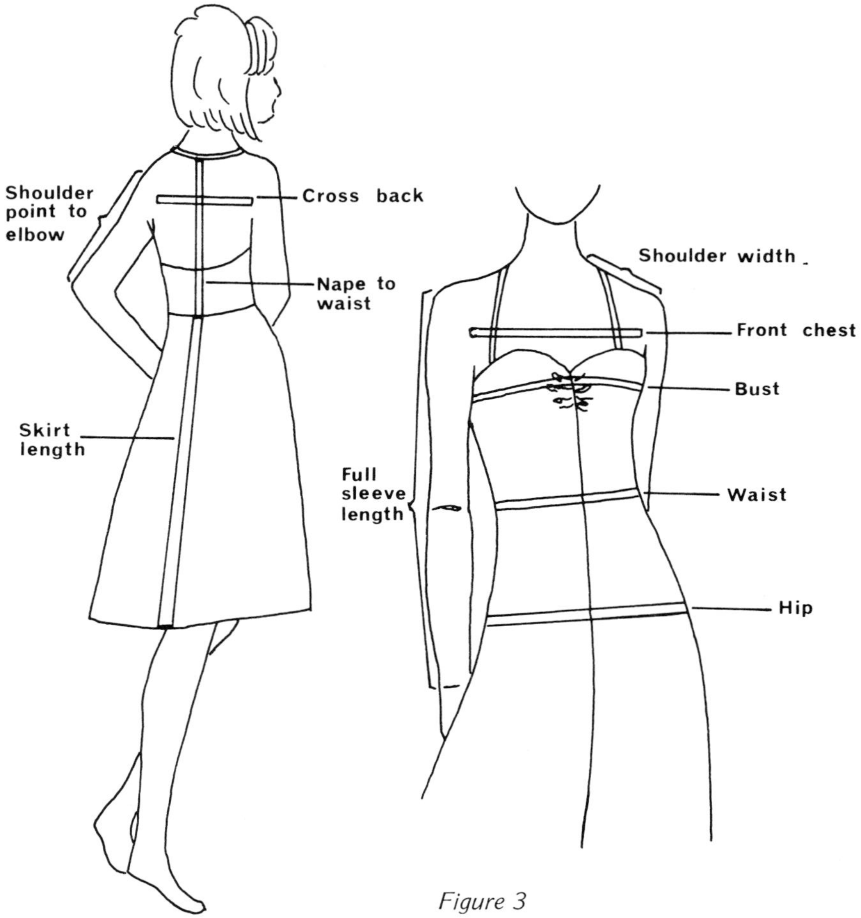

Figure 3

Measure the bust and hip circumferences around the fullest part. When measuring your waist, the tape should be comfortable around the natural waist. The nape-to-waist length is measured down the centre back from the nape of the neck to the natural waist line. The sleeve length is measured from the shoulder point to elbow and from the shoulder point to wrist. The shoulder width is measured on the top of the shoulder from the neck to the end of the shoulder (shoulder point). For the skirt length, measure from the waist at the centre back to the back of the knee. All these measurements are straightforward enough to take with the assistance of another person, but the cross back and front chest measurements are not so easily defined and the chart should be used for guidance. For example, if the bust measurement is 88cm, then upon reference to the chart you will find the cross back is given as 35cm and the front chest as 37cm. A check of your body measurements against those given in the size chart will indicate any serious discrepancies that may have occurred in your measuring.

This size chart is a table of measurements representing the 'typical' proportions of women of average height (160–170cm). It is reasonable to assume that the girth measurements (i.e. bust, waist and hip) increase systematically, but this is not necessarily so with height measurement. Therefore, the nape-to-waist length may possibly be shorter on a large-busted woman than that of a small-busted woman depending upon the overall height of the woman. Also the length of the arm varies considerably, and the chart can only serve as a rough guide. This, or a similar size chart, would be used commercially when manufacturing for the wholesale trade, and the garments would be size labelled according to the customary style of the wholesale house. However, to construct a block to fit yourself, use your own personal measurements.

A good well-fitting block is essential because it is unreasonable to expect future styles to be satisfactory if the block upon which they are based is incorrect.

Theoretical size chart

Bust	Hip	Waist	Nape to waist	Cross back	Front chest	Shoulder width	Sleeve wrist	elbow
78–82	84–88	62–64	38–40	33.5	35	12	53	30
84–86	90–92	66	40	34–35	36	12	55	31
88	94	68	40	35	37	13	56	32
90–94	96–98	70	41	36–37	37.5	13	56	32
96	102	72	40–42	37.5	39	13.5	56	32
100	106	76	40–42	38.5	40	13.5	57	33
102–104	108–112	78–80	40–43	39–40	42	14	57	33
108	114	84	40–43	41	43	14	57	33
112	118	88	40–43	41.5	44	14.5	58	34
116	122	92	40–44	42	45	14.5	59	35

BODICE AND SLEEVE BLOCKS

To construct these blocks you will require a sheet of plain paper approximately 1m x 75cm. The measurements required for the bodice are nape to waist, bust, cross back, front chest, waist and shoulder width. Start the construction at point A which should be 4cm from the top and 4cm from the left-hand edge of the paper. Bear in mind that only half a back and half a front bodice is to be constructed. The block in this book is made to quarter-scale for size 88 bust measurement.

Bodice

The starting point is A. This point represents the nape of neck.

A to B is the nape-to-waist measurement. This line is the centre back of the block, and future lines across the sheets to the right, must be at right angles to this centre back line.

C is midway between A and B.

C to D is half the bust measurement plus 4cm ease.

D to E is 2.5cm for sizes up to a 96 bust. Sizes above 96 should add 0.2cm for every 4cm bust increase, i.e. for bust 100 it is 2.7cm, for bust 104 2.9cm and for bust 108 3.1cm. This is to allow greater width on the front bodice as it is assumed that this is where the figure is fullest.

F is midway between C and E. Place the square at D on line CD, and draw a line up and down at right angles to CD. This is the centre front line. Draw a line from A to the centre front line; the intersection is G. This line should be a right angles to line AB. Draw a line from B to the centre front line. H is at the intersection. A rectangle, measuring nape to waist x half bust plus ease, should now have been formed.

A to I is 2.5cm. This is a guide to the shoulder slope position. Draw a line from I across to the centre front line.

A to J is 6.5cm. This is the back neck width. For sizes above 96 bust, add 0.2cm for every 4cm bust increase, i.e. for bust 100 it is 6.7cm, for bust 104, 6.9cm and for bust 108 7.1cm. It is assumed that a fuller-busted person is corre-

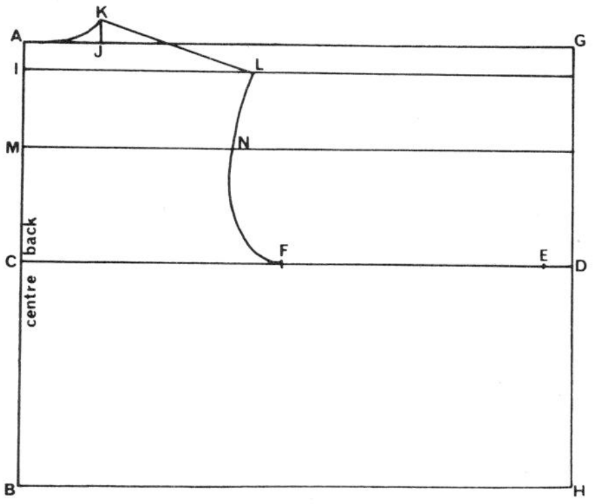

Figure 4

spondingly larger at the neck, and hence the extra allowance.

J to K is 2cm at right angles to line AG. Connect K to A with a suitable curve to form the back neck.

K to L is the shoulder width measurement plus 1cm ease (14cm for size 88 bust). Point L falls on the line I to centre front.

M is midway between A and C.

M to N, the half cross back measurement plus 0.5cm ease. Connect L through N to F with a suitable curve to form the back scye.

G to O, 6.5cm. This is the front neck width, and, as with the back, sizes above 96 will need to be increased by 0.2cm for every 4cm bust increase.

O to P, 3cm. This is the front neck point.

Figure 5

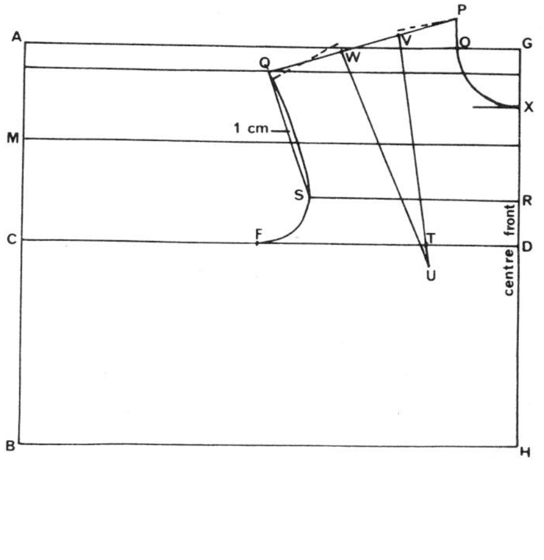

P to Q, shoulder width plus 6cm dart allowance. This is measured to the shoulder line in the same way as for the back. For sizes above 96 an extra 0.2cm for every 4cm bust increase should be added to the dart allowance, i.e. bust 100 will measure shoulder width plus 6.2cm and bust 104 will be shoulder width plus 6.4cm.

D to R is 5cm.

R to S is half the front chest plus 2cm ease. This line is at right angles to line GH. Sizes above 96 should add an extra 0.2cm ease for every 4cm bust increase.

Connect Q through S to F with a suitable curve, using the suggested line and offset shown in the quarter-scale block as a guide, to form the front scye.

D to T is 9cm. For sizes above 96 bust add 0.2cm for every 4cm bust increase.

T to U is 2cm. Generally the bust point is approximately 2cm below the underarm line, but this does depend to a large extent on foundation garments, the 'fashionable figure of the day' and a woman's age. However, for the purpose of the block assume that U is the bust point towards which all shaping should be directed.

P to V is 6cm.

V to W is 6cm—being the value of the dart allowance up to size 96. Sizes above 96 rise accordingly by 0.2cm for every 4cm bust increase.

Connect U to W and U to V to form the dart. Drop the shoulder point at Q by one cm. Raise W and V slightly (0.2cm), and redraw shoulder line. This is to allow for an even shoulder slope when the dart is closed.

G to X is 6cm. This is the centre front neck. For sizes above 96 bust add 0.2cm for every 4cm bust increase.

Connect P to X with a suitable curve to form the front neck. The back and front neck curves should be drawn at right angles to the centre front and centre back for approximately 2cm to avoid a bad shape.

The basic bodice block is now almost complete, having covered the shoulder area, scye, neck line and chest. The amount of suppression at the waist is more or less dependent on fashion and is not so essential to the basic block. However, before the block may be made up for a personal fitting, some suppression must be used. To find the amount of suppression required, take the waist measurement from the bust measurement, and halve the answer, i.e. bust 88 less waist 68 equals 20cm—this must be halved as only half the block is being constructed. Therefore, for the example in this book 10cm must be taken away at the waist, for the purpose of fitting the block. This reduction is brought about by the use of darts and side seam shaping. The example used is 3cm from the back, 3cm from the side and 4cm from the front. The position of the centre of the back dart is found by dropping a perpendicular line from midway between M and N onto the waist line. The amount to be taken out is divided equally either side of this line, and the apex of the dart is approximately 3cm below the underarm line. The centre of the front dart is a perpendicular line dropped from U to the waist line, and the value of the dart is divided either side of this line. The apex of the dart is 4cm from U. The side seam shaping is divided equally either side of a line from F to the waist line. This waist measurement still has 4cm of ease (added to the bust at C to D), and for many styles a greater amount of suppression may be required.

The apex of the shoulder dart should be approximately 4cm from the bust point to allow for fullness of the bust, as shown by broken lines on the quarter-scale block diagram. It is helpful to draw a circle around U (bust point) of radius 4cm (5cm on larger sizes). This gives some indication of bust fullness, and any future style shaping should be directed towards this area.

It is important to record clearly the cross back line, bust or underarm line, chest line, centre back and centre front. Mark points N and S for balance notches to give guidance when fitting in the sleeve.

The centre front line will need to be lengthened at H to allow for contour. For sizes up to 96 bust add 1cm, and above this size add an extra 0.2cm for every 4cm bust increase.

Sleeve

From the bodice, extend the underarm, chest and cross back lines by approximately 40cm to the right of the sheet. The measurements required for the sleeve draft are – length from shoulder to wrist (56cm) and length from shoulder to elbow (32cm).

1 is the starting point for the sleeve draft to the right of the sheet.

1 to 2 is 36cm for sizes up to 96 bust. Sizes above 96 should add 1cm for every 4cm bust increase, i.e. for bust 100 this is 37cm and for bust 104 38cm.

3 is midway between 1 and 2.

3 to 4 is 14cm (crown height). Add 0.2cm to this measurement for every 4cm bust increase above 96.

Connect 1 to 4 and 2 to 4. These lines are guide lines for the sleeve head shaping. Find the centre of the guide line between the chest line and the underarm line from both 1 and 2. As illustrated, measure inwards from the guide line at this point by 1cm for the back-sleeve and 1.5cm for the front sleeve. (Although this is a one-piece sleeve, the words 'front' and 'back' are used for identification purposes.) On the cross back line, measure outwards from the guide lines by 2.5cm for the back sleeve and by 3cm for the front sleeve. Draw in the sleevehead using these offsets for guidance. It may be easier to use a broken line in the first instance to obtain a good shape.

4 to 5 is the sleeve length (56cm). This line must be at right angles to the underarm line.

5 to 6 is 12cm.
5 to 7 is 12cm. } Average cuff.

Connect 2 to 6 and 1 to 7

4 to 8 is the length from shoulder to elbow (32cm).

Line 8 to 9 is a right angles to line 4 and 5.

9 to 10 is 1.5cm. This is the value of the dart or the amount of ease required for the elbow movement. The lower dart line is at right angles to line 10 to 6.

6 to 11 is 1.5cm. The extra length is to allow for elbow ease.

Connect 11 to 5 with a slight curve.

To find the position of the balance notches in the sleeve head, measure from F to N on the bodice block, and then measure this distance plus 1cm ease along the back sleeve head from 2. Measure F to S on the bodice block and record this distance plus 0.5cm ease along the front sleeve head from 1.

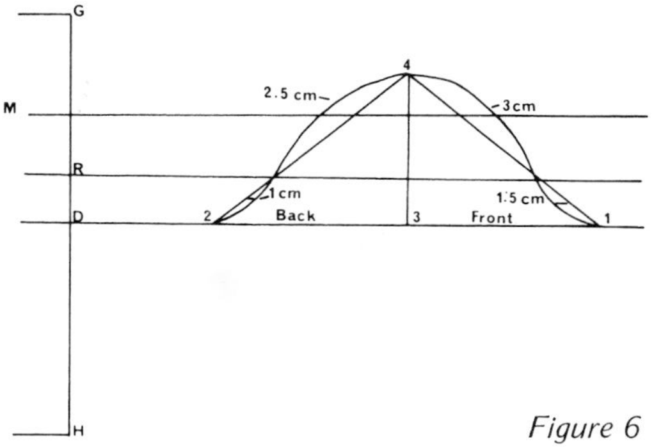

Figure 6

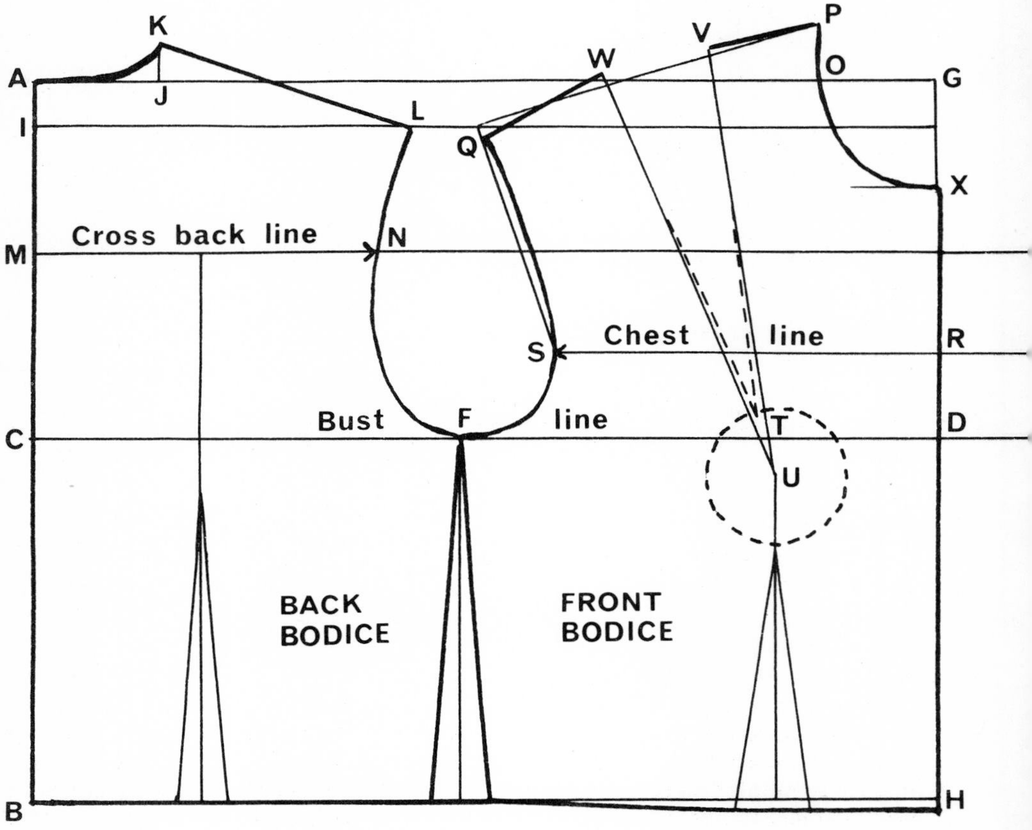

Figure 7 *Quarter-scale bodice and sleeve block, size 88 bust*

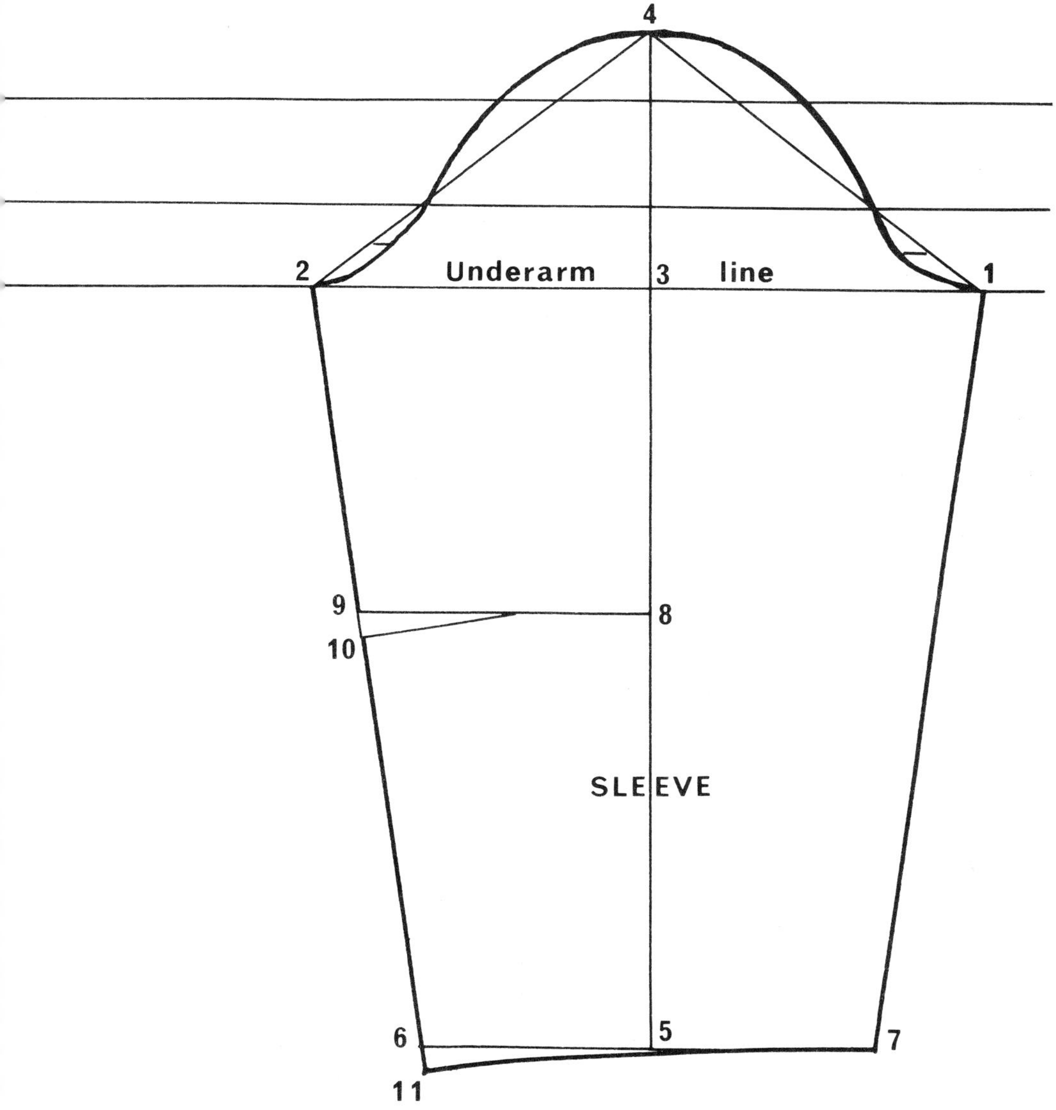
4
2
Underarm
3
line
1
9
8
10
SLEEVE
6
5
7
11

BASIC TWO-PIECE SKIRT BLOCK

To construct this block you will require a piece of plain paper approximately 75cm square.

The measurements required are waist, hip and skirt length. Skirt lengths vary considerably according to fashion trends, but for the purpose of the block construction it is desirable to use the body measurement from waist to knee. This provides a well-proportioned balance for the foundation block. The actual skirt length may be decided upon when making the style patterns. The skirt in this book is made to quarter-scale to fit hip size 94cm.

The starting point is A, which should be approximately 4cm from the top and 8cm from the left-hand edge of the paper.

A to B is half the hip measurement plus 2cm ease.

A to C is a quarter of the hip measurement plus 1.5cm.

C to D is 1cm.

Connect A to D and D to B.

A to E is the skirt length. This line is at right angles to the line AD (60cm).

B to F is the skirt length. This line is at right angles to the line BD (60cm).

Connect E to F.

C to G is a line perpendicular to the line AB.

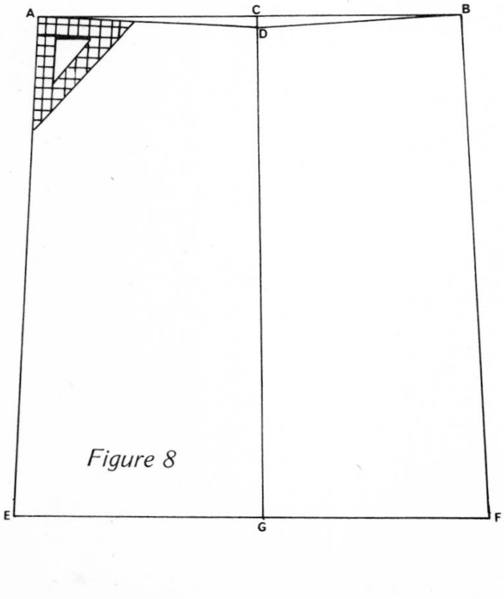

Figure 8

A to H is 20cm.
D to I is 20cm. } Hip level.
B to J is 20cm.

If the body measurements, waist to knee, is less than 55cm, the hip level should be adjusted to 18cm.

Connect H to J through I.

G to K is the 3cm stride room.

G to L is the 3cm stride room.

Connect K and L to I respectively.

The back and front skirts now overlap at the hem. Because the seam line is now slightly on the bias, K and L are raised 0.5cm from the original line as shown.

The difference between half the hip and half the waist has to be taken away at the waist by means of darts and side seam shaping.

In this example the hip is 94 and the waist 68, and the difference therefore is 26cm. Since only half the block is being constructed, the amount to be suppressed is 13cm. 3.5cm is taken out at each side of C, thus accounting for 7cm. The dart in the back skirt is 4cm, leaving 2cm for the front skirt suppression. These suppression details can only serve as an example and will vary with different sizing, i.e. hip 98 and waist 70 will leave 14cm to be suppressed on half a block; hip 102 and waist 72cm will leave 15cm. In all cases, apportion the suppression between side seam and darts accordingly.

The centre of the back dart is at right angles to line A and B and is positioned 12cm from the centre back for size 94 hip. Add 0.2cm to this for every hip increment of 4cm. The length of the dart should be 12cm long (on a short person the length of the dart should be reduced accordingly). Although a front dart is included in the block draft, it is not always essential to use one. To ease away the fullness often creates a more flattering effect. The centre of the front dart is positioned 13cm from the centre front for size 94 and is at right angles to the line A–B. The length of the dart is 8cm.

Draw in the side seam, using a suitable curve from I. Raise this seam by 1cm at the waist, and reshape the waist with a curve as shown.

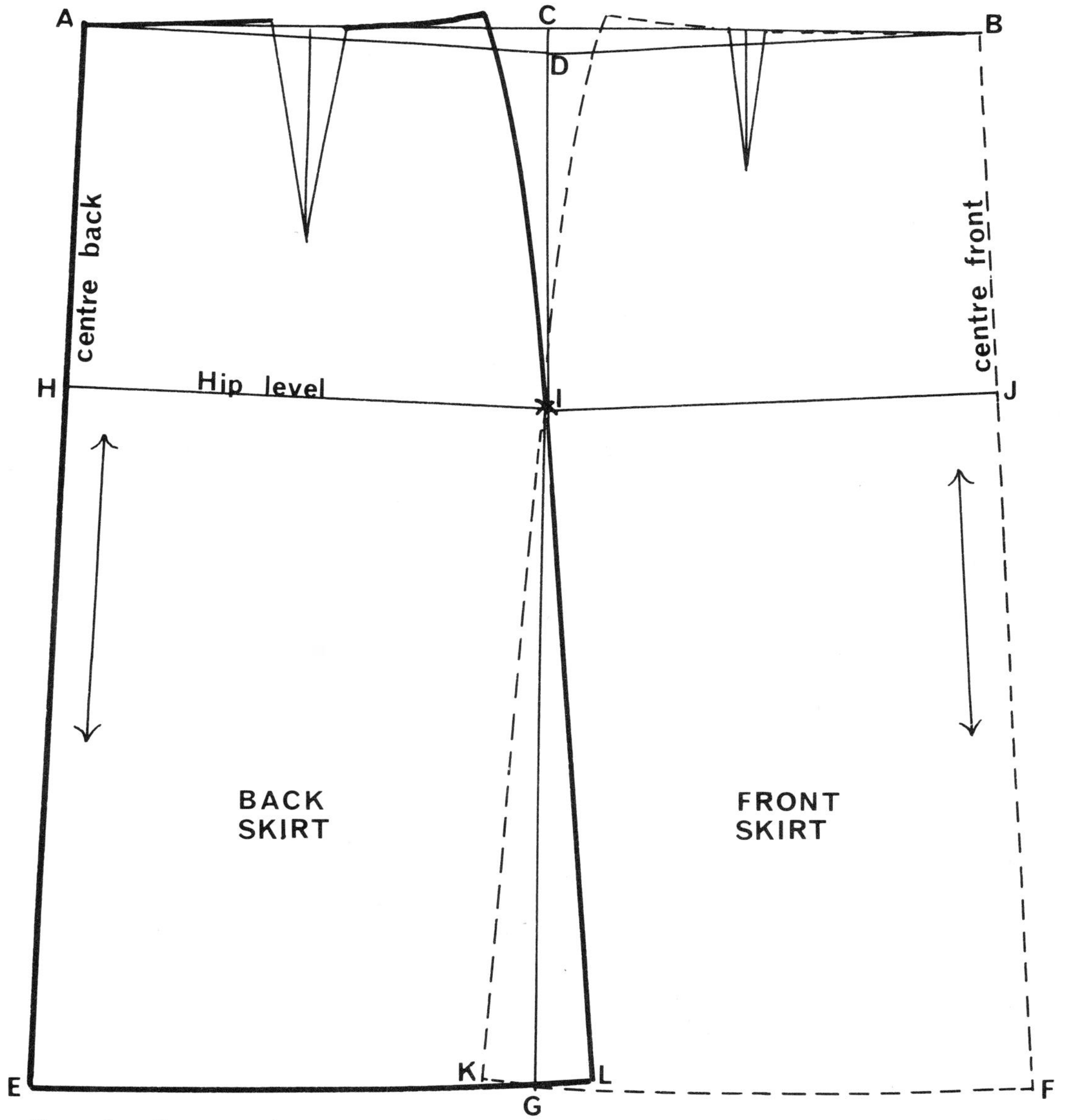

Figure 9 Quarter-scale skirt block, size 94 hip

At this stage the back skirt has been constructed to overlap the front skirt and must therefore be traced off to separate the two pattern pieces. The tracing off is carried out by placing the draft over a clean sheet of paper and by running the tracing wheel around the outer edge of the back skirt (outlined in bold print on the quarter-scale block). This creates perforations on the clean sheet and enables you to produce a fresh outline. The process may then be repeated for the front skirt (outlined by a broken line on the quarter-scale block) on a separate sheet of paper. Record the darts; mark the centre front and centre back on each pattern piece together with the hip level. Grain lines should be marked to run parallel with the centre front and centre back. Balance notches are necessary at point I on the side seam (hip level).

PREPARING THE PATTERNS FROM THE DRAFTS

Having completed the draft of the sleeve, bodice and skirt blocks, a pattern of each must be prepared to enable you to cut them in cloth for making up.

Seam allowances are not included in the block but must be added to all style pattern pieces cut from the block. The amount of seam allowance is dependent to a large extent on the type of fabric being used. As a general rule, 2cm on all seams and a 6cm hem allowance is sufficient. However, if the fabric is likely to fray, a greater amount should be allowed.

For the purpose of fitting the basic pattern, trace the block, and add the seam allowances as illustrated, *figure 10.* As indicated, the darts and seams are shaped to ensure that they lie flat when made up. Note that no allowance has been added at this stage to the neck edge or for the hem, since this is not necessary for a trial fitting.

The skirt block as it is drafted is intended as a separate skirt. However, if you wish to fit the

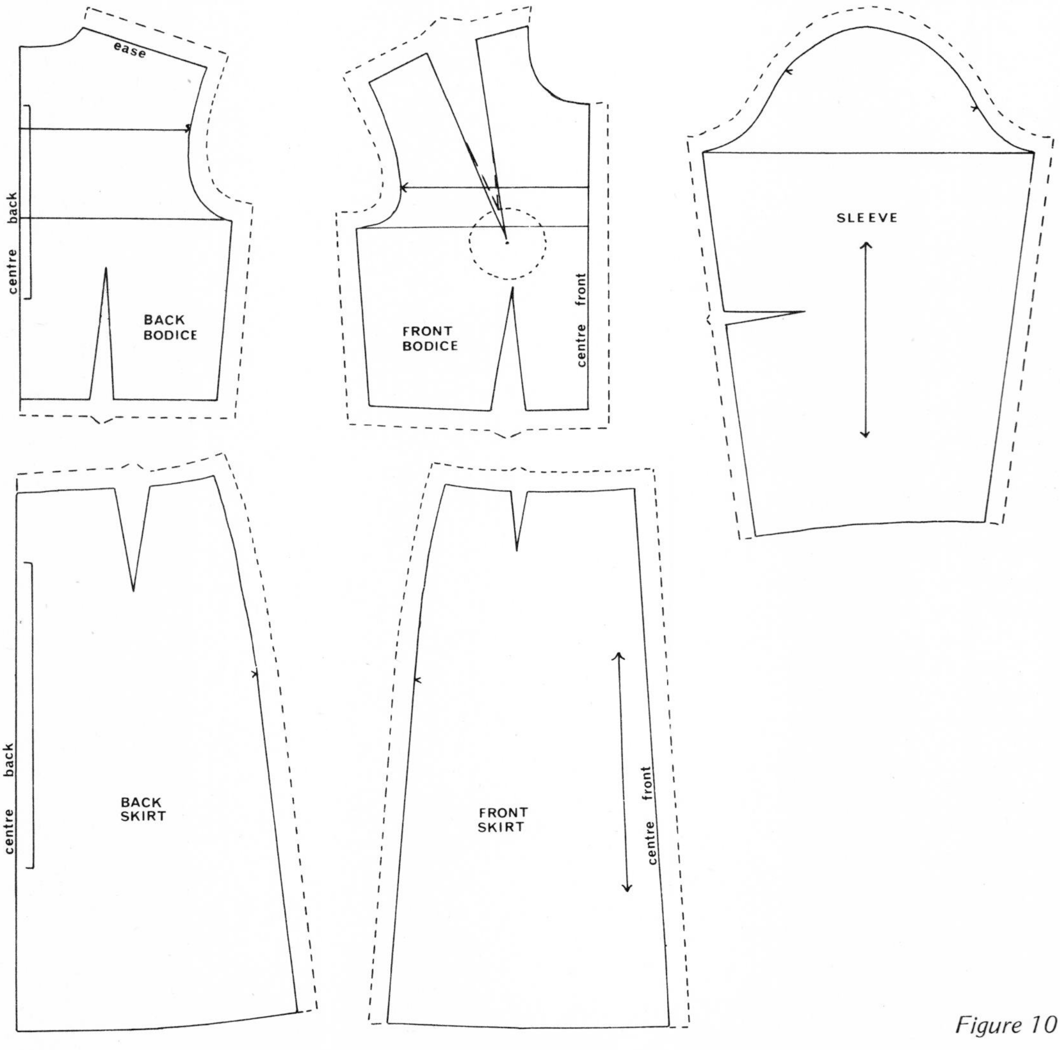

Figure 10

skirt and bodice together with a waist seam, an adjustment must be made to enable the skirt darts to line up with the bodice darts. To do this, measure the distance from the centre back of the bodice to the dart. This is 7.5cm in the example given as a guide in *figure 11.* Now measure the distance from the side seam to the back dart—10.5cm in the example. The back skirt darts must be arranged to correspond with the bodice dart; therefore measure (7.5cm) from the centre back and (10.5cm) from the side seam. Draw in a new dart accordingly. The measurements are only given as examples, and individual patterns may differ. The front bodice and skirt darts are lined up in just the same way. Measure from the centre front to the dart and from the side front to the dart on the bodice; then move the skirt dart accordingly. There is no reason why the dress dart and the skirt dart should not both be recorded on the same block, as long as they are clearly marked as such. You must remember of course that only one dart should be marked onto the cloth.

The back shoulder is 1cm longer than the front. This extra length should be eased onto the front when making up to allow a slight fullness over the shoulder blade.

For fitting purposes the centre front should be left open from the neck to 14cm below the waist. The centre back is placed to the fold. Mark balance notches at the scye, sleevehead and hip level on the pattern and test cloth, in order that these points may be observed when fitting. Use calico or a similar plain weave fabric for the test fitting. Knitted fabric is unsuitable for trial fitting since it will give a distorted result, and it is essential that the block pattern is made up exactly as it is cut, in order to make the correct alterations.

Personal adjustments will undoubtedly need to be made to the block draft after a fitting. These may include, for example, raising or lowering the shoulder slope positions, deepening the scye at the underarm position or adjusting the neck line to achieve a correct fit at the base of the neck. The skirt side seam should fall vertically, and, if the seam swings to the front, the back waist line will require lifting. It is advisable to pencil any alterations directly onto the calico test garment and to modify the original block construction accordingly.

Having satisfied yourself that the simple blocks are the correct fit for your body they can now be cut out in card, without seam allowances, to be used for the basis of all designs. Punch holes at the bust point and along the dart lines at regular intervals to make future marking simpler.

Figure 11

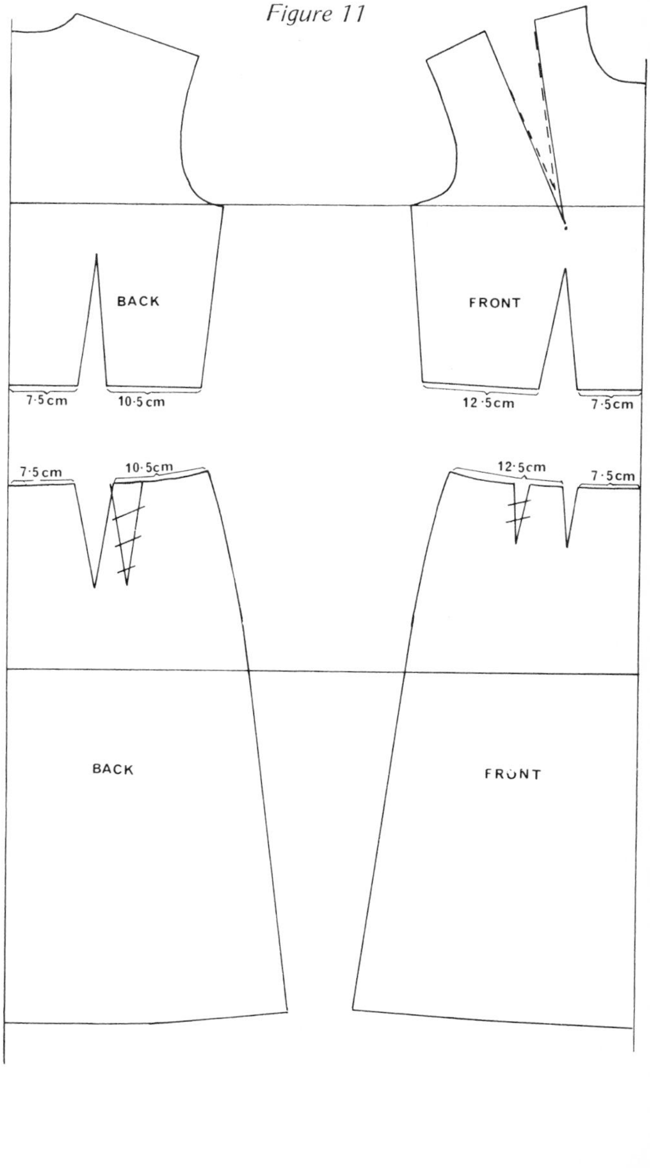

TWO

Dart manipulation

The shoulder dart, although valuable when drafting the block, is not always acceptable for certain styles. However, the shaping must be incorporated in the bodice to ensure the correct balance. Provided the dart is directed towards the bust area previously marked, it can take many forms.

This first example of dart arrangement shows the bust dart in the underarm position.

Figure 12

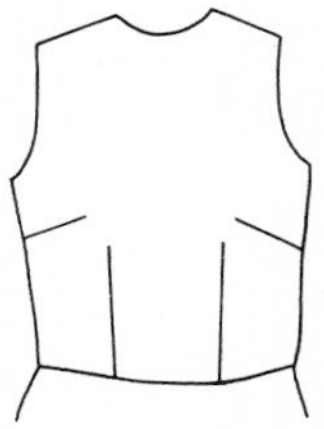

Using the front bodice block as a template, copy the outline onto a sheet of paper marking the darts clearly. Cut out this bodice and the shoulder dart. Mark the position of the new dart approximately 8cm below the scye. Ensure that this new dart line (shown by a broken line) meets the apex of the shoulder dart (the bust point).

Figure 13

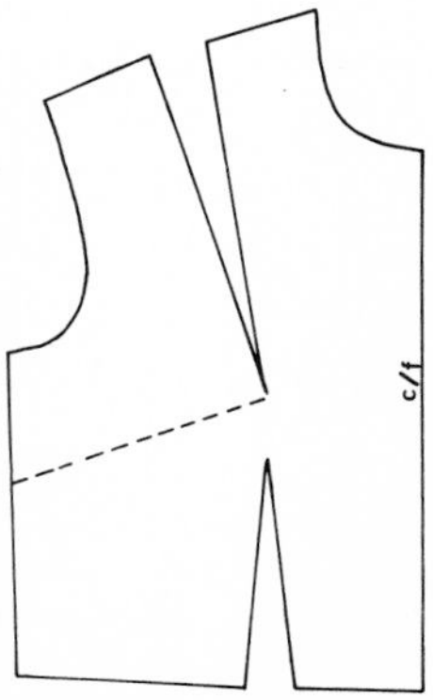

Cut along the broken line to within approximately 0.2cm of the bust point. Close the shoulder dart, and in so doing the fullness is transferred to the new position, *figure 14*.

Figure 14

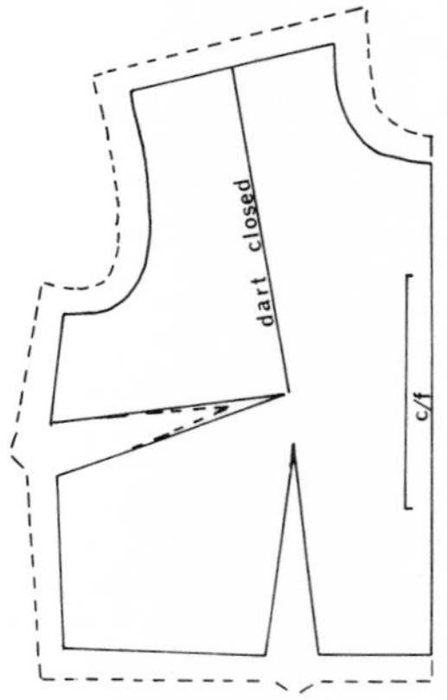

Copy this new outline onto a fresh piece of paper. Reduce the underarm dart to a length approximately 4cm from the bust point. Add seam allowances to the finished pattern piece.

This block is one of the most used, and therefore it could be cut in card without seam allowances. It may then be used as a template for other styles.

SIDE WAIST SHAPING

With the style shown in *figure 15* the shoulder and underbust darts are both closed out, and the shaping is transferred to the side waist.

Figure 15

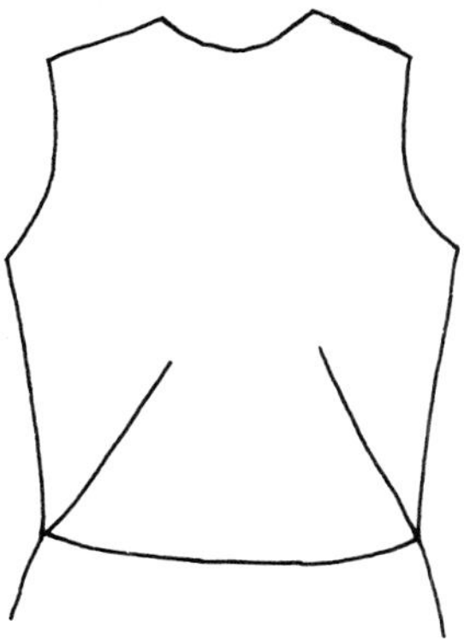

Draw around the front bodice block, marking the darts as before. Cut this out and mark the required position of the new dart, shown as a broken line in *figure 16.* Extend the apex of the underbust dart towards the bust point and the broken line.

Figure 16

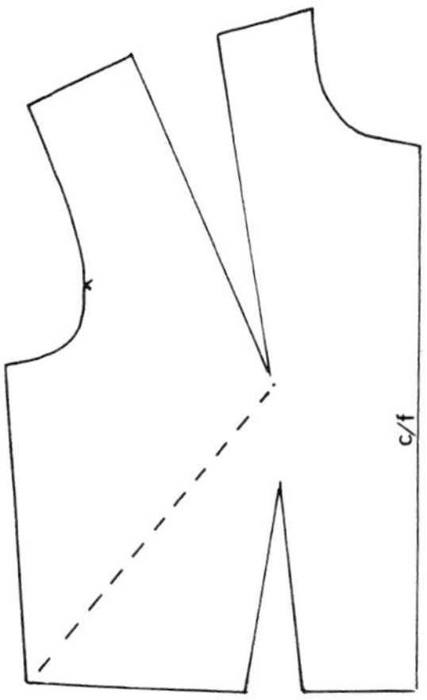

Cut out the shoulder dart and the underbust dart to within 0.2cm of the bust point. Cut along the broken line to within 0.2cm of the bust point. Take care not to cut the portion out completely. Close the shoulder and underbust darts, thus creating fullness in the new dart position, *figure 17.*

Figure 17

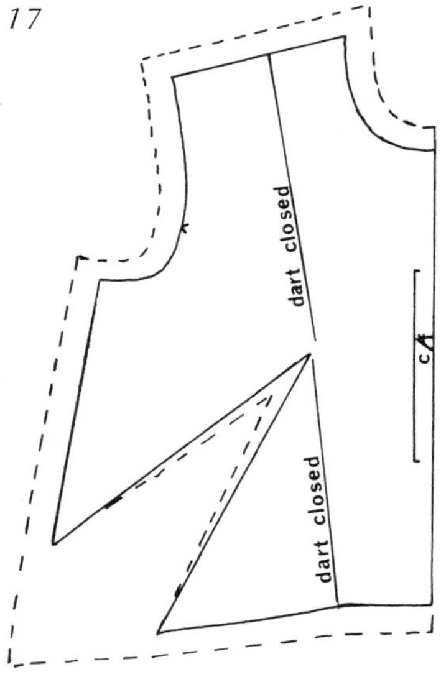

Transfer this outline onto a new sheet of paper, and shorten the side waist dart to finish about 4cm from the bust point.

Add seam allowances to the finished pattern piece.

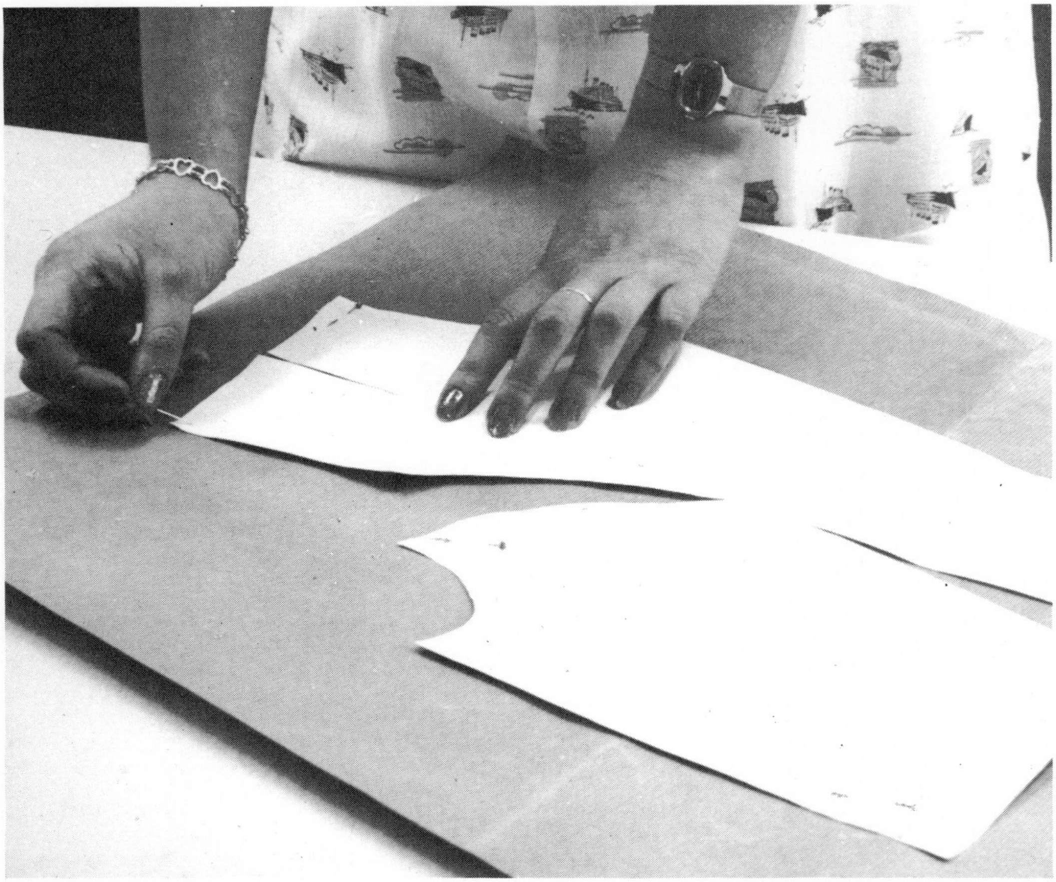

Figure 18 Manipulating the shoulder dart

MOVING THE SHOULDER DART
Here the shoulder dart is moved to a position approximately half-way round the front scye.

Cut along the broken line towards the bust point—avoid cutting the section out completely. Close the shoulder dart, thus opening up a dart in the scye as shown in *figure 21*.

Figure 19

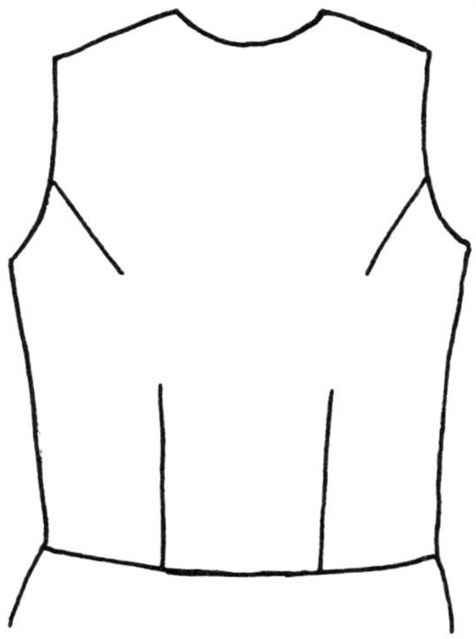

Draw round the front bodice block marking the darts, and cut this out as before. Draw a line from the scye to the bust point as shown by a broken line. Cut out the shoulder dart.

Figure 20

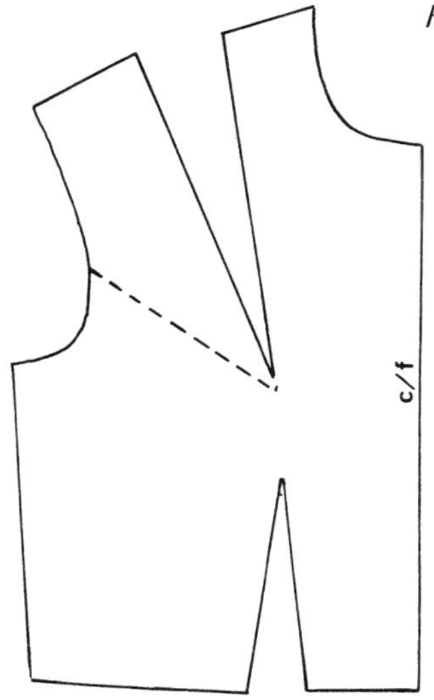

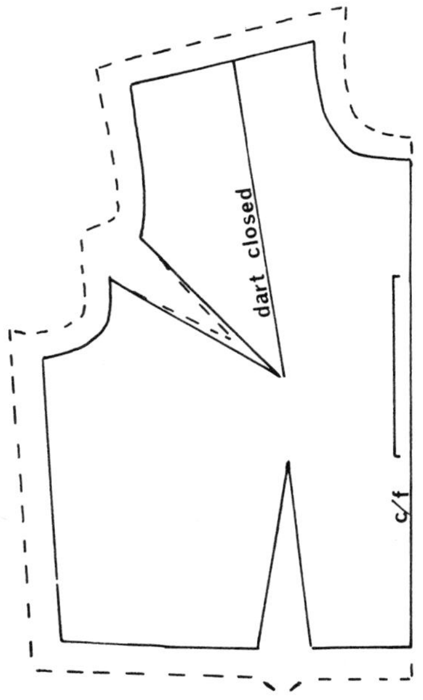

Figure 21

Draw round this new outline on a fresh sheet of paper. The new dart should be adjusted in length to finish approximately 4 to 6cm from the bust point. Add seam allowances to complete the pattern piece.

DART AT THE NECK LINE

In this style a dart at the neck line is used instead of the shoulder dart. The underbust dart remains the same.

Figure 22

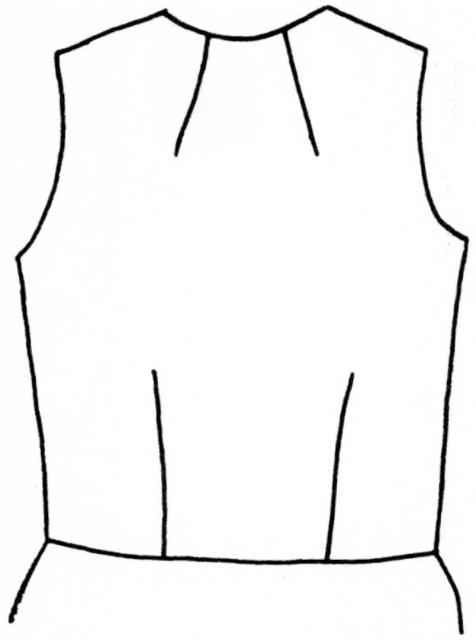

Copy the outline of the block including the darts as before. Cut out the shoulder dart. Draw a line for the new dart position from the neck line to the bust point. Cut along this line to within 0.2cm of the bust point.

Figure 23

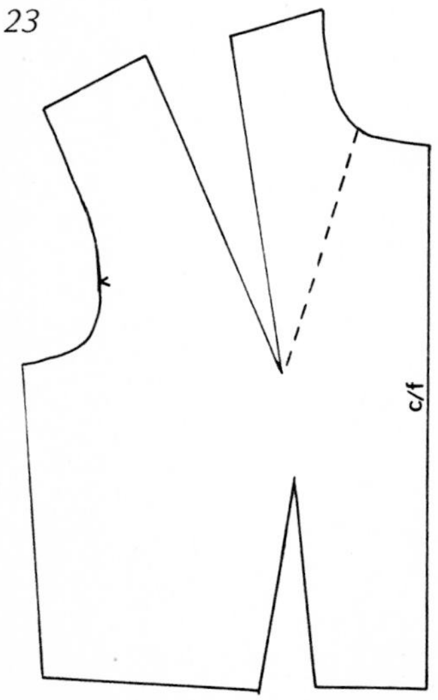

Close the shoulder dart, transferring the fullness to the neck area. Draw around the new outline onto a fresh sheet of paper. Shorten the neck dart to the desired length, and add seam allowances to the finished pattern.

Figure 24

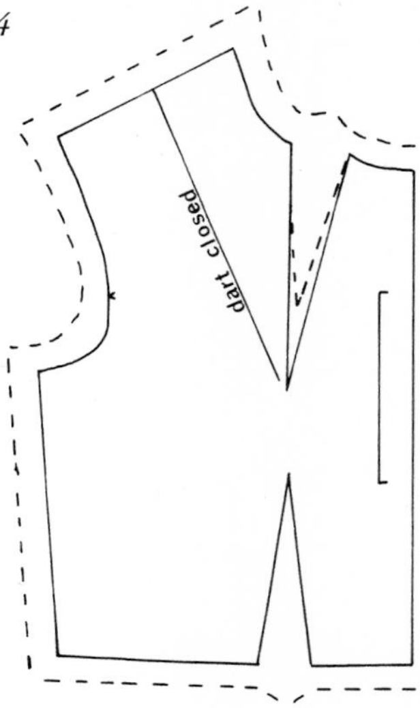

CURVED DARTS

The bodice darts need not necessarily be straight. A more flattering effect is often created by using a curved line. An example is given here, where the shoulder and underbust darts are substituted by a curved dart from the side seam.

Figure 25

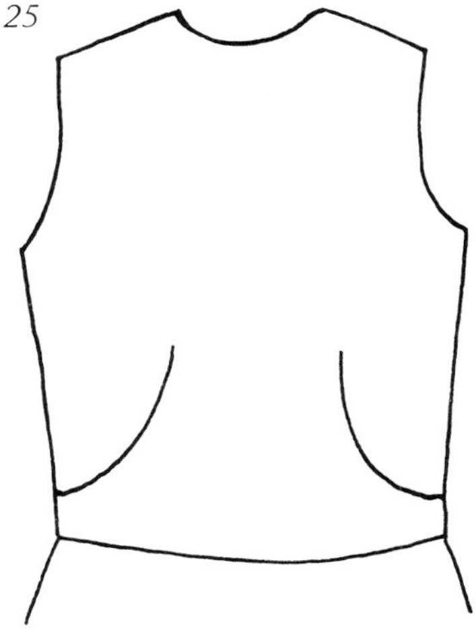

The principles are similar to those on the previous pages. Draw round the block extending and marking the darts. Cut out the block and darts to within 0.2cm of bust point. Draw in the curved line to mark the position of the new dart, and cut along this curved line to within 0.2cm of the bust point.

Figure 26

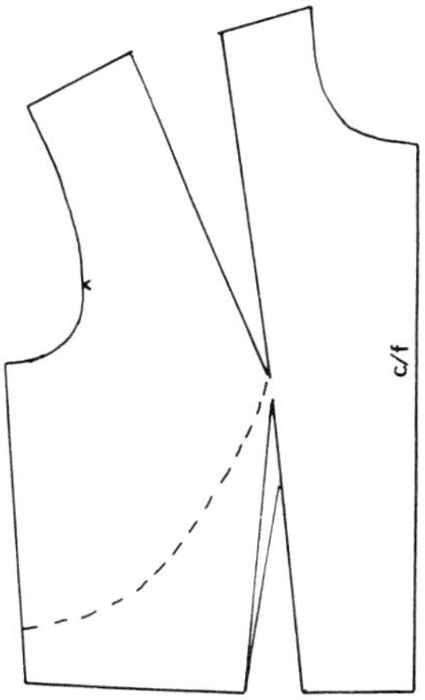

Close the original darts, transferring the fullness to the side seam. Draw around the new outline, marking the curved dart, and shorten this accordingly. Add seam allowances to the finished pattern piece. Shape the side seam in order that the dart lies flat when made up. If desired, some of the dart fullness may be cut away, and the dart may be pressed open during making up.

Figure 27

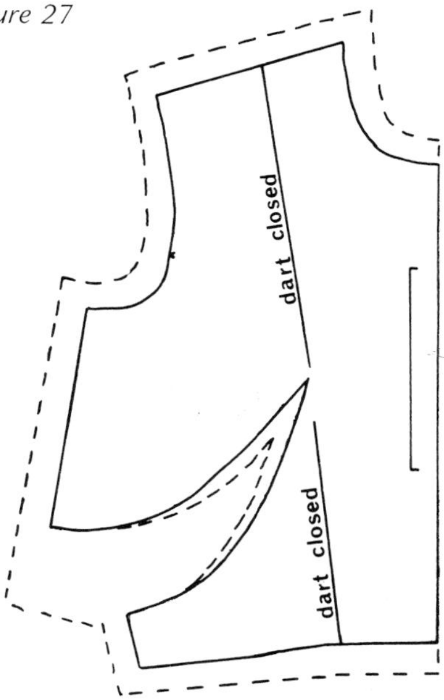

CUTTING PANELS

A variation of dart manipulation is to cut panels which incorporate the dart suppression in the style seams. These panels can be most attractive as well as functional. Top stitching or contrasting fabrics may be used to emphasize a particular cut.

Figure 28

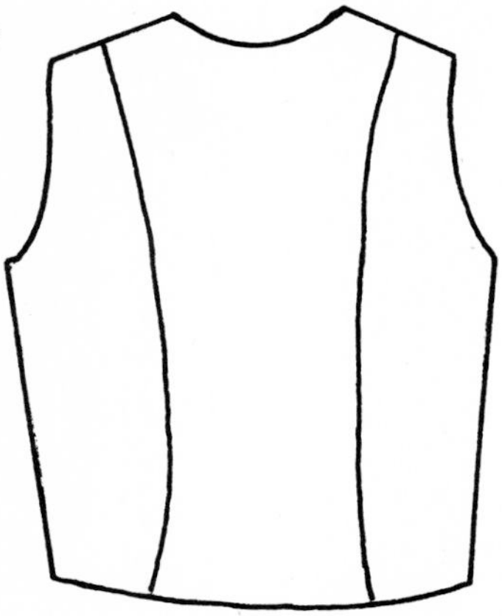

Figure 28 has a seam running from the shoulder, over the bust to the waist line. To construct this, draw around the front block, marking the darts. Extend the underbust dart to the point as shown in *figure 29.* At this stage, mark the position of the notches at the chest line and the underarm line to ensure correct matching of the pattern pieces. Also mark a grain line on the side section of the block—running parallel to the centre front as this represents the straight grain.

Figure 29

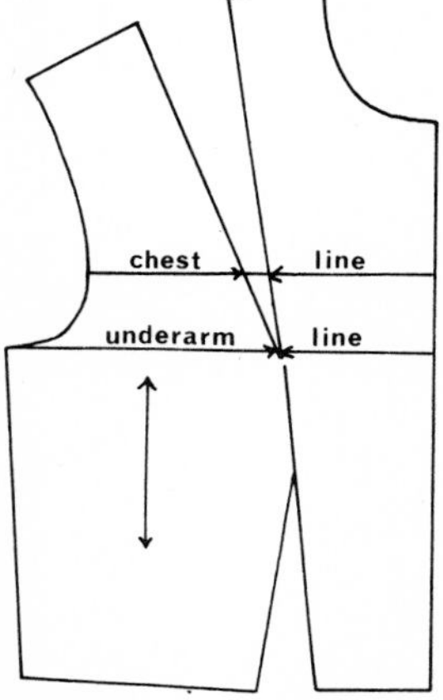

Cut out the darts to the bust point, separating the side front section from the centre front in order to produce the panels as shown in *figure 30.* The side front panel will require reshaping slightly to allow for the bust fullness.

Figure 30

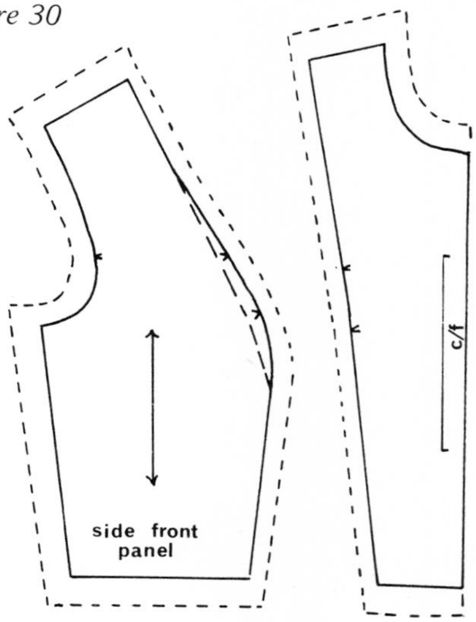

Redraw each panel, and add seam allowances. Record the grain line and notches. It will be necessary to ease away the side front slightly when making up.

WING SEAMS

A wing seam running through the bodice from the scye to the waist is another popular example of shaping being incorporated in the style seam.

Figure 31

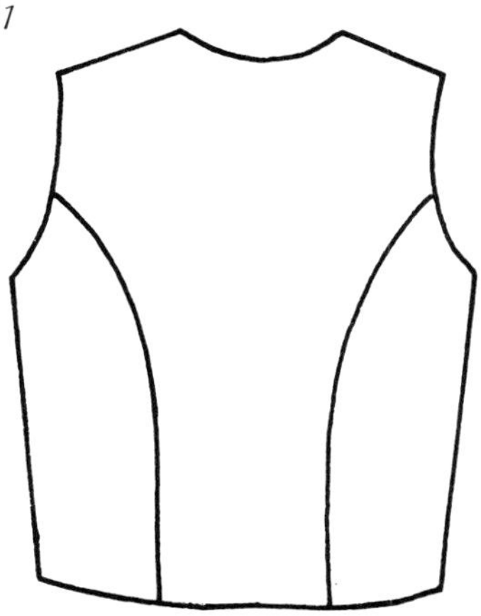

Draw round the front bodice block, marking the shoulder and underbust darts clearly. Cut this out, and draw in the position of the wing seam required, ensuring that this runs through the bust area, shown by a broken line in *figure 32.* At this stage, mark the grain line and the balance notch positions as illustrated in *figure 32.*

Figure 32

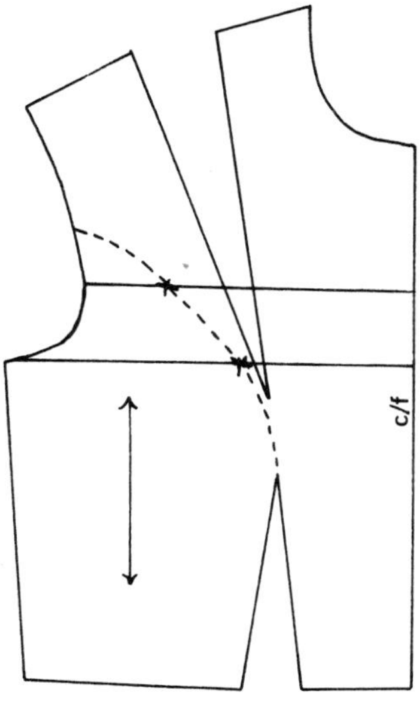

Cut out the underbust dart, and cut along the wing seam line (broken line), separating the side section from the centre front section.

Close out the shoulder dart on the centre front section piece. The shaping suppression will now have been transferred to the scye area.

Figure 33

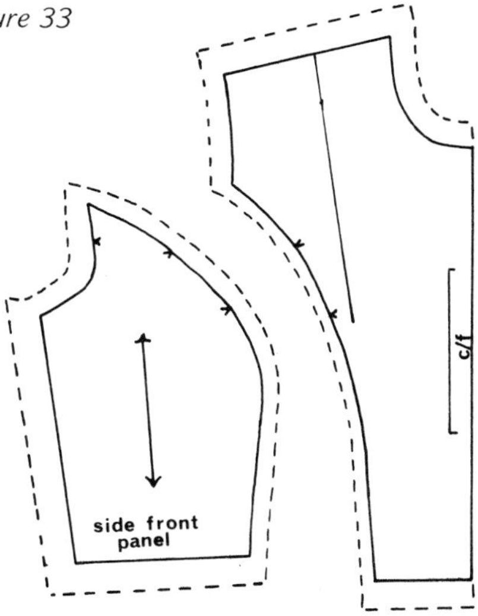

Draw around the new outline of each piece, recording the notches and the grain lines. Re-shape the side front panel slightly to allow for the bust fullness. Add seam allowances to both panels.

To cut the back of this style, follow the same procedure.

SHAPING INCORPORATED IN YOKE SEAM

The shoulder dart has been closed out on this style so that the shaping is directed from the scye and is incorporated in the yoke seam.

Figure 34

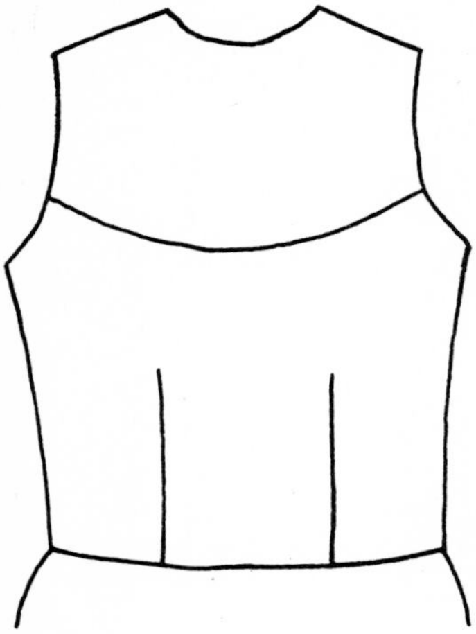

Outline the front bodice, marking the darts as before. Draw in the position of the seam line (broken line), ensuring that this runs through the bust area. Mark a notch at the bust area. Cut along the broken line, separating the shoulder area from the underarm section.

Figure 35

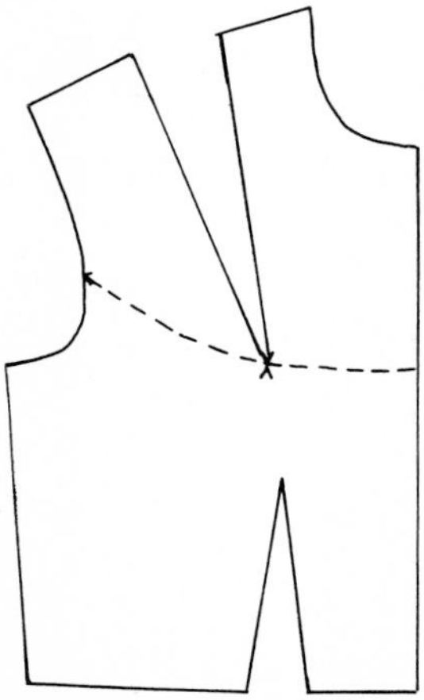

Close out the shoulder dart on the appropriate section. Note that the broken line in *figure 36* represents the yoke line before the shoulder dart closure. This is shown only to indicate how the suppression is being transferred to the seam and must not be mistaken as part of the new pattern piece.

Figure 36

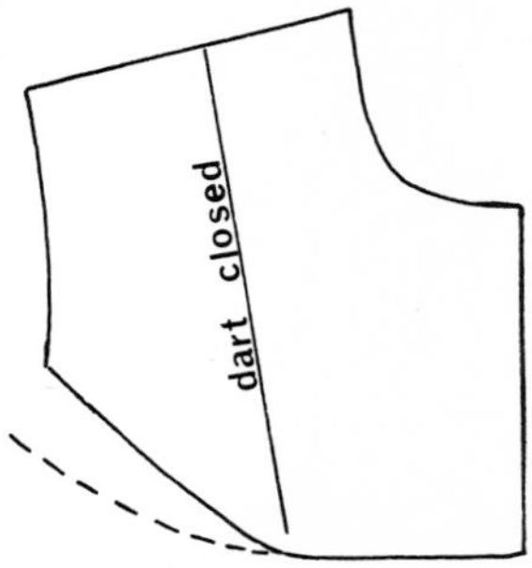

Redraw each section, and add seam allowances. Record the balance notches along the yoke seams.

Figure 37

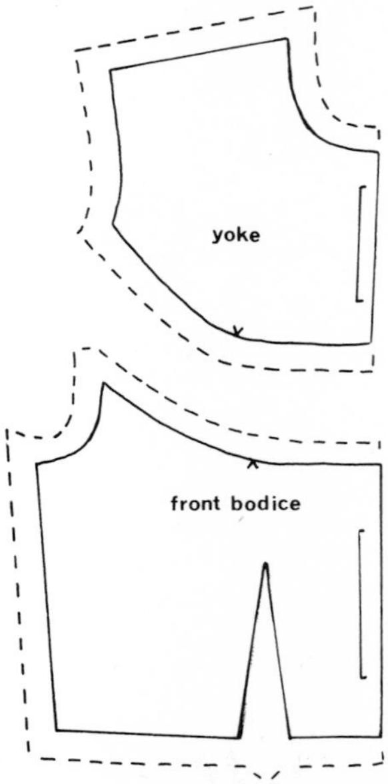

'BIB' INSERTION

A seam from the shoulder dart to the centre front forms a 'bib' insertion in this style. The 'bib', when cut in a contrast fabric, makes an additional feature.

Figure 38

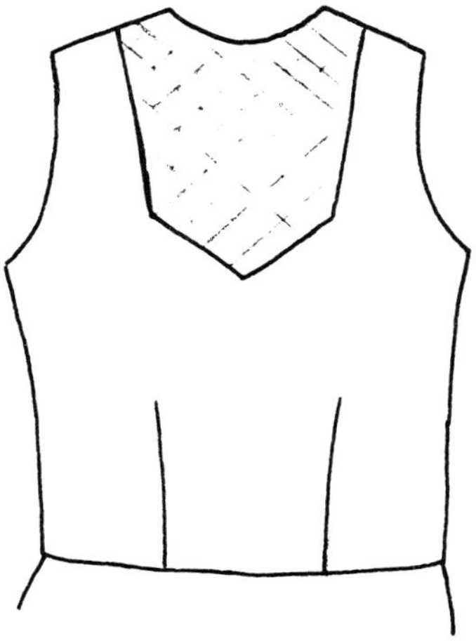

Draw round the front bodice block, marking the darts. Shorten the shoulder dart to finish at the chest line. From the apex of this shortened dart, sketch in the style line, (shown by a broken line in *figure 39).* Mark the notches on the chest and underarm lines.

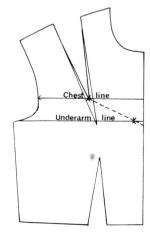

Figure 39

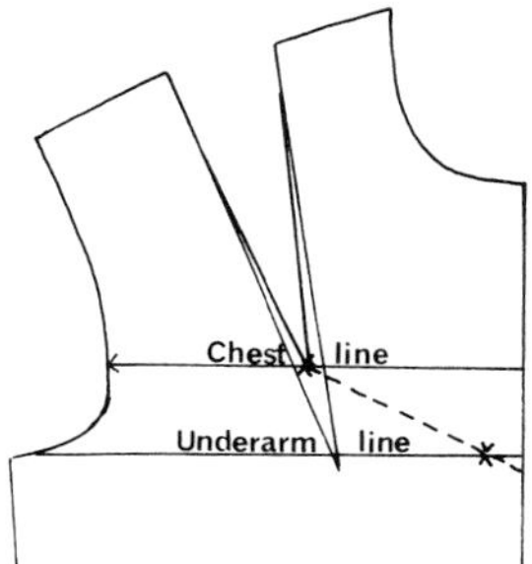

Cut along the broken line, and cut out the shoulder dart. Draw around the outline of each piece, and add seam allowances to finish the pattern pieces. Finally mark the notches and centre front positions.

Figure 40

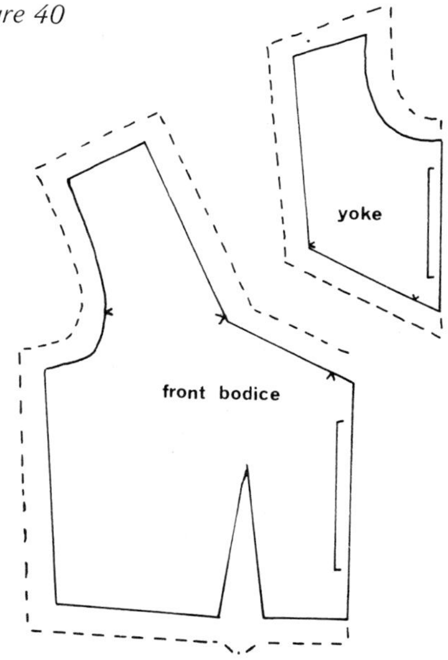

EMPIRE BODICE

In this Empire type of bodice the shoulder and underbust darts are closed out to transfer the suppression shaping to the side bodice.

Figure 41

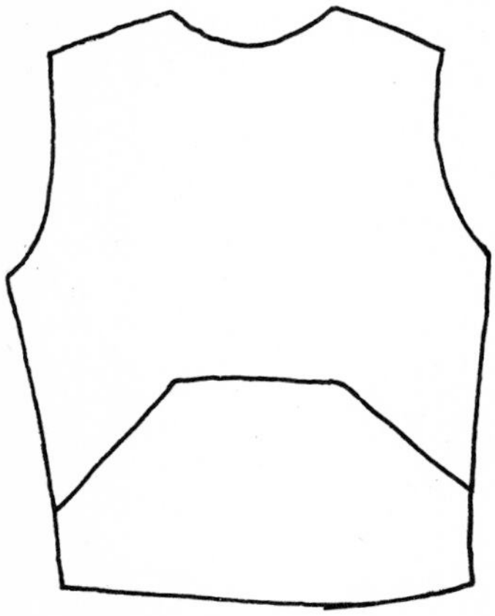

Outline the front bodice block. Mark the position of the Empire style line, and indicate notches for guidance when making up. The apex of the underbust dart should be adjusted in length if necessary so that it is on the new style line. Draw a line from the apex of the underbust dart to the apex of the shoulder dart.

Figure 42

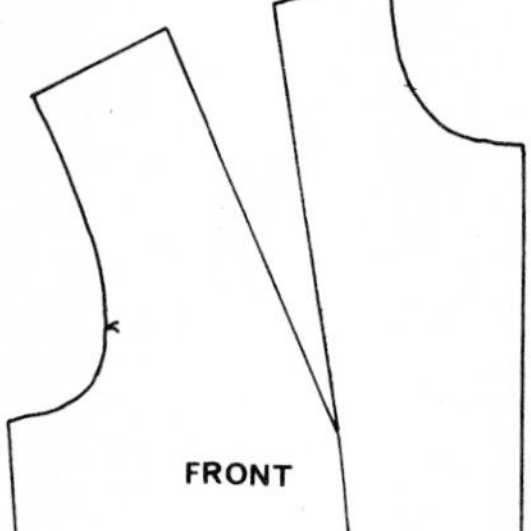

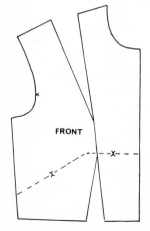

Cut out the bodice, and cut along the style line, separating the shoulder section from the waist section. Close out the underbust dart, and redraw this section, transferring the shaping to the side seam. The broken line represents the style line before the closure of the dart indicating the transfer of the shaping, *figure 43.*

Figure 43

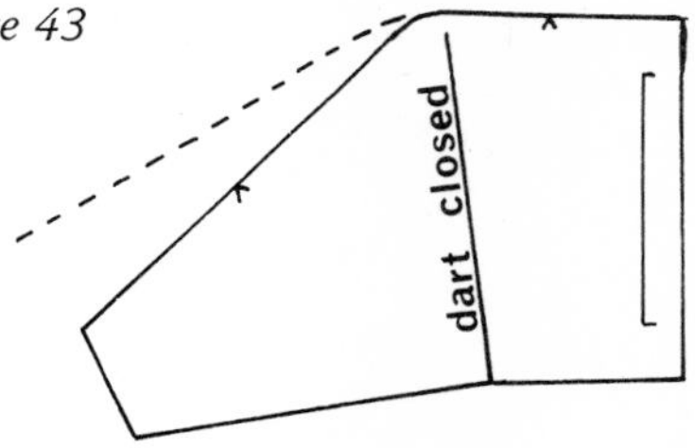

Cut along the underbust line that previously connected the two darts to within 0.2cm of the apex of the shoulder dart. Close the shoulder dart, thus transferring the shape to the side seam and an amount to the underbust position, *figure 44.* The amount of fullness created at the underbust position may be eased away in make-up.

Redraw each pattern piece, and add seam allowances in the usual way.

Figure 44

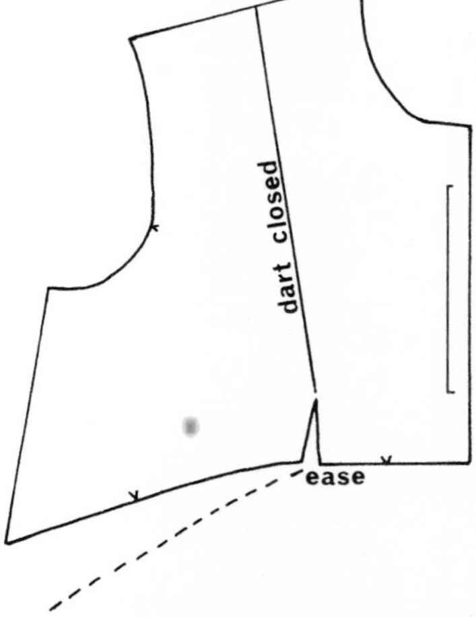

GATHERING

Examples have been given of shaping by the means of darts and style seams. A further method is to use gathering, thus creating a more gentle draped effect. This method is particularly popular when designing blouses. This style has the fullness gathered onto a neck yoke seam.

Figure 45

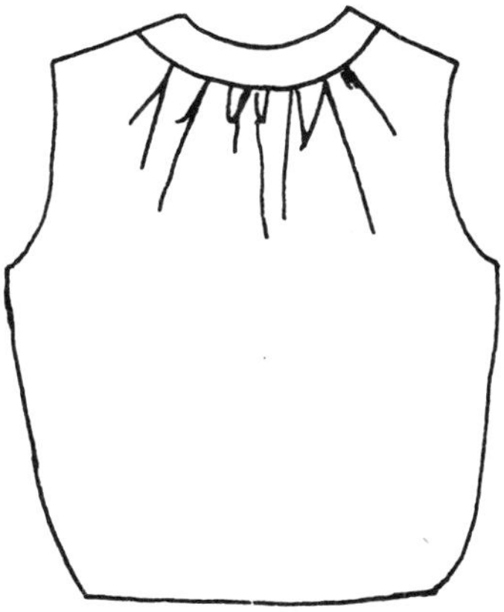

Using the front bodice with the underarm dart as a template, copy the outline, marking the darts. Draw in the desired line of the neck yoke. Mark a notch approximately 6cm from the shoulder. Draw a line from the apex of the underarm dart to this notch and a second line from the apex of the underbust dart to a point approximately 3cm from the centre front at the neck.

Figure 46

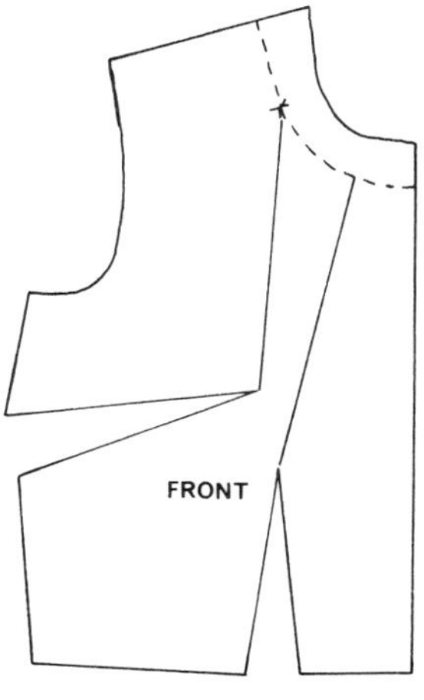

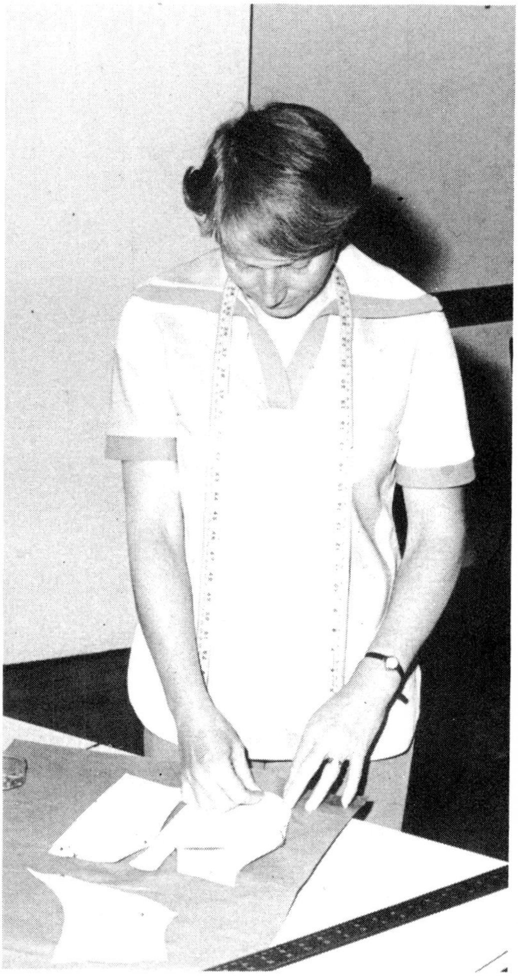

Figure 47 Manipulating the front bodice dart

Cut off the neck yoke, and add seam allowances; also record the centre front position, and balance notches.

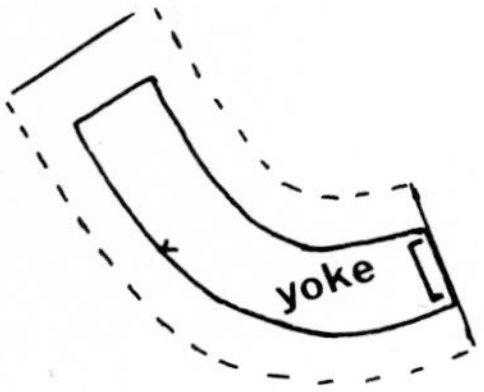

Figure 48

Cut out the main section, and cut down each line from the neck to within 0.2cm of the apex. Cut out and close the underarm and underbust darts, transferring the fullness to the neck area.

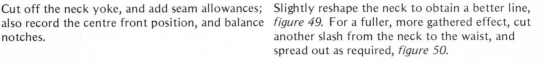

Figure 49

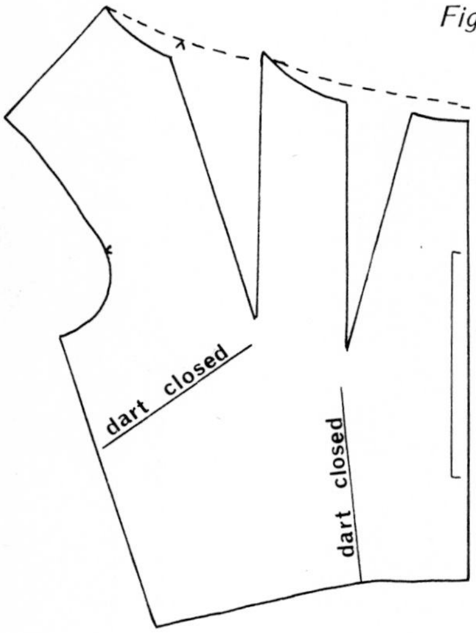

Slightly reshape the neck to obtain a better line, *figure 49.* For a fuller, more gathered effect, cut another slash from the neck to the waist, and spread out as required, *figure 50.*

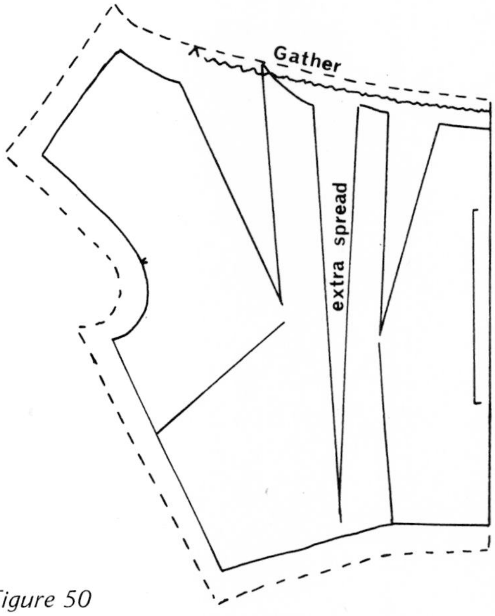

Figure 50

Redraw the pattern on fresh paper, and add seam allowances to finish the pattern piece. Record the notches, and indicate that the gathering is arranged from the notch through the centre front.

CENTRE FRONT GATHERS

Here a centre front seam is used, with gathering at the bust area instead of darts.

Figure 51

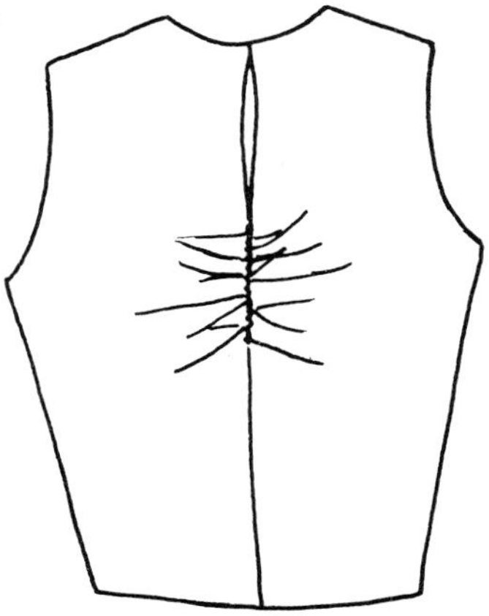

Draw around the front block, marking the shoulder dart and underbust dart. Cut this out. From a position marked on the centre front, 2cm above the underarm line, draw a line to the bust point or the apex of the shoulder dart. Draw a second line from a position marked on the centre front, 6cm below the underarm line, to the apex of the underbust dart. Mark a grain line between the side seam and the underbust dart parallel to the centre front as shown. This grain line is marked at this stage because the centre front is to be reshaped to a curve and because it is essential that the true grain be retained around the scye area.

Figure 52

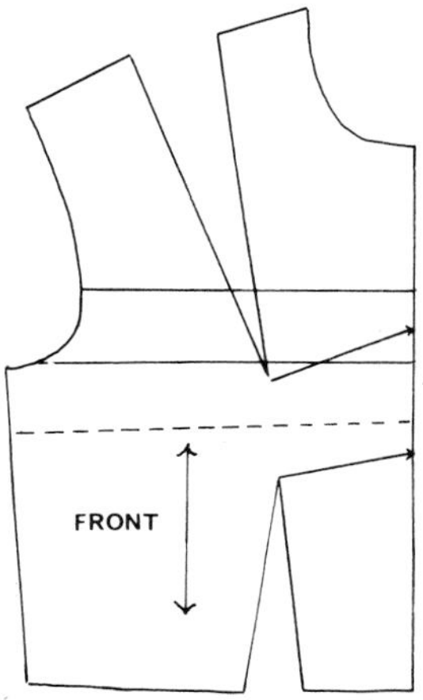

Cut along the two lines from the centre front to within 0.2cm of the apex of the darts. Close the shoulder dart and underbust dart to create fullness at the centre front.

If a greater amount of gathering is required, a line may be cut from the centre front to within 0.2cm of the side seam (broken line). This may then be opened giving extra length to the centre front.

Figure 53

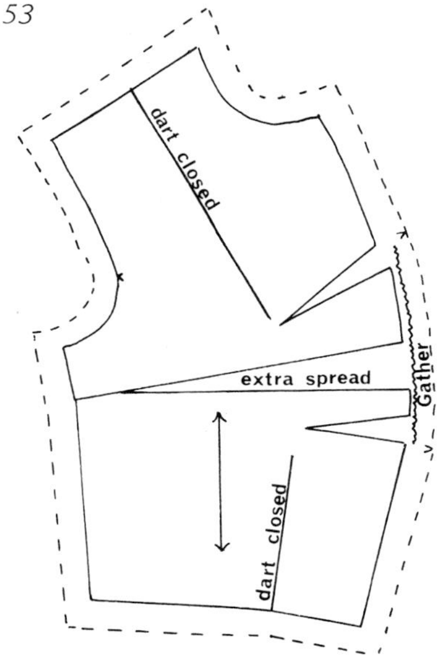

Redraw the outline onto fresh paper, and reshape the centre front at the gathering area. Record the grain line and use notches to mark the position of gathers. Finally add seam allowances.

When gathered, the centre front length should be the same as the length on the original foundation block.

THREE

Facings

The finish of the neck line plays an important part in designing. The neck line may be cut to almost any shape and may be faced; alternatively a collar may be used.

ROUND NECK LINES
This round neck is suitable for a pinafore dress. Because this is a sleeveless bodice, the armhole facing is cut in one piece together with the neck facing.

Figure 54

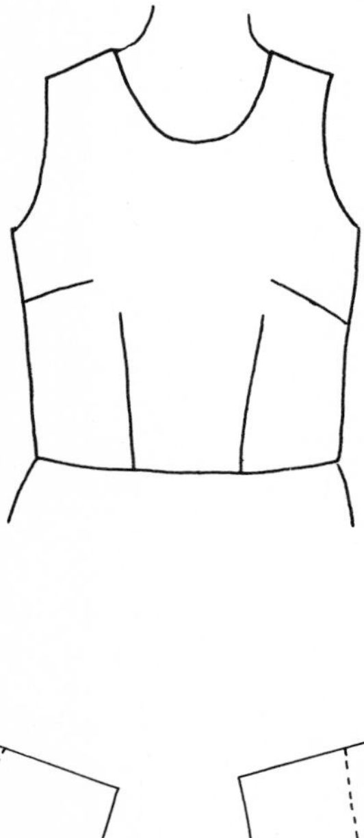

Figure 55

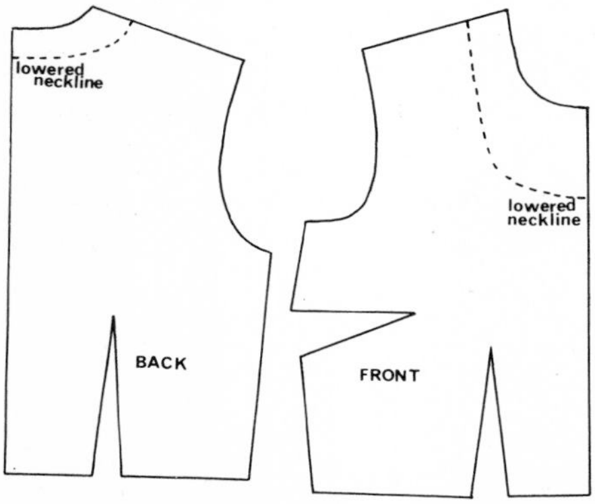

Mark the desired neck line shape on the back and front bodice block. Ensure that the new shapes are both the same distance from the neck point along the shoulder line.

Trace off the main pieces, and add seam allowances to complete the patterns. On these completed pattern pieces, mark the outline of the facings (broken line). The facings should be approximately 5cm wide plus seam allowances.

Figure 56

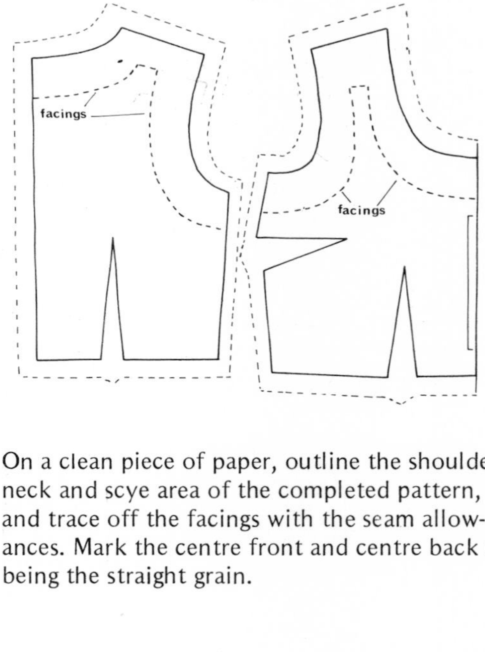

On a clean piece of paper, outline the shoulder, neck and scye area of the completed pattern, and trace off the facings with the seam allowances. Mark the centre front and centre back as being the straight grain.

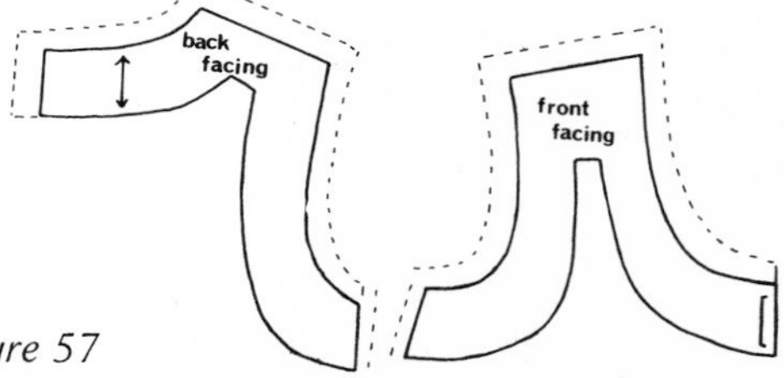

Figure 57

V-SHAPED FRONT NECK LINE

This is a V-shaped front neck line with a round back neckline. The line is cut away from the neck slightly.

Figure 58

As before, draw the shape required onto the back and front blocks, ensuring that both the back and front lines are the correct distance from the neck point.

Trace off the main pieces, and add the seam allowances to complete the pattern pieces.

On the completed pattern, mark in the lines of the facings. This style is intended to have a sleeve inserted—therefore only neck facings are required.

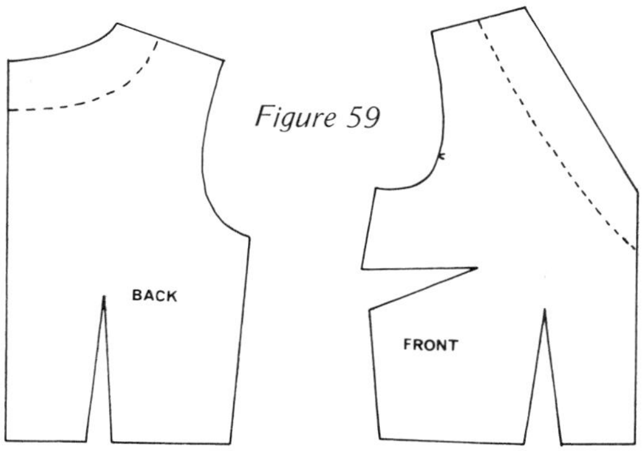

Figure 59

Using the completed pattern as a template, outline the neck and shoulder area, and trace off the facings, with the grain lines and seam allowances.

Figure 60

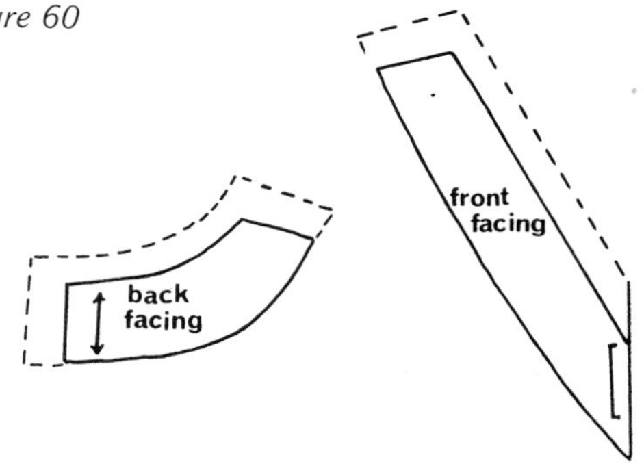

FRONT OPENING

Where a dress has a front opening, the neck and front facings are cut all in one piece.

Figure 61

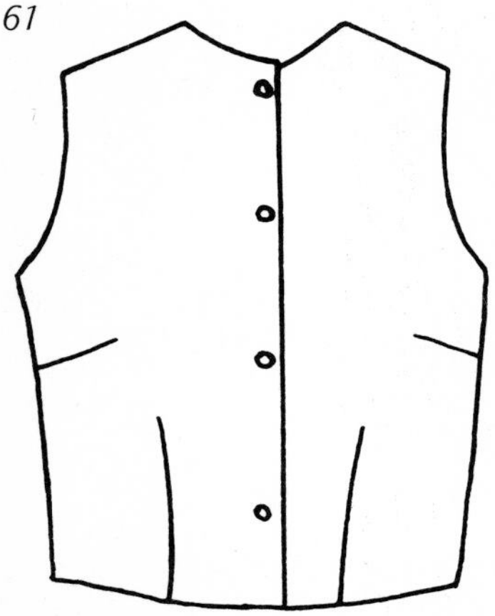

Draw around the front bodice block. Extend the front for button clearance. This clearance should be measured with regard to the diameter of the intended button, so that, when the button is placed on the centre front, half the amount is clear, i.e. if a 2cm button is to be used, then 2cm must be added for clearance. On a single-breasted dress the button should be sewn on at the centre front position.

Figure 62

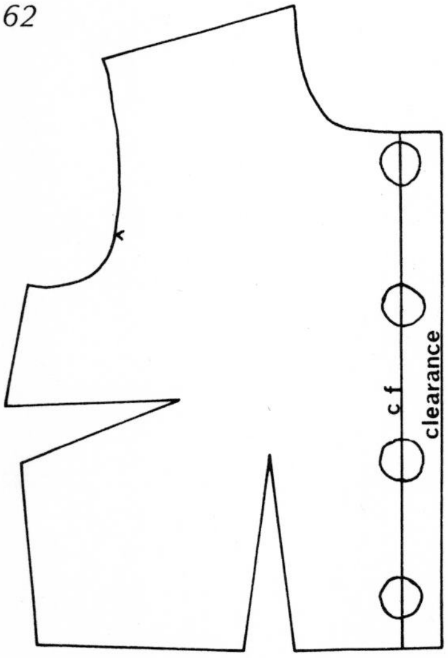

Add seam allowances to finish the pattern piece. Record the centre front position, and mark the button hole positions. On the finished pattern mark in the facing line; bring this line at least 5cm to the left of the centre front to allow for the button holes, *figure 63*.

Figure 63

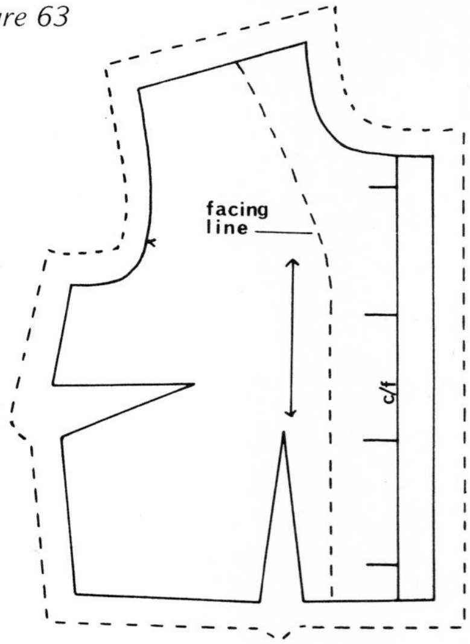

Using the pattern as a template, outline the neck, shoulder and front, and trace off the facing with seam allowances, *figure 64.*

Figure 64

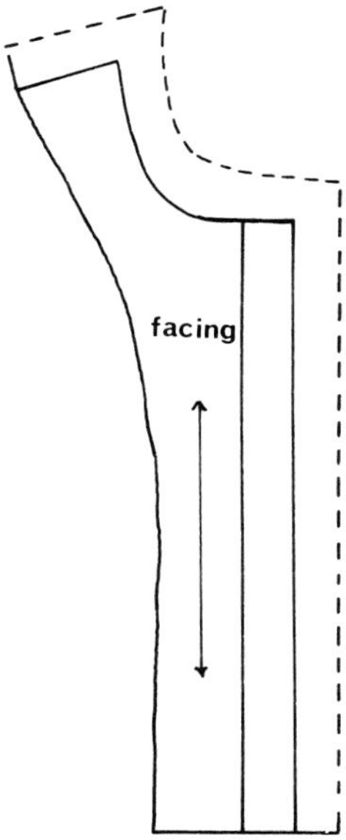

A better effect is sometimes created if the facing is built on—avoiding a seam at the clearance area. To obtain this pattern, space must be available to the right of the centre front after clearance has been added. The paper is then folded along the clearance line underneath the pattern, enabling the facing line (broken line) to be traced through with the use of a tracing wheel. The pattern is then opened out and is cut along the perforations, *figure 65.*

Figure 65

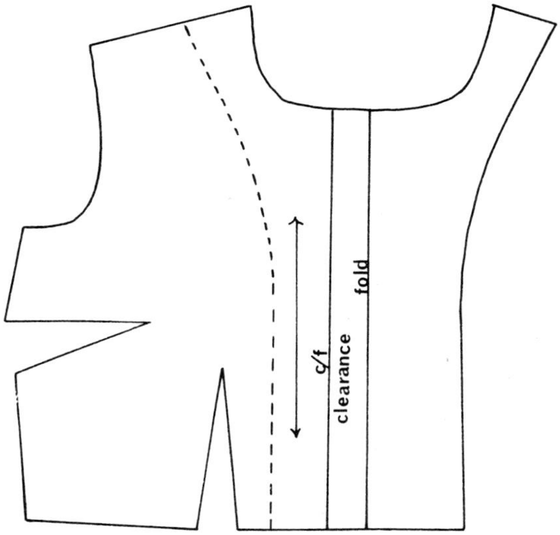

FOUR

Collars

When a collar is used by the dress designer, it is usually intended that this feature should be a focal point of the garment. Many women have personal reasons for preferring a collar—to disguise a long thin neck, to hide tell-tale age lines, to detract from broad shoulders or for extra warmth around the throat, to name but a few.

The shapes and type of collars change frequently according to fashion trends, but the main principles and cutting techniques remain the same. The inner edge of the collar, which is sewn to the neck edge of the garment, must measure the same as the neck line of the bodice. However, this inner edge need not necessarily be the same shape as the neck outline. The shape of the outer edge determines the set of the collar and the amount of roll. This outer edge is called the fall edge. If the fall edge fits around the body area, lying flat over the back, shoulder and front of the body, this is a flat collar. However, if the outer circumference of the collar is shortened, tightening the fall edge around the body, the collar will be forced to a new level, and an amount of stand or roll will be created at the neck area.

Before constructing a collar, adjust the neck line of the bodice to accommodate a collar. The amount of adjustment is dependent upon the type of collar and whether it is intended to fit close to the neck or stand away. The bodice is cut to fit comfortably around the base of the neck; therefore for a flat collar or close-fitting collar it should only be necessary to drop the centre front by about 1cm and to take off approximately 0.5cm at the neck point, the centre back remaining unchanged. For a stand-away collar 2 to 3cm may be taken off at the neck point, and the line may be reshaped accordingly.

FLAT COLLAR

To construct a flat collar, place the back and front bodice blocks together at the neck point. Overlap the shoulder line at the shoulder point by 3cm. If this amount is not taken out, the collar will not lie flat against the body in wear. Lower the neck edge of the collar by 1cm at the centre front. Decide upon the desired depth of the collar, and measure guide lines from the neck edge as shown (8cm in this example).

Figure 66

Draw in the fall edge of the collar as shown by the broken line, and mark a notch at the shoulder position. Mark the centre back on the collar piece, *figure 67.*

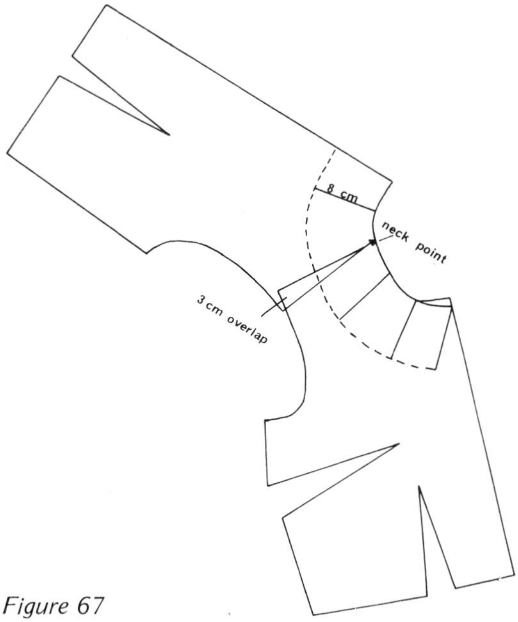

Figure 67

Trace off this collar, recording the notch and the centre back. Add seam allowances and cutting instructions to complete the pattern. Centre back is the straight grain and should be placed to the fold. A top collar and under collar will be required.

Figure 68

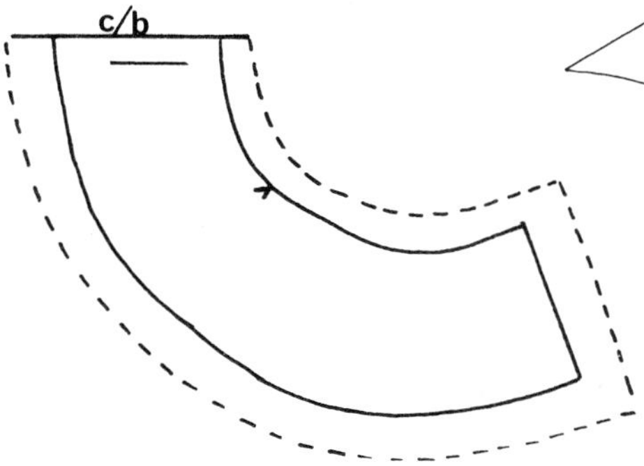

To achieve a more rolled effect from the flat collar, draw around the collar, and add 2cm to the fall edge to allow for stand. Slash the collar from the fall edge to within 0.2cm of the neck edge, in four places.

Overlap each of these cut lines by 2cm to shorten the fall edge and to change the shape but not the size of the neck edge. Redraw this new shape, and add seam allowances to finish the collar, *figure 69.*

Figure 69

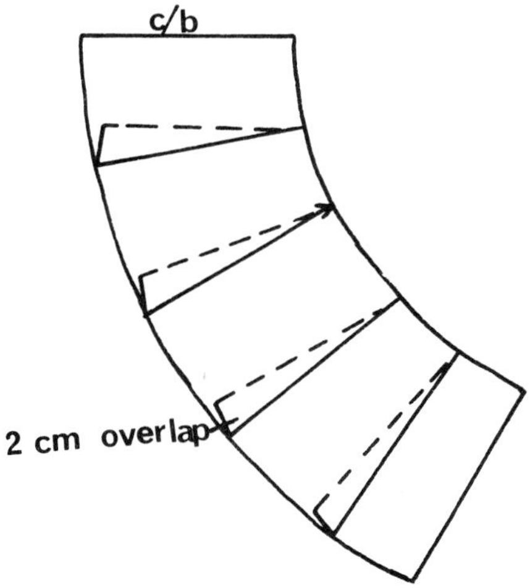

The fall edge of this collar may be cut to any desired shape as illustrated.

Figure 70

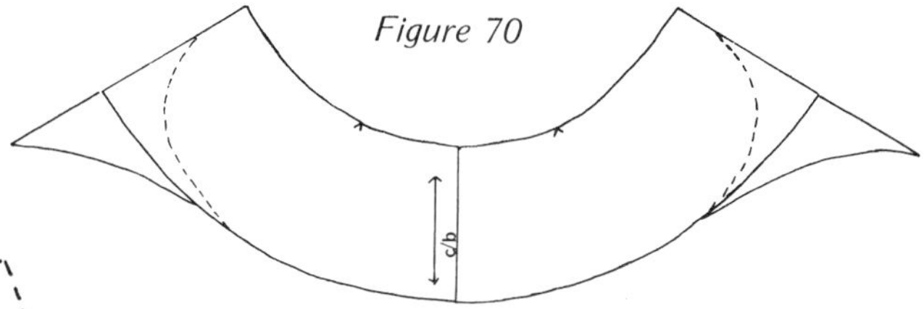

V-SHAPED COLLAR

Using the same basic principles as for the flat collar, it is possible to cut collars to fit V-shaped neck lines.

Arrange the back and front blocks to meet at the neck point, and overlap at the shoulder point. Decide upon the depth of the V neck, and redraw the neck edge, widening this slightly. Add the necessary button clearance to the front bodice, and draw in the collar shape as shown by a broken line.

Trace off the collar, and add seam allowances. Record the centre back and the notch. For a more rolled effect, cut from the fall edge to within 0.2cm of the neck edge, and overlap to shorten the fall as previously described.

Figure 71

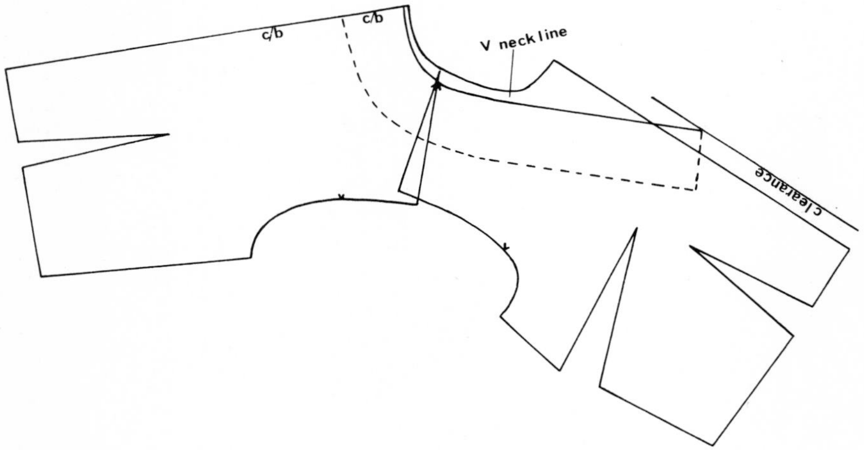

SAILOR-TYPE COLLAR

A sailor-type collar with a V front is cut on the same principle.

Figure 72

Arrange the bodice blocks as before. Draw in the shape of the required collar, adjusting the neck line accordingly. Notch the collar at the shoulder, and mark the centre back.

Figure 73

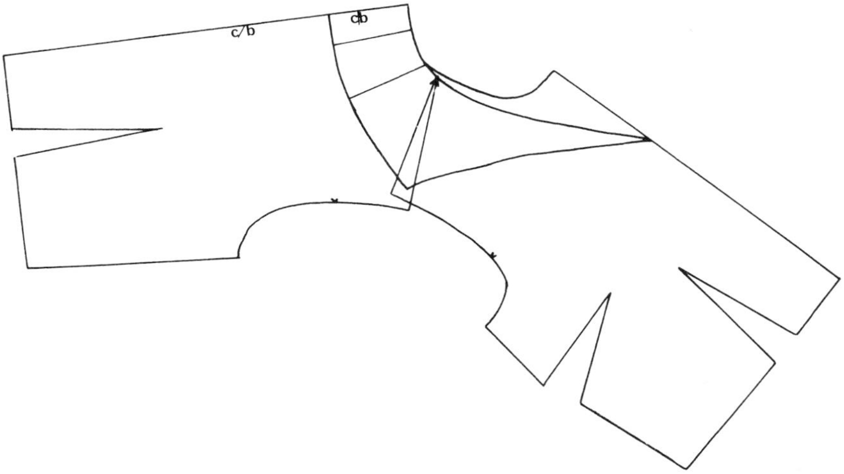

Trace off and cut out the collar; then cut from the fall edge to within 0.2cm of the back neck in two places as shown, and overlap as described before. This is to create a slight tightness across the back and thus to achieve a back neck roll. Reshape the fall edge if necessary.

Figure 74

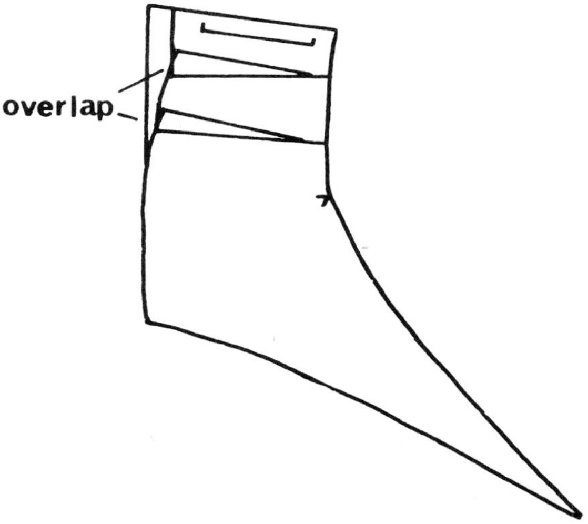

STRAIGHT SHIRT COLLAR WITH A GROWN-ON STAND

Figure 75 is a straight shirt collar with a grown-on stand.

Figure 75

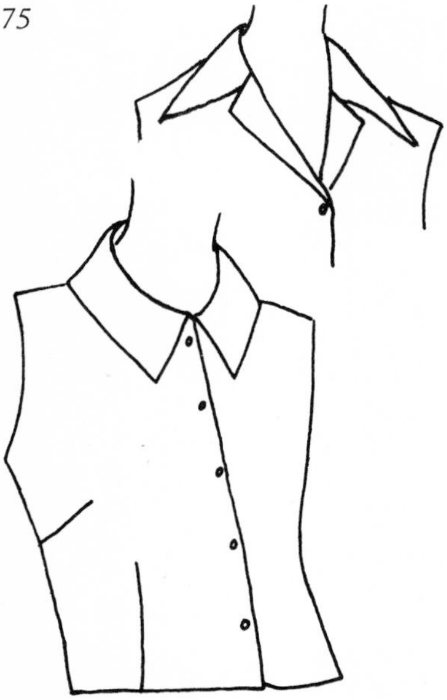

Draw around the front bodice block, and add the required button clearance. Lower the front neck slightly to allow the collar stand to fit comfortably. Draw a line from the centre front to the neck point; this is the crease line. Fold along this line, and trace the front neck curve, transferring this curve to the right-hand side as shown by the broken line.

Extend the crease line beyond the neck point to measure half the back neck circumference (take this measurement from the back bodice pattern). Draw a line at right angles to the crease line, measuring 3cm to the right for the stand and 5.5cm to the left for the fall. Draw in the desired shape of the fall. For this example, the bold line is used and the other lines are intended as suggestions only. Connect the centre back stand to the curved broken line as shown.

Figure 76

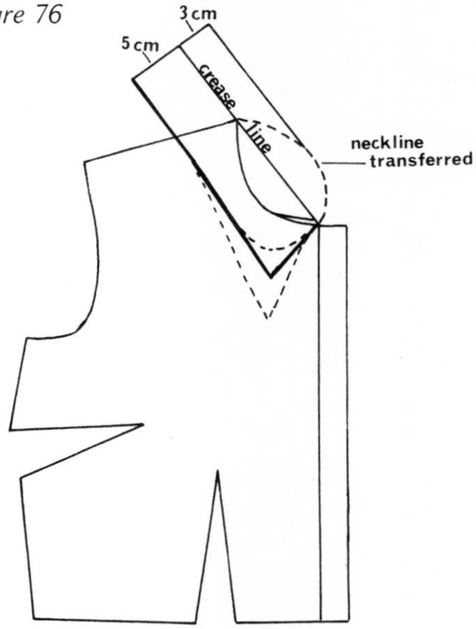

Trace off the collar piece, recording the crease line. Reshape the centre back of this collar, taking 0.5cm away from the neck edge, *figure 77*.

Figure 77

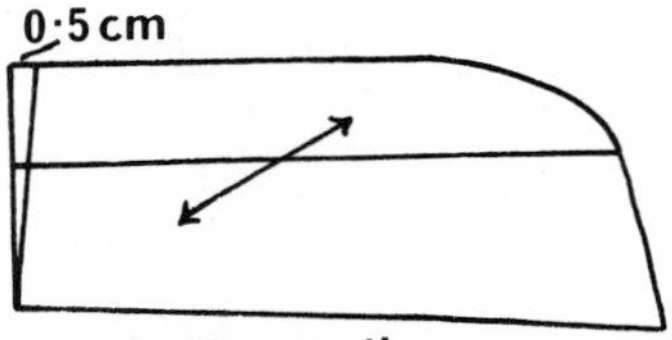

Under Collar

Add seam allowances to complete the collar pieces. A top and an under collar will need to be cut. The under collar may be cut on the bias with a back seam allowance, but the top collar should be cut without a seam.

This is a useful collar and may be worn with or without a neck fastening.

Figure 78

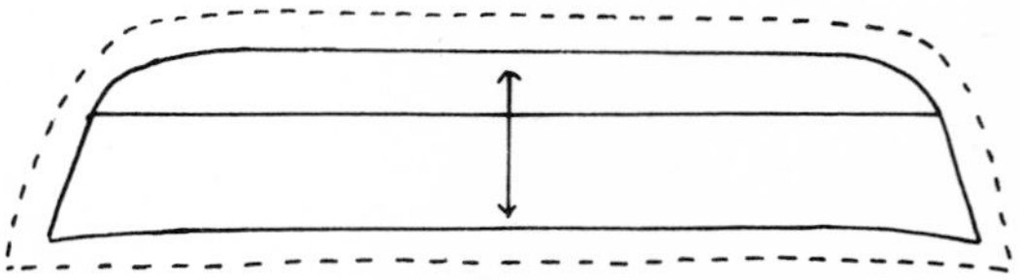

Top Collar

REVERS

A rever is part of the front bodice which is usually faced and turned back along the crease line. The shape and size of a rever varies according to vogue, but, as with collars, the construction techniques change very little.

Figure 79

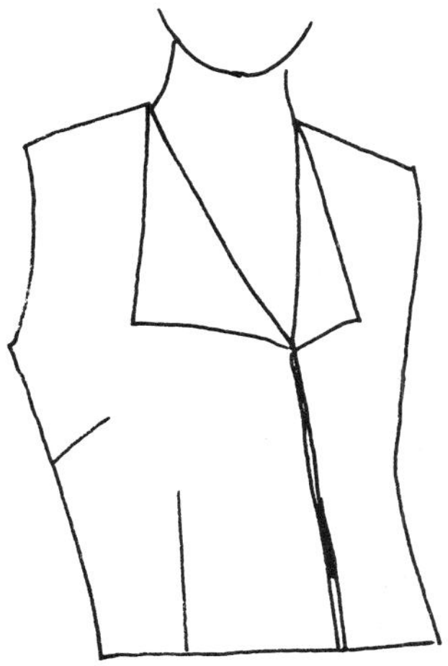

To construct the style illustrated, draw around the front bodice block. Adjust the neck line to a V front, and draw in the shape required for the rever. Mark the crease row along the V front.

Figure 80

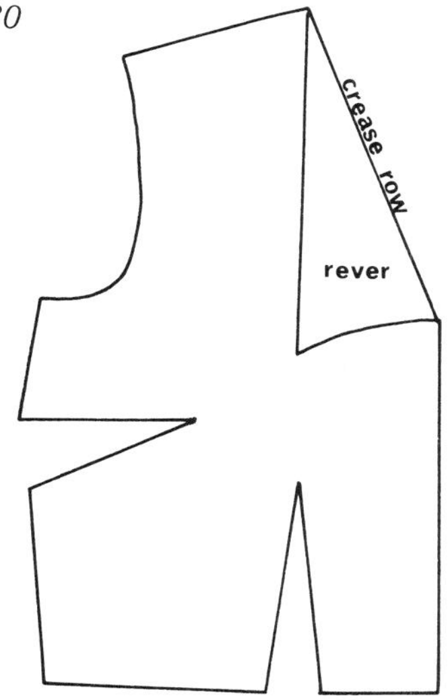

Have sufficient paper on the right-hand side to fold along the crease row underneath the drawn rever outline. Trace off the rever shape, thus transferring the rever to the right-hand side, *figure 81*. Add seam allowances to complete this pattern piece.

Figure 81

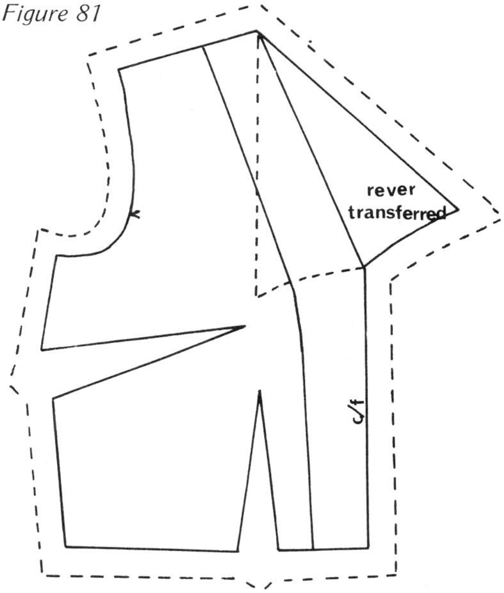

This rever, which is built onto the bodice, will form the under part when it is folded back. A top rever, therefore, should be cut together with the facing. To do this, mark the facing edge, and trace off the rever and facing in the usual way.

Figure 82

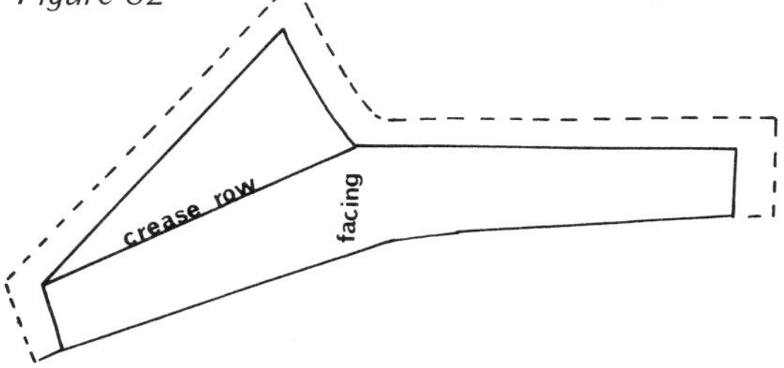

Record the crease row on the top rever and facing piece. A zip fastener may be inserted in this style for a centre front opening.

SHAWL-TYPE COLLAR

This is a shawl-type collar which has revers and includes a back collar. The rever and back collar are built onto the front bodice and are faced for a top collar.

Figure 83

Draw round the front bodice block. Adjust the neck to a V front, and add the button clearance. Place the back block to the front at the neck point, overlapping at the shoulder point by 3cm. Widen the neck by approximately 1.5cm. Draw in the required collar shape, marking the crease row and notch at the neck point.

Figure 84

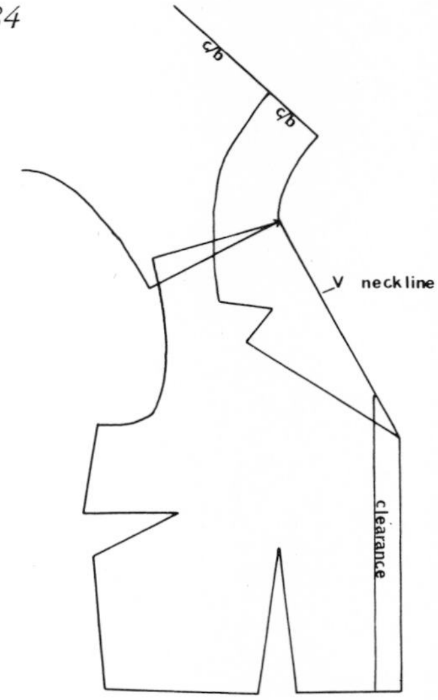

Trace off the rever and back collar, recording the notch and crease row (*figure 85*), then place the crease row of the rever onto the V front of the main bodice (matching the neck point notches). Transfer the outline of the rever and collar to the right of the bodice, *figure 86.*

Figure 85

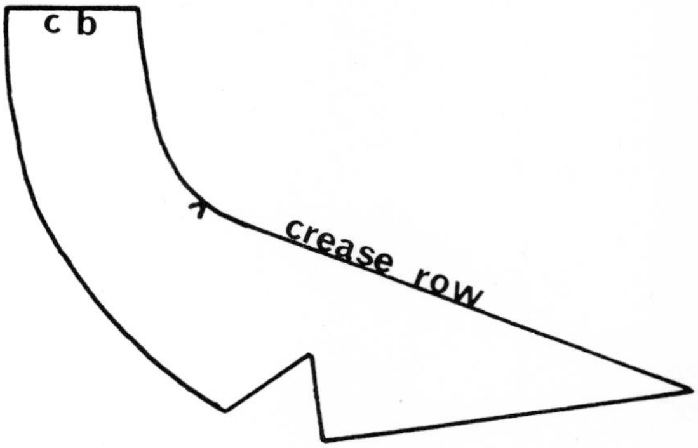

Figure 86

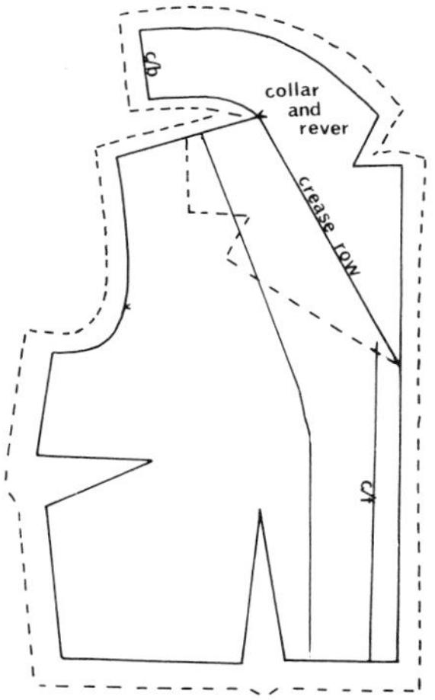

Where a more rolled effect is desired, the fall edge of the back collar may be shortened before placing this against the crease row. To do this, make two cuts from the fall edge to the neck edge, and overlap these cuts by 2cm. An amount may also be taken off the centre back. Reshape the fall edge slightly. The neck edge of this collar must remain the same size and only the shape should be altered. As the neck edge of the collar is sewn to the bodice, the fall edge will find its own level and will automatically create a back stand.

Various shapes may be constructed by this method. It is just a matter of drawing in the correct rever shape at the first stage.

Mark the outline for the front facing, and trace off the collar, rever and facing piece. Add seam allowances to bodice pattern piece and facing pattern piece. Record notches, crease rows and centre fronts on both pattern pieces. The centre back of the collar should be placed to the fold when cutting to avoid a seam in the top collar.

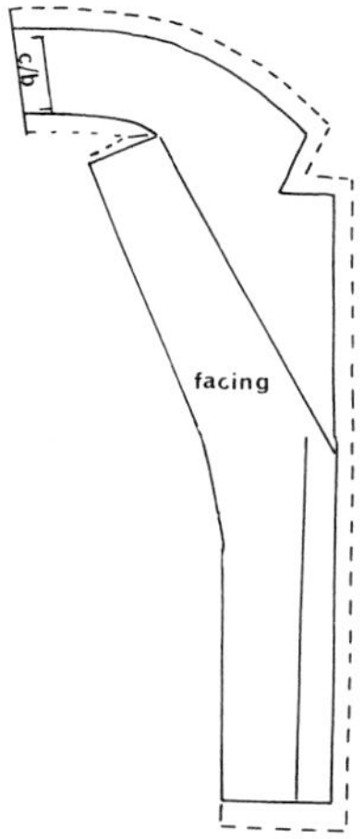

Figure 87

Figure 88

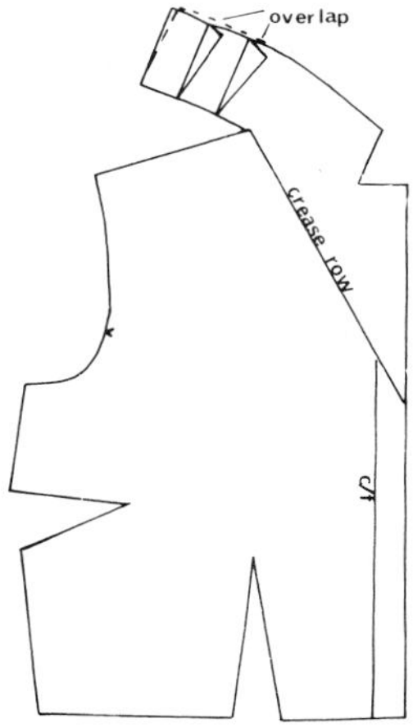

COLLAR WITH A FLARED OR FLOUNCED EFFECT

The examples of collars on the previous pages have had a roll or stand produced by shortening the fall edge. It is possible to reverse this and to create a flared or flounced effect by lengthening the fall edge.

Figure 89

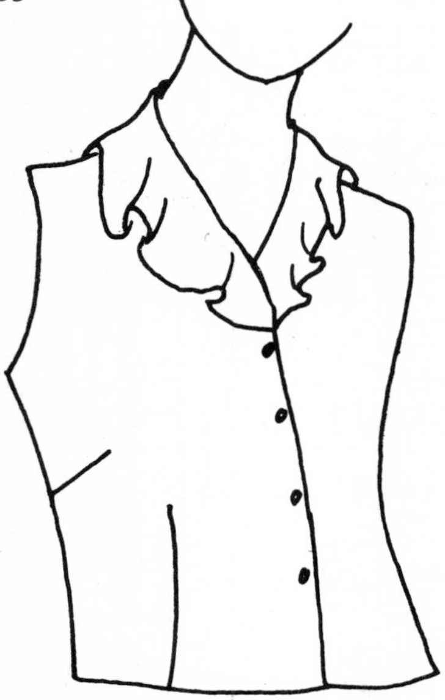

Figure 90

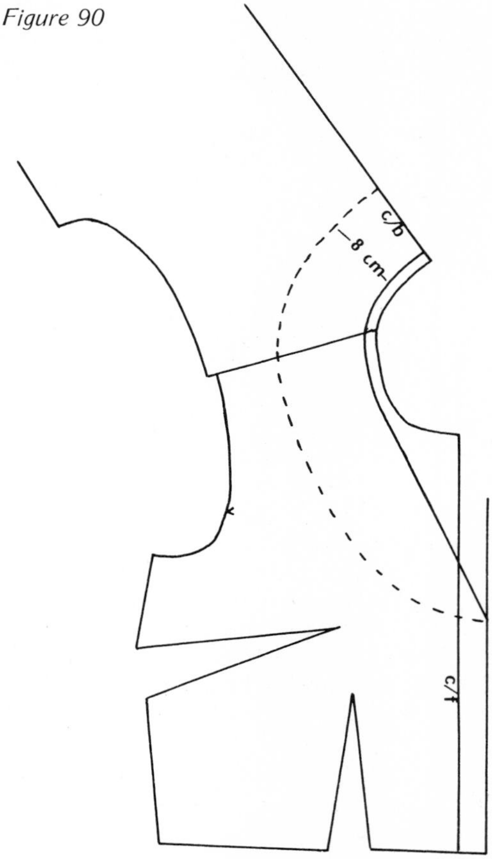

Place the back and front blocks together along the shoulder line. It is not necessary to overlap the shoulder points for the style. Widen the neck and adjust the front to a V, incorporating a front clearance. Draw in the collar shape required; the example here is 8cm deep at the centre back.

Figure 91 *The author with a student discussing the amount of flare required in the collar*

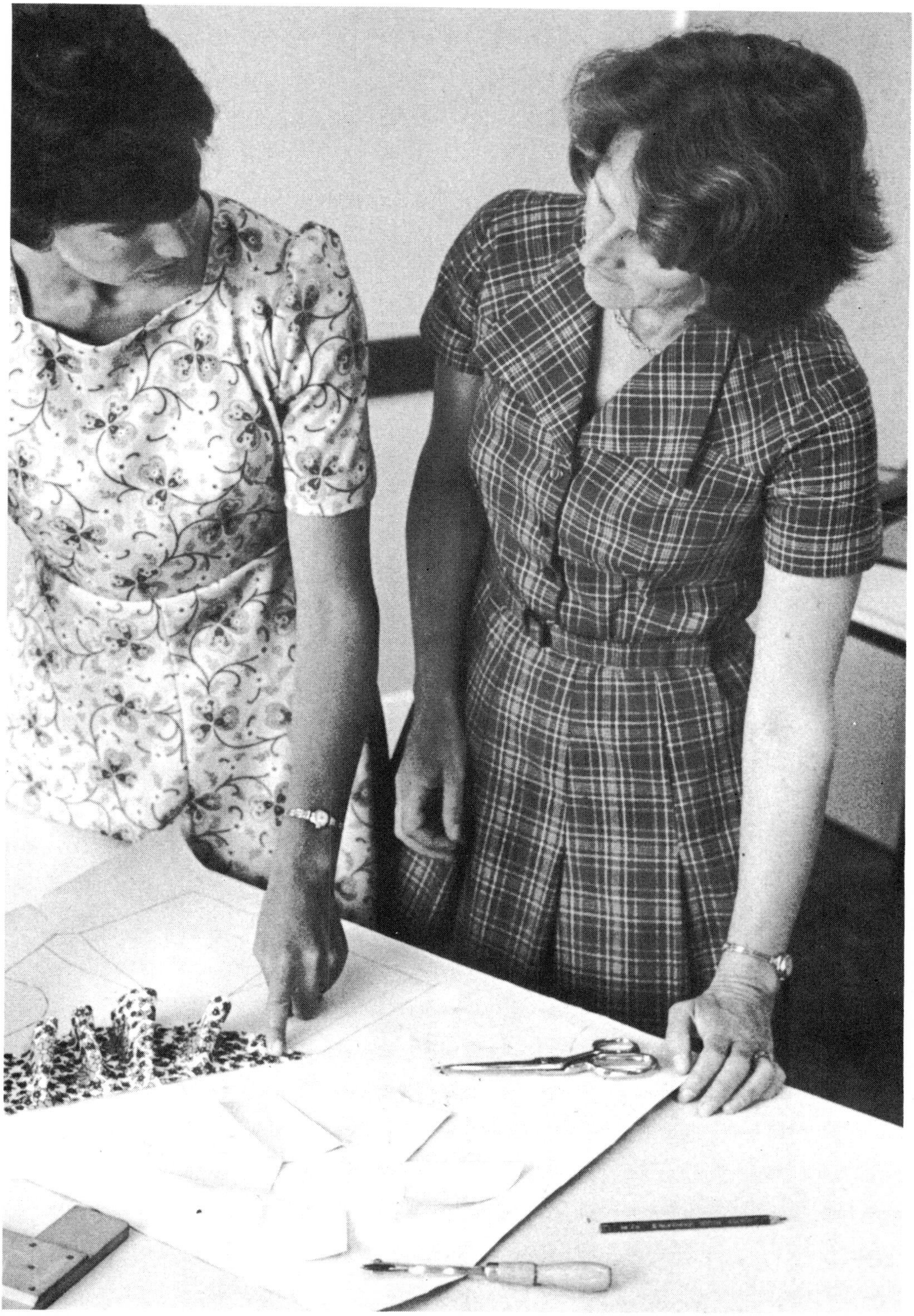

Figure 92

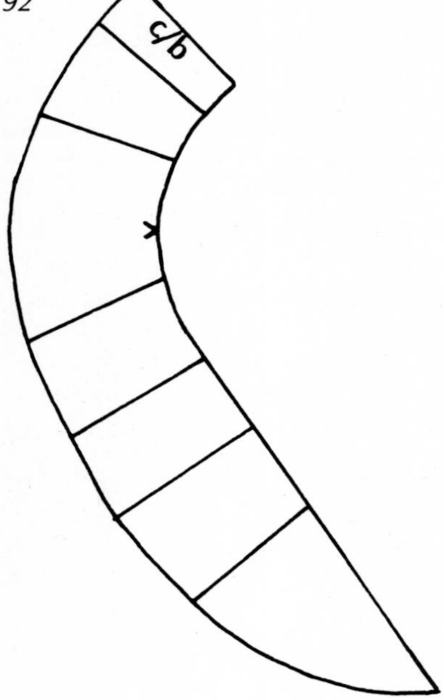

Trace off the collar, recording the neck point notch. Draw in about six lines, avoiding the shoulder line as shown, and cut this out. Cut each line from the fall edge to within 0.2cm of the neck edge. Now spread the pattern piece, allowing approximately 4cm to 5cm at each cut, and with the aid of pins redraw this. Record the centre back position and the neck point notch.

Figure 93

Finally add seam allowances to the finished pattern piece.

Figure 94

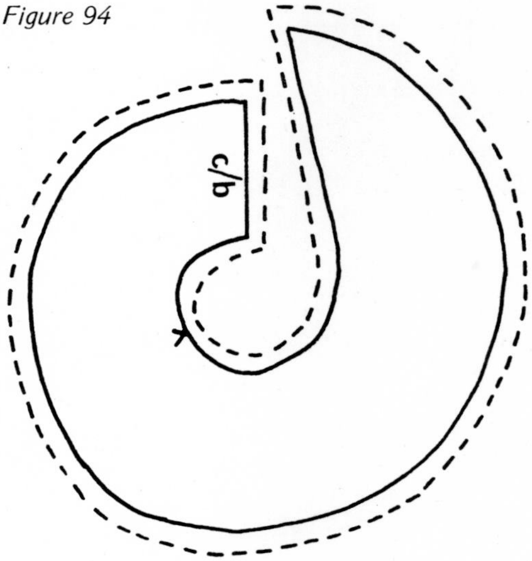

When the neck edge of the collar, which still measures the same as the bodice, is sewn to the bodice, the fall edge will fold into gentle flounces. It will of course be necessary to have a centre back seam in this collar.

FIVE

Sleeves

STRAIGHT SLEEVE

The straight sleeve may be made up using the elbow dart as originally planned. Alternatively the dart may be omitted, and the back part of the sleeve may be eased onto the front within the elbow region.

Another variation is to transfer the dart from the elbow to the back wrist position. From a point approximately 10cm from the back, draw in a line from the wrist to the apex of the elbow dart. Cut along this line to within 0.2cm of the dart apex. Close the elbow dart, opening up the wrist dart, *figure 95.* If a small wrist measurement is required, a greater amount may be taken out at the dart.

To shorten the straight sleeve block, measure down the underarm seams for the length required, and connect with a straight line. The example used is 6cm for the underarm length. Measure 2cm, from the line, up the centre line towards the crown height, and connect this point to the side seam with a suitable curve, *figure 96.*

Trace off the new shortened sleeve. It is useful to have a short sleeve block cut in card as it is frequently used.

Figure 95

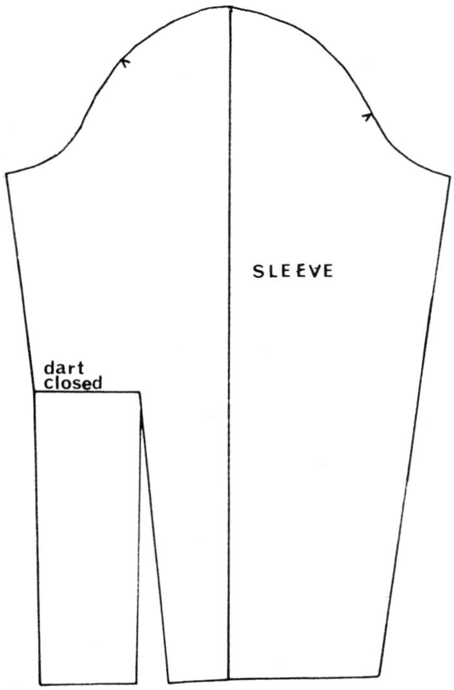

Figure 96

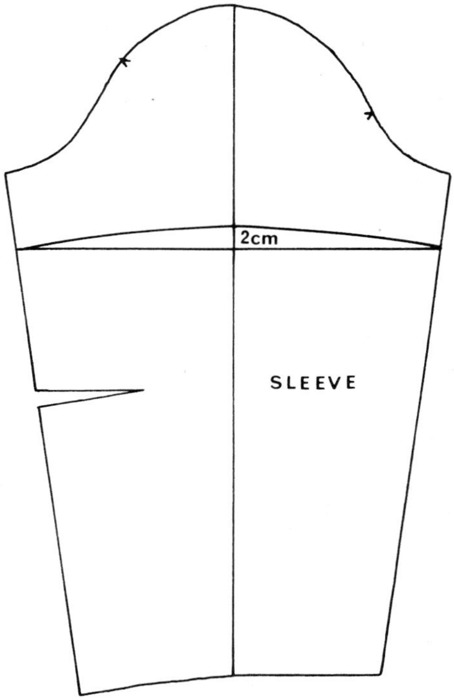

TWO-PIECE SLEEVE

A two-piece sleeve has the shaping incorporated in the seams, dispensing with the need for a dart at the elbow or the wrist. The sleeve comprises an under piece and upper piece, the under piece being the smaller of the two. These pieces are so shaped that, when joined to form the complete sleeve, the sleeve swings slightly forwards, in keeping with the natural arm position.

To construct the two-piece sleeve, copy the straight sleeve, and cut this out. The dart of the straight sleeve may be virtually disregarded, except for giving guidance to the elbow position. The 2cm added to the back sleeve length to allow for the dart may be removed. The wrist line therefore should be at right angles to the centre line running from the crown height to the wrist.

Fold the underarm seams (1 to 7 and 2 to 6 on the block) inwards to meet along the centre line. Draw a line across the folded sleeve at the elbow level, and, at this stage, mark the centre line above the elbow line as being the straight grain. The sleeve head balance notches must also be recorded now.

Measure 3cm inwards from the fold line around the sleeve head as shown in *figure 97*, and measure 2cm from the fold at the wrist, this too being shown in *figure 97*. Connect these points to mark the outline of the under sleeve, as illustrated by the broken line.

Cut the elbow line through the folded 'back' line to within 0.2cm of the 'front' folded line.

Figure 97

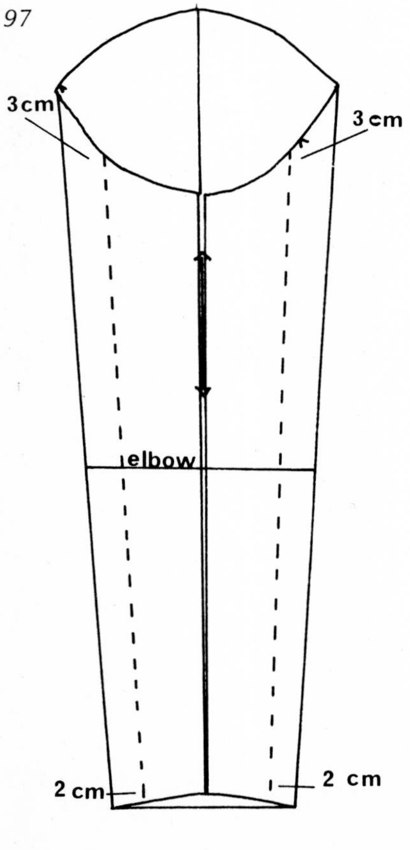

Figure 98

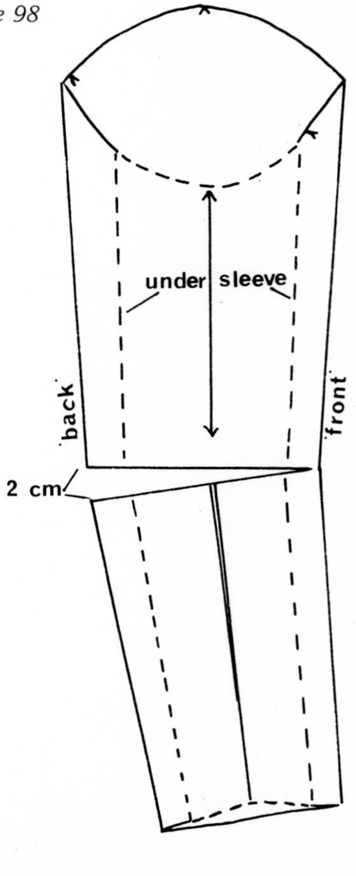

Place this sleeve over a clean sheet of paper, and spread the sleeve, opening the back line by 2cm. Now trace off the under sleeve recording the centre line as the grain line, *figure 99.*

Having traced off the under sleeve, return to the folded sleeve, and cut away the under sleeve piece, leaving the upper sleeve. Open out the folded lines, and outline the upper sleeve, being certain that the slash line is open by 2cm at the back fold position, *figure 100.*

Record the grain line and the notches, and add seam allowances to both sleeve pieces.

Figure 99

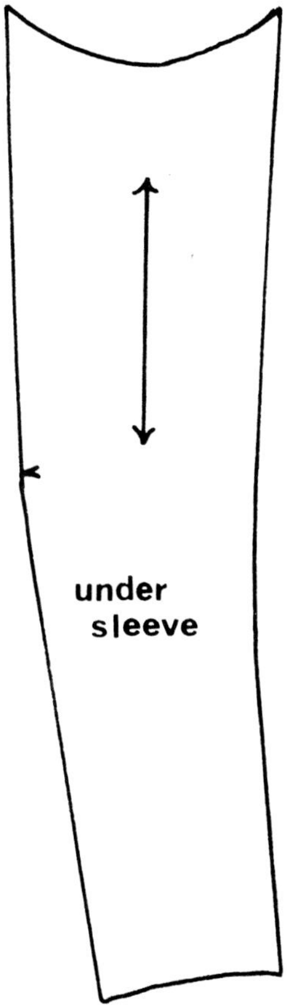

Figure 100

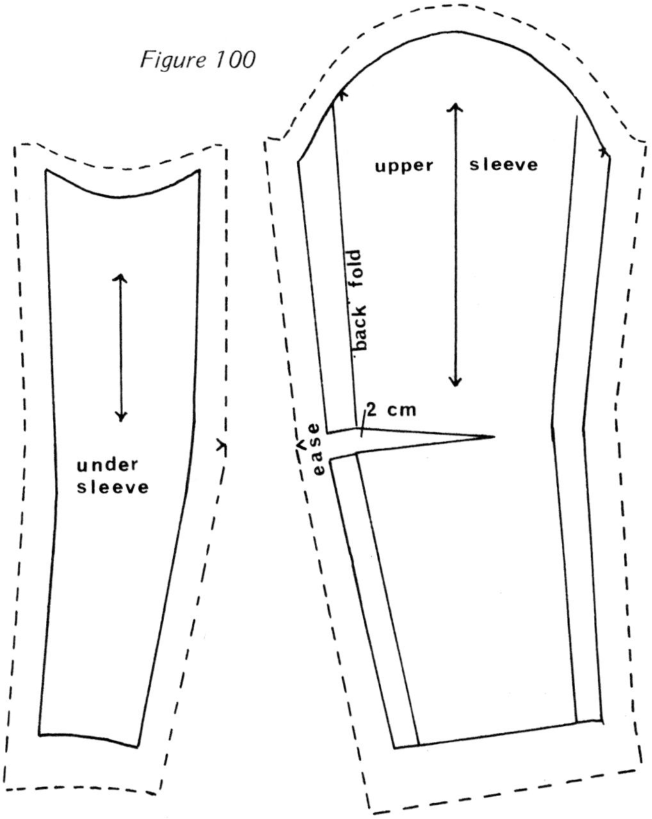

FLARED SHORT SLEEVE

In general the straight sleeve block may be adapted to contend with changing fashion. The first style used to illustrate this is a flared short sleeve, fitted into the armhole without being gathered.

Figure 101

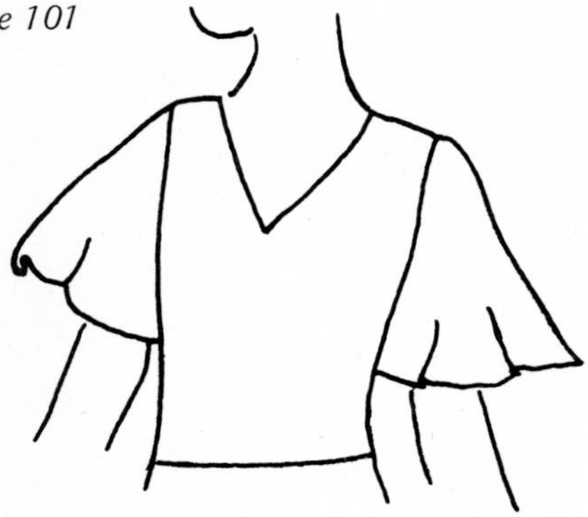

Using the short sleeve block as a template, copy the outline onto a sheet of paper. Mark the notches, and cut this out. Divide the sleeve into four equal sections by drawing three lines from the sleeve head to the lower edge as illustrated, *figure 102.*

Figure 102

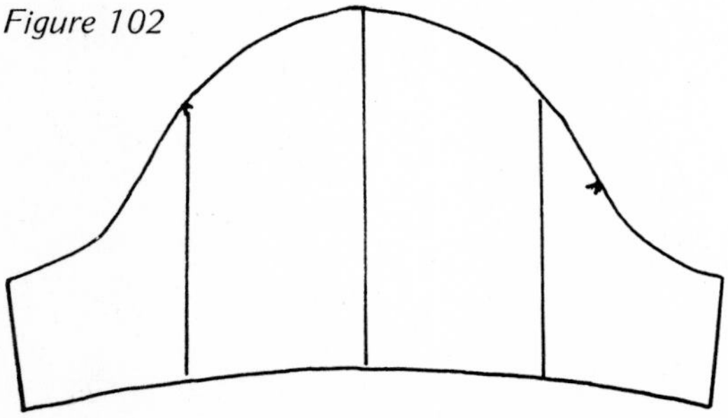

Cut each line from the lower edge to within 0.2cm of the sleeve head. Place this on a clean piece of paper, and spread the lower edge evenly adding the flare required (approximately 8 to 10cm). Copy the outline, and add a small amount to the side seams for extra flare. When spreading the pattern piece, it is advisable to pin each section into position before outlining the flared sleeve.

Figure 103

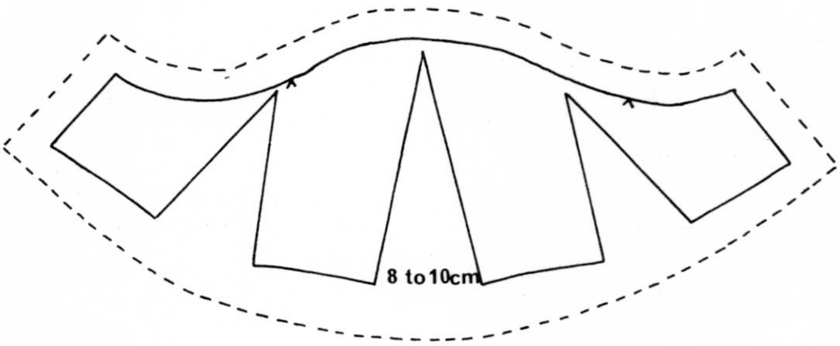

Note that, although the sleeve head shape has been changed, this still measures the same as the block. When it is sewn into the bodice, the lower part of the sleeve will hang in gentle flounces.

Add seam allowances, and record the notches to finish the pattern.

Figure 104 Outlining a flared sleeve

SLEEVE WITH FULLNESS AROUND THE CROWN

Here the sleeve has fullness around the crown but no extra width in the lower part of the sleeve.

Figure 105

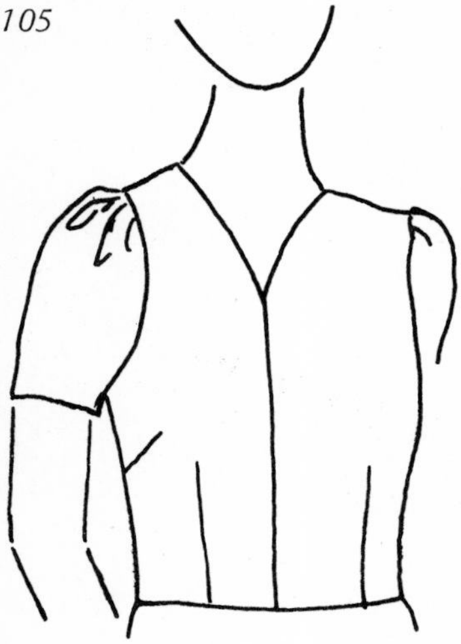

Use the shortened sleeve block, and as before divide the sleeve into four equal sections.

Cut each line from the sleeve head to within 0.2cm of the lower edge. Place this on a clean sheet of paper, spread the sleeve head evenly and draw round the outline. To achieve a more raised crown, add 5cm at the crown height. Form a new outline from this point as illustrated by a broken line, *figure 106.*

Figure 106

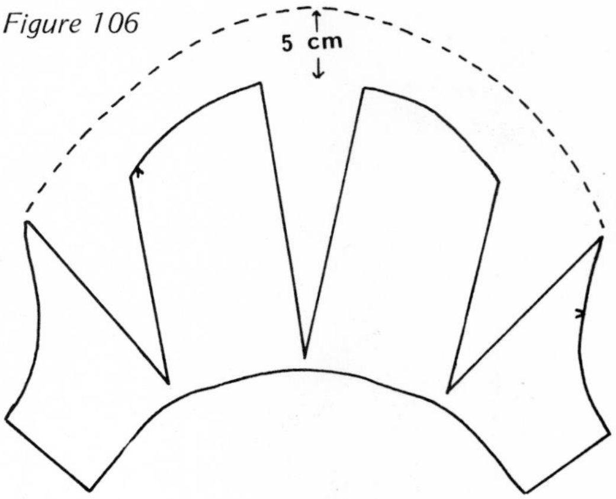

Add seam allowances to the finished pattern, and record the notches. Indicate on the finished pattern that the gathers should be arranged between the left and right slash lines.

Figure 107

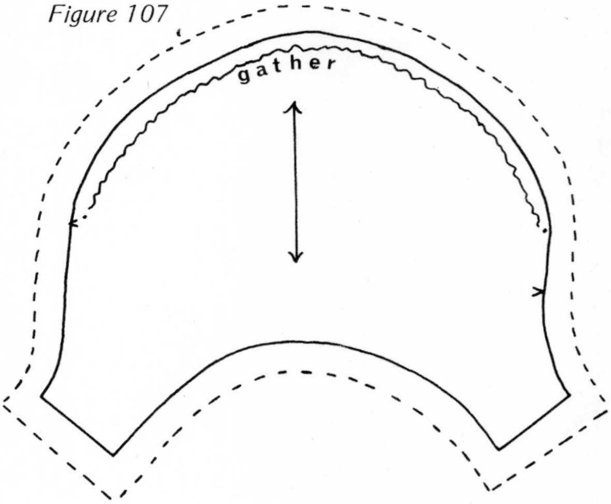

STRAIGHT SLEEVE WITH FLOUNCED CUFF

Interest may be added to the straight sleeve by the addition of a flounced cuff.

Figure 108

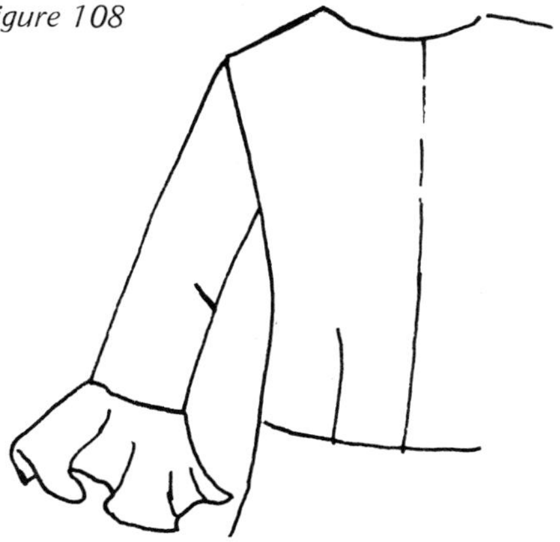

Draw around and cut out the full-length straight sleeve. Draw in the line marking the required depth of the cuff (approximately 12cm). Mark a notch on this line to aid subsequent sewing, and divide the cuff piece into five equal sections as shown.

Figure 109

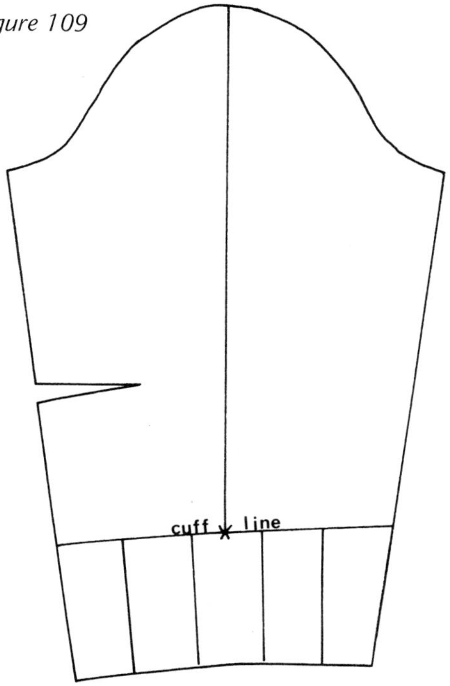

Trace off and cut out the cuff piece. Cut the lines marked on the cuff from the direction of the wrist, to within 0.2cm of the seam line. Place this over a clean sheet of paper, and spread the cuff to obtain the flounced effect. The degree of flare is dependent upon the amount of spread. The example illustrated is almost circular.

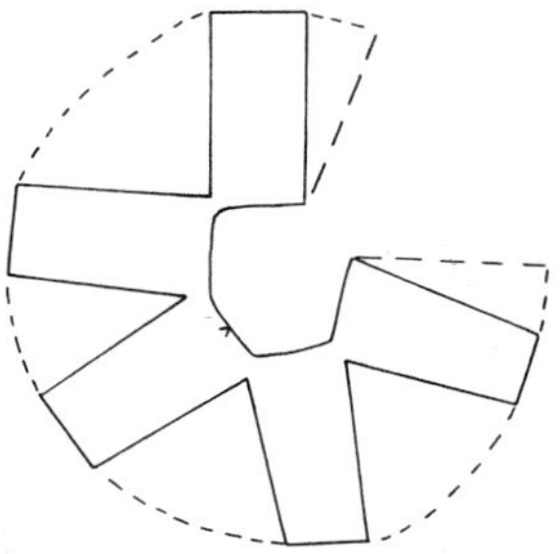

Figure 110

Draw around the new outline of the cuff, and add seam allowances. Add seam allowances to the main sleeve from which the cuff piece was traced. Record the notches on both pieces.

Figure 111

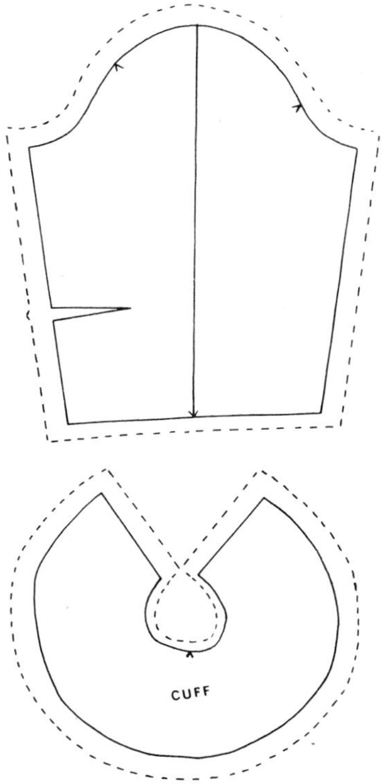

LONG FULL SLEEVE

This long sleeve has fullness at the crown, and at the wrist the fullness is gathered into the cuff.

Figure 112

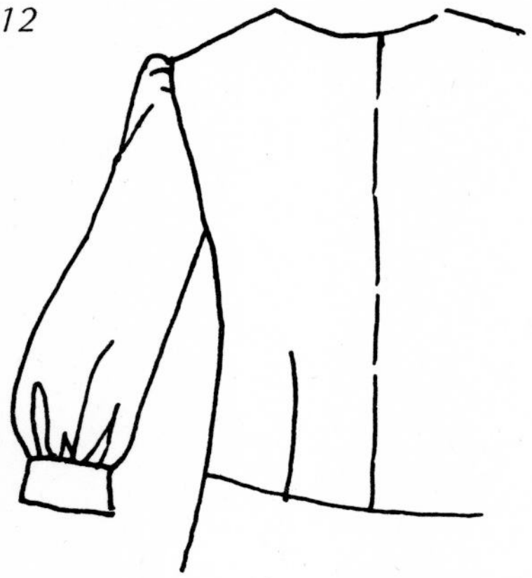

Draw around the full-length sleeve block, and cut this out. Connect the underarm points with a straight line, and divide the sleeve head into four sections, *figure 113.*

Cut down from the crown height to the underarm line, and cut along this line to within 0.2cm of the underarm points. Cut the remaining two lines from the sleeve head towards the horizontally cut line. Spread the crown as illustrated, and redraw the outline, *figure 114.*

Shorten the sleeve to allow for the cuff. Draw a line vertically from the crown height to the wrist line. Decide upon the width required to be gathered into the cuff (approximately 40cm). Divide this width equally either side of the vertical line, and extend the wrist line accordingly. Connect the underarm points to the ends of this lower line with a guide line. To avoid excessive fullness at the upper arm position, reshape the seam as suggested with a curved line. Reshape the lower edge of the sleeve by lengthening the back part by approximately 2cm to allow for contour, *figure 115.*

Mark the position for an opening, and add seam allowances to finish the pattern piece.

The cuff pattern is a rectangle measuring twice the depth of the required cuff by the length of circumference plus overwrap allowances.

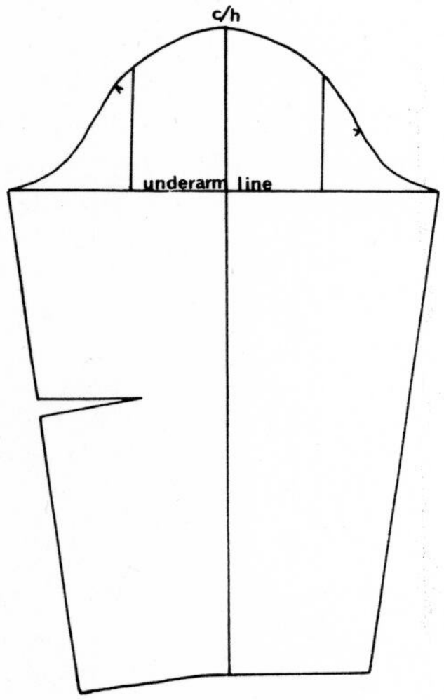

Figure 113

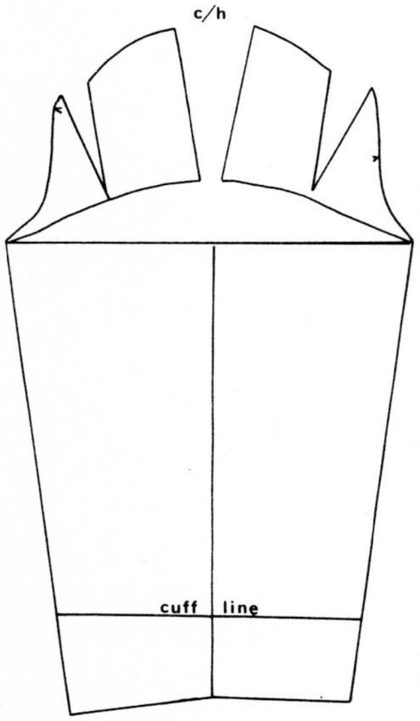

Figure 114

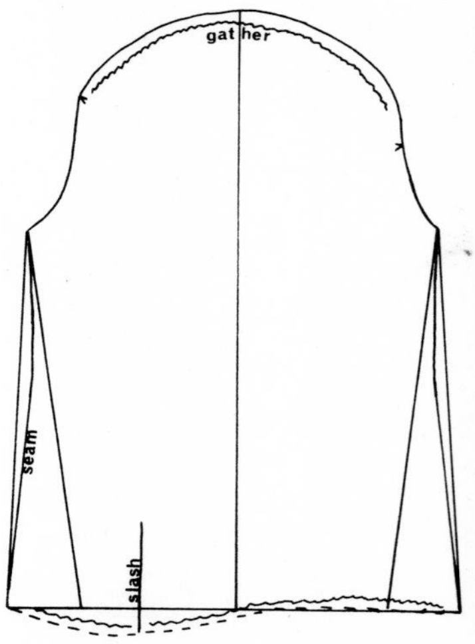

Figure 115

TOP SLEEVE GATHERS
Top sleeve gathers are featured in this style.

Figure 116

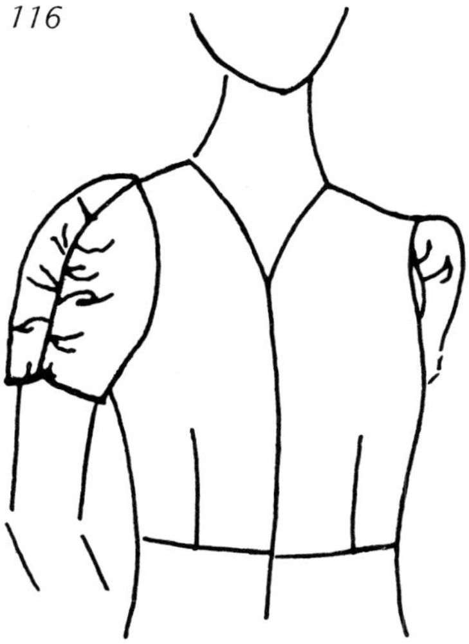

Draw around the short sleeve, marking the notches and the vertical line from the crown height. Cut out the sleeve, and draw three lines across the sleeve as shown.

Figure 117

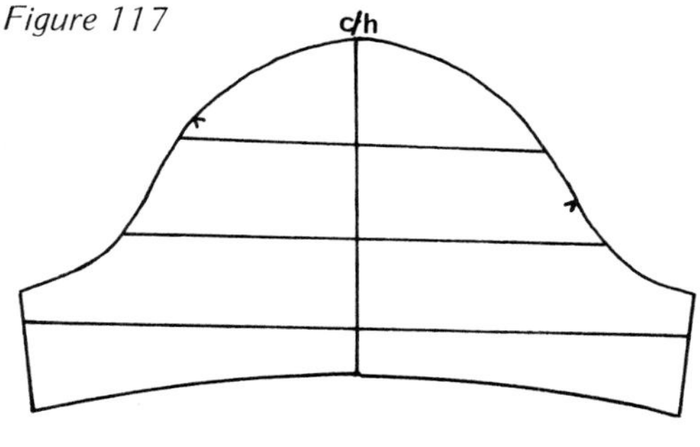

Cut the vertical line from lower edge to within 0.2cm of the crown height; then cut from the vertical line along each horizontal line to within 0.2cm of the sleeve head. Spread the sleeve allowing approximately 4cm at each cut, and with the aid of pins redraw the new shape.

To allow for the fullness along the gathering line, add 4cm at the lower sleeve, and gradually shape this off towards the crown height as shown by a broken line, *figure 118.*

Figure 118

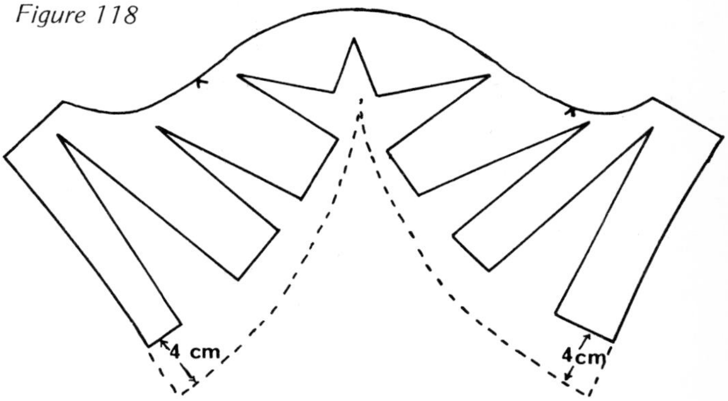

Add seam allowances, and record the notches. Indicate that the gathering runs from the position of the horizontal cut, nearest to the crown height, to the sleeve edge.

Figure 119

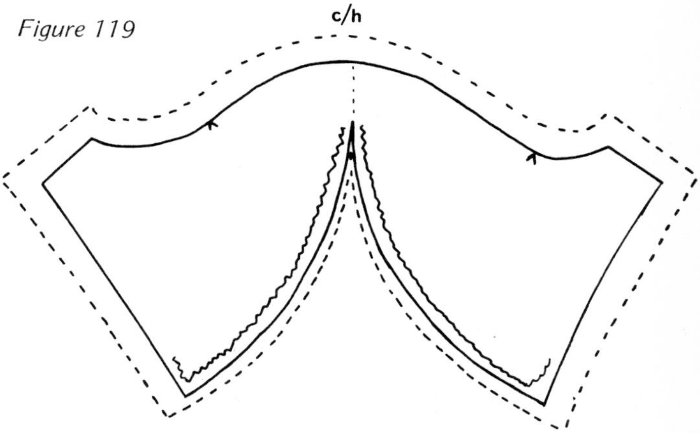

The illustrated sleeve is finished at the edge with a binding strip. To enable this sleeve to be cut more economically in cloth, it could be made into a two-piece sleeve by cutting through the crown height and by adding the necessary seam allowance.

RAGLAN SLEEVE

With a raglan sleeve the shoulder part of the bodice is included in the sleeve head.

Figure 120

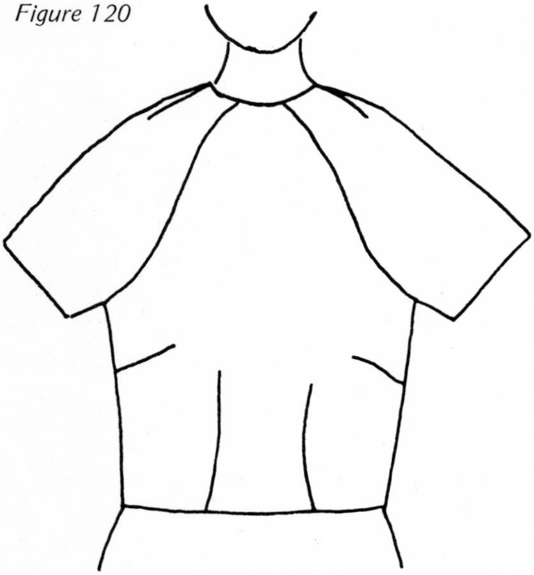

Draw around the back and front bodice blocks. Mark the notches at the scye on the bodice. Starting approximately 3cm from the neck point, draw in the required line for the raglan seam. A curved line is more commonly used for this style, and in the example illustrated it will be noted that the line meets the front scye notch. The back line meets the scye at a point approximately 6cm below the back scye notch. Mark notches across this raglan line about 5cm from the neck—two for the back and one for the front to avoid confusion, *figure 121.*

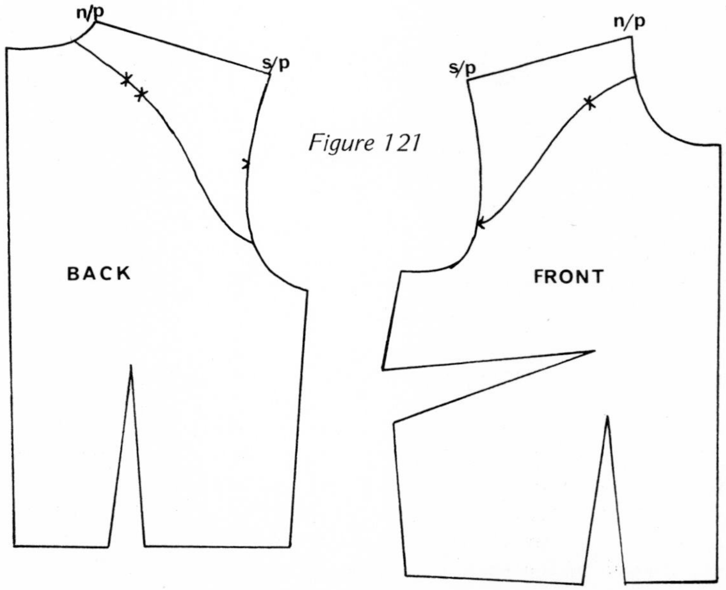

Figure 121

Trace off and cut out the shoulder pieces above the raglan line, recording the notches. Place these pieces on the sleeve head of the shortened sleeve as shown in *figure 122*. Match the shoulder point to the crown height, and allow the scye to rest against the sleeve head. A shoulder dart is formed when both back and front pieces are in position.

Redraw the new outline, mark notches and add seam allowances to the sleeve and bodice pieces. It will be necessary to ease the sleeve/shoulder part onto the bodice between the notches when making up.

Figure 122

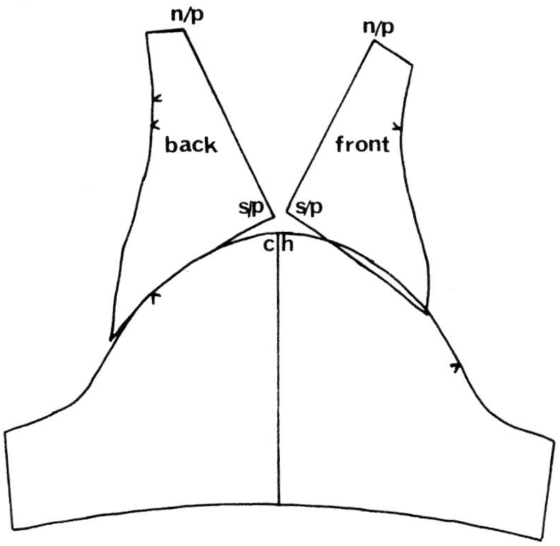

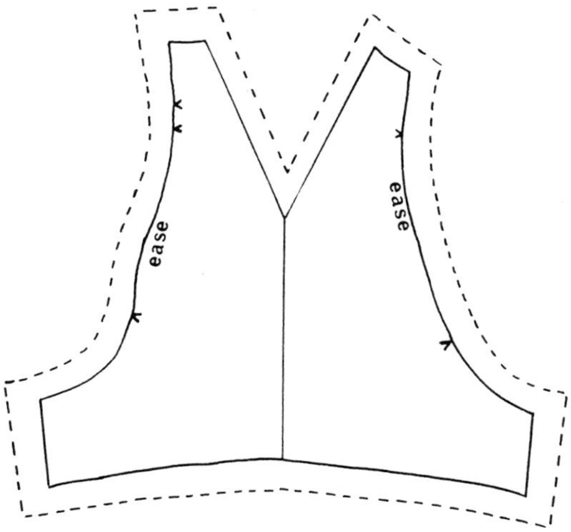

Figure 123

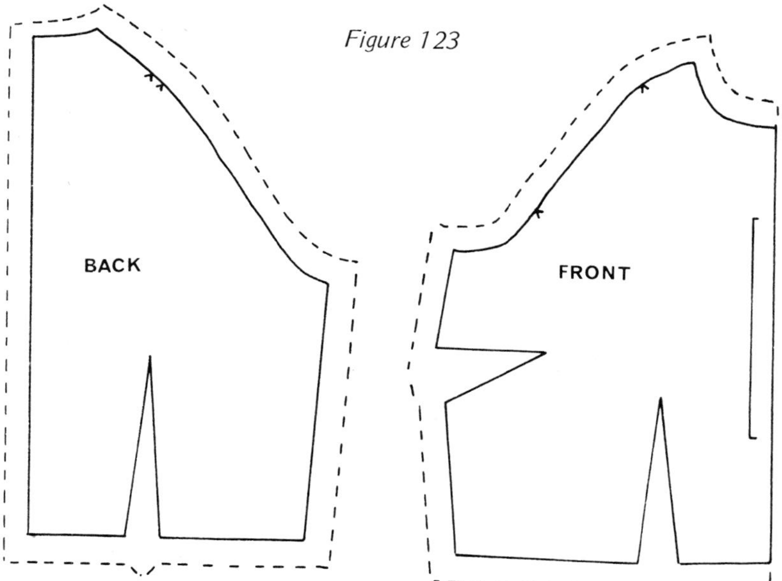

MAGYAR STYLES

A true Magyar style is loose fitting around the chest and arm, the bodice and sleeve being cut all in one piece.

Measure 14cm along the underarm seam of the front sleeve, and connect this point to the waist line of the bodice. Find the centre of this line, and measure inwards 5cm; using this point as a guide, draw in a suitable curve. Add seam allowances to complete the pattern pieces.

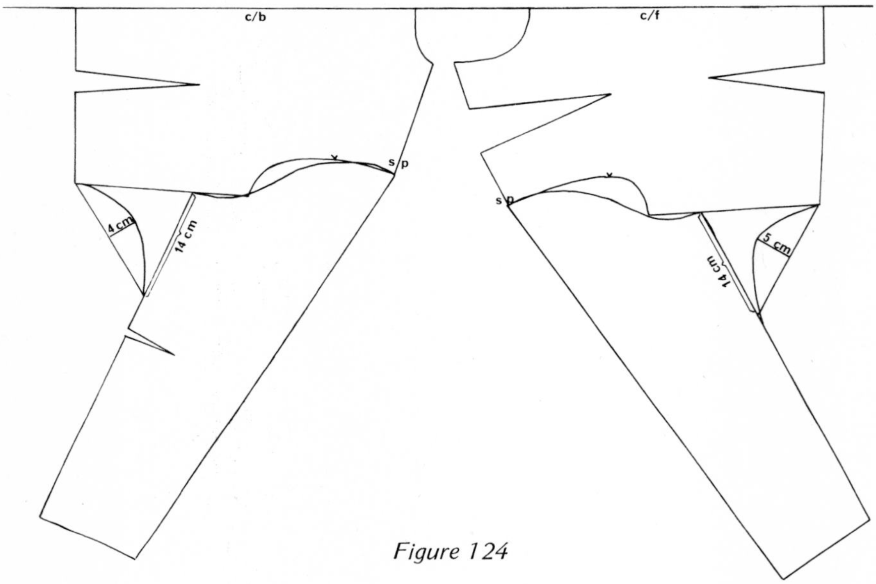

Figure 124

Place the back and front bodice blocks with the centre front and centre back along a straight line, and draw around these. Take a copy of the straight sleeve block, and cut this along the centre line (4 to 5, crown height to wrist). Place the back sleeve to the back bodice so that the shoulder point and crown height meet. The underarm part of the sleeve should be arranged to touch the side seam of the bodice as shown.

Place the front sleeve to the front bodice in the same way, meeting shoulder point to crown height with the underarm of the sleeve touching the side.

Measure 14cm from the underarm point of the back sleeve towards the dart. Draw a line from this point to the waist line of the bodice. Find the centre of this line, and measure 4cm inwards towards the underarm position. Using this mark as a guide, draw the new underarm seam line with a suitable curve.

If a greater amount of movement is required at the underarm area, cut a line from the underarm position to within 0.2cm of the shoulder point on the back and front, and spread the pattern. The example shown gives an extra 6cm.

Figure 125

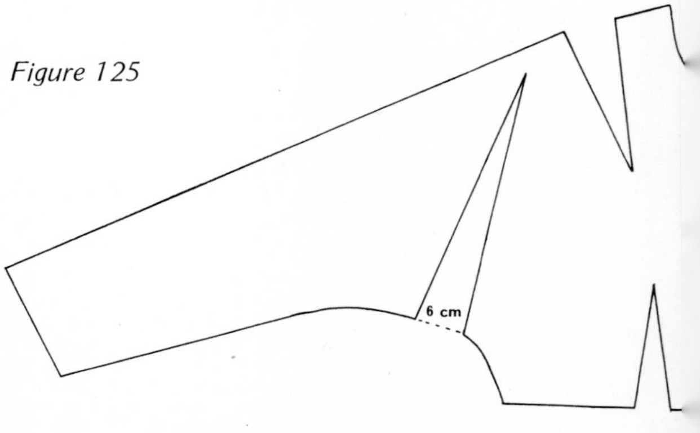

GUSSET INSERTION

This Magyar style has a gusset insertion at the underarm and is not so loosely fitted as the true Magyar.

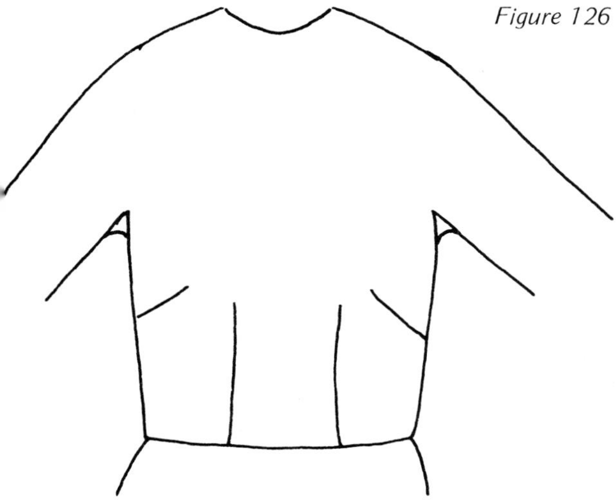

Figure 126

Place the back and front blocks with centre back and centre front along a straight line. In this example the front block with the underarm dart is used. Record the scye notches when drawing round the blocks. As with the true Magyar, arrange the back and front sleeves to meet at the shoulder point, and touch the underarm of the sleeve to the side bodice. Add 1.5cm to the front shoulder, and draw in a new shoulder and top sleeve line, gently curving this towards the elbow level. Reposition the back shoulder by 0.5cm, and gently curve towards the elbow. Adjust the slant of the sleeve by 2cm at the wrist on both the back and the front pieces. This is shown by a broken line in *figure 127.*

A gusset must be inserted at the underarm position to allow for easy movement and to prevent pulling from the waist. To mark the position of the gusset, draw a line from the underarm position to the balance notch on both back and front patterns. The gusset slash should be 9cm long from the underarm position.

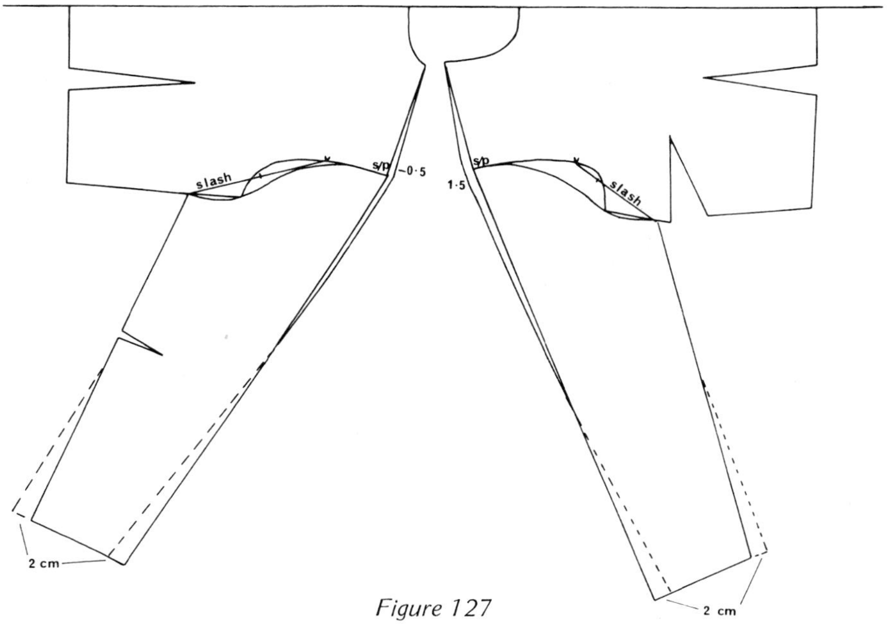

Figure 127

Add seam allowances to the finished pattern pieces, and mark the slash for the gusset insertion. This pattern may be useful cut in card without seam allowances for adaptation to other styles.

Figure 128

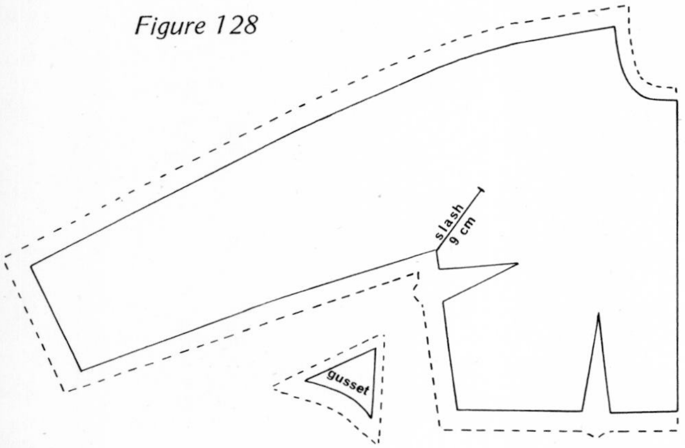

For the gusset, draw a triangle with each side 9cm long. The lower line of the triangle should be slightly curved as shown to form a better underarm line. Add seam allowances to the gusset.

Figure 129

SQUARE SLEEVE

It is not always necessary to insert a gusset if a style is cut with a seam running from the under-arm area to the top arm area around the shoulder point or neck line. However, it is always necessary to allow extra length to the underarm seam to substitute for a gusset. This is obtained by cutting and spreading the under-arm part of the sleeve as in the following examples.

The square sleeve is an adaptation of the Magyar sleeve. The underarm dart on this style has been transferred to the underbust position.

Figure 130

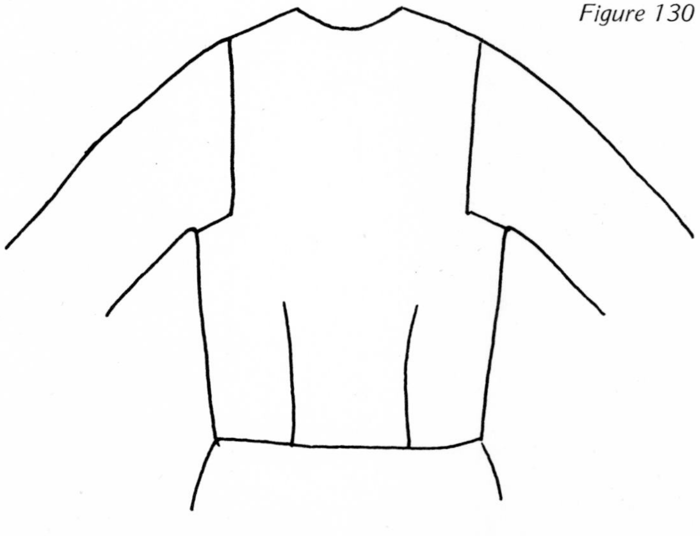

Draw around the Magyar sleeve block, transferring the dart to the underbust position.

Figure 131

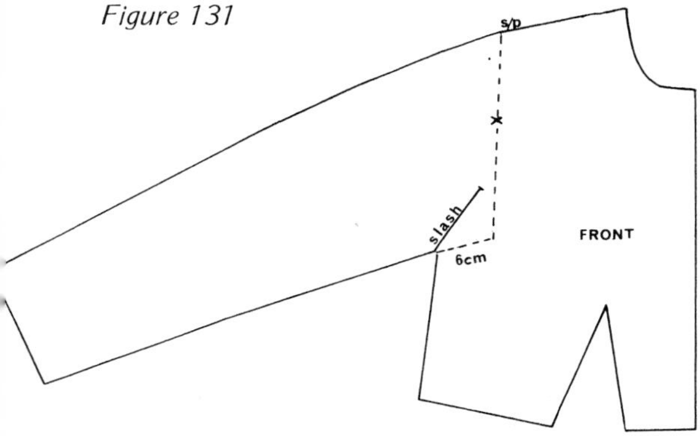

Record the slash position. Mark in the square style line (broken line). This comes from the shoulder point down to meet the extended underarm line. The underarm line is extended by approximately 6cm in this example. Cut along the style line, separating the sleeve from the bodice, *figure 132.*

Figure 132

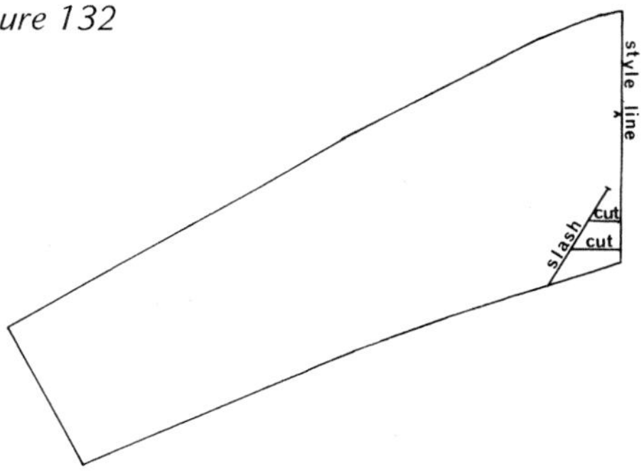

Cut along the slash line to within 0.2cm of the style line. Make two cuts from the slash line to within 0.2cm of the vertical style line, and spread the pattern as shown, allowing approximately 10cm extra length in place of a gusset. Reshape the underarm seam, and add seam allowances.

Figure 133

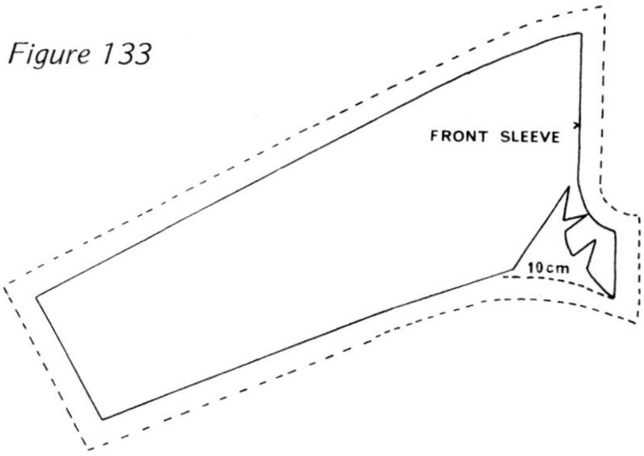

Redraw the bodice piece, and add seam allowances.

The back of this style is constructed in the same way as the front.

Figure 134

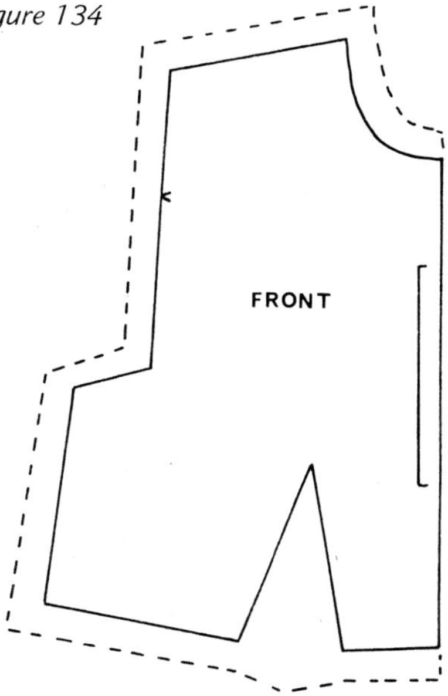

YOKE SLEEVE

Here the style line runs from the underarm through the chest area to the neck, to form a yoke. A short sleeve has been used and a V neck line.

Draw around the Magyar block, adjust the neck line to a V and shorten the sleeve. Draw in the style line (broken line) and the slash line. Mark a grain line on the yoke piece to run parallel with the centre front. Now mark a balance notch approximately 10cm from the underarm position. Cut along the style line, separating the shoulder area from the lower bodice.

Figure 135

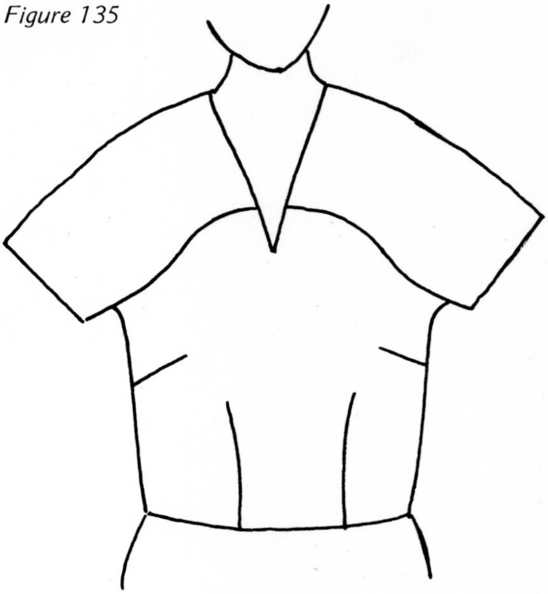

Figure 136

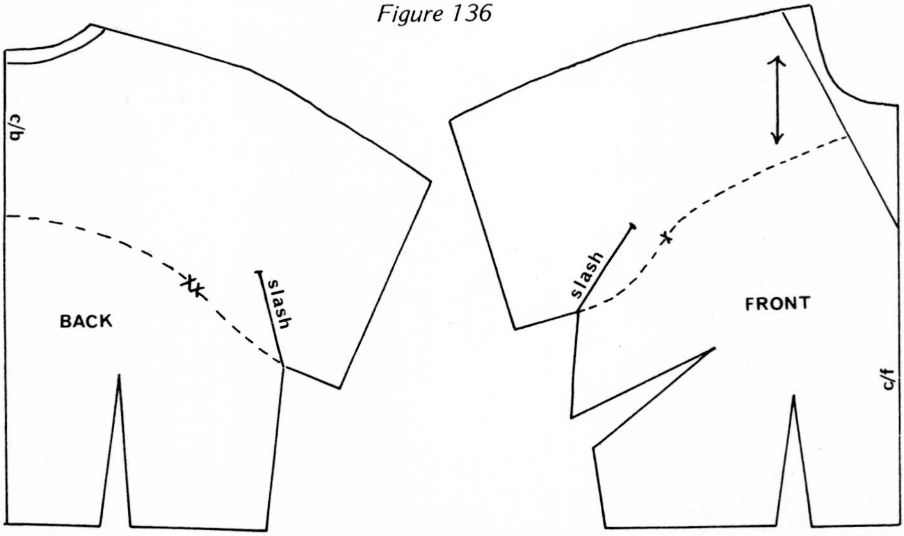

Using the slash line as a guide, draw a curved line from the underarm position to within 0.2cm of the yoke line (broken line), *figure 137.*

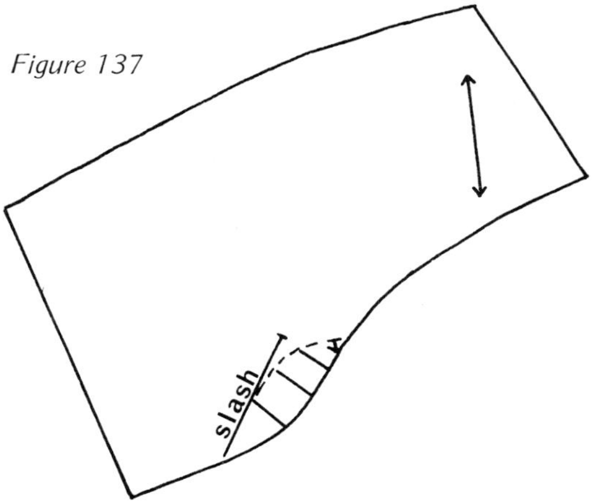

Figure 137

Cut along this curved line, and make three cuts from this line towards the yoke line. Spread the pattern as shown allowing approximately 8cm extra length to the underarm seam, *figure 138.*

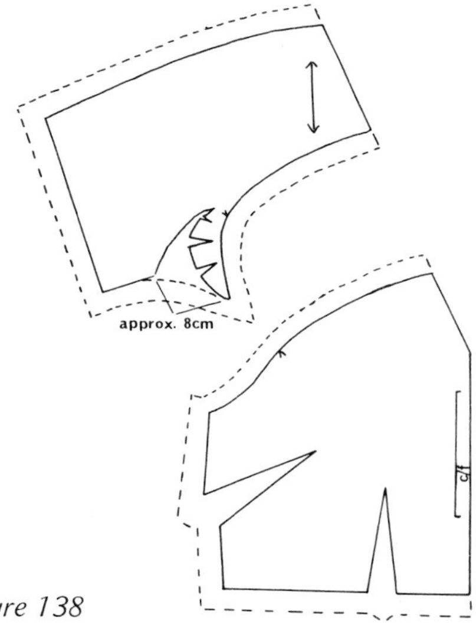

Figure 138

Redraw the yoke, and add seam allowances, recording the notch and grain line. Add seam allowances to the lower bodice piece, and record the notch.

The back of this style may be cut in the same way. The yoke, however, may be drawn from the underarm position to the centre back as shown in *figure 136.*

The back and front sleeve may, if desired, be placed together, eliminating a top seam and using a dart for the shoulder shaping as in a raglan style, *figure 139.* Seam allowances will be required as usual.

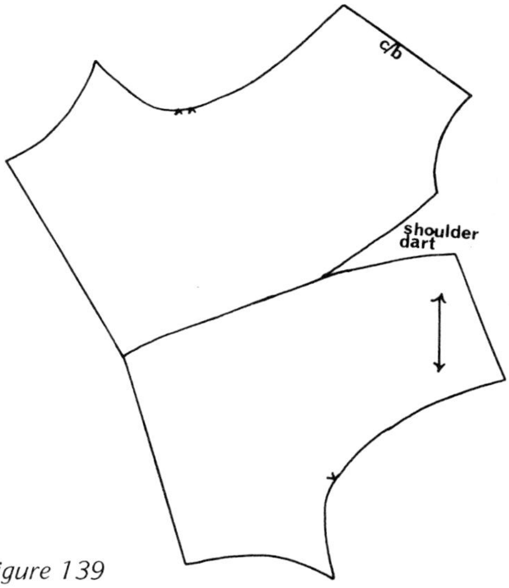

Figure 139

SIX

Skirts

The basic two-piece skirt block given in this book may easily be adapted to other styles.

SIX-PIECE GORED SKIRT

The first example of skirt adaptation is a six-piece gored skirt.

Figure 140

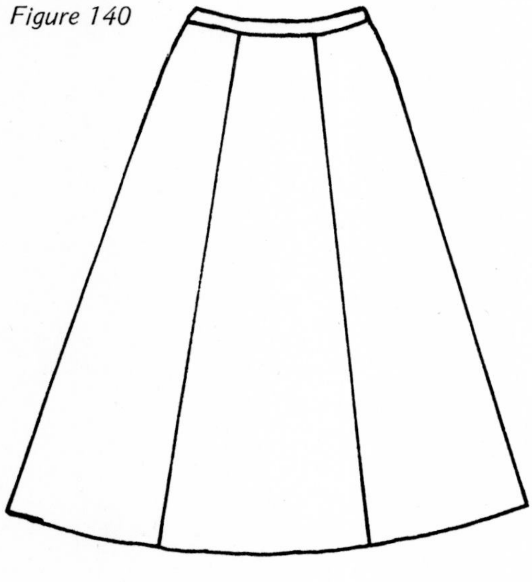

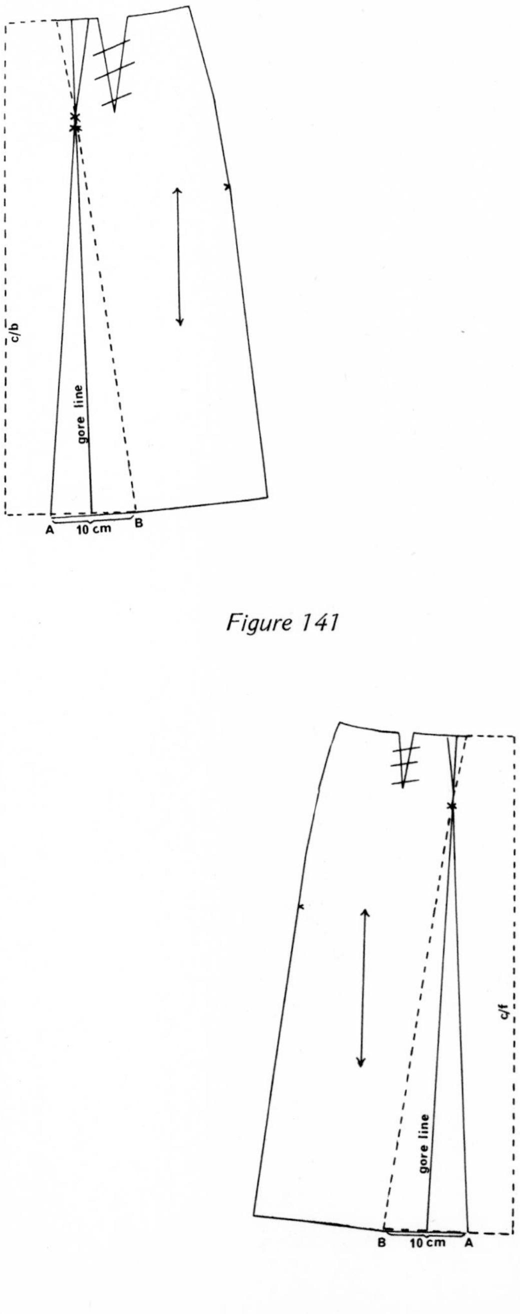

Figure 141

Copy the outline of the back and front skirts. Draw in a line on each block to mark the position of the gore. (This should be approximately one-third of the way from the centre front and centre back so that, when the skirt is completed, the gores appear to fall in three equal sections). Reposition the waist darts so that the apex falls on the gore lines.

At the hem position, decide upon the amount of flare required (10cm in this example) and divide this equally either side of the gore line (points A and B in *figure 141*). Connect points A and B to the apex of the waist darts. Mark a grain line on the side sections parallel to the centre front and centre back. Mark notches as shown, two for the back pieces and one for the front to avoid confusion when making up.

Trace off each panel, recording the notches and grain lines. The panels do of course overlap at the hem and must therefore be separated. The centre front and centre back panels are illustrated by broken lines to avoid confusion. Note that the waist suppression is taken out in the panel seams.

Add seam and hem allowances to the finished pattern pieces. Record the notches, grain lines and centre front and centre back.

Figure 142

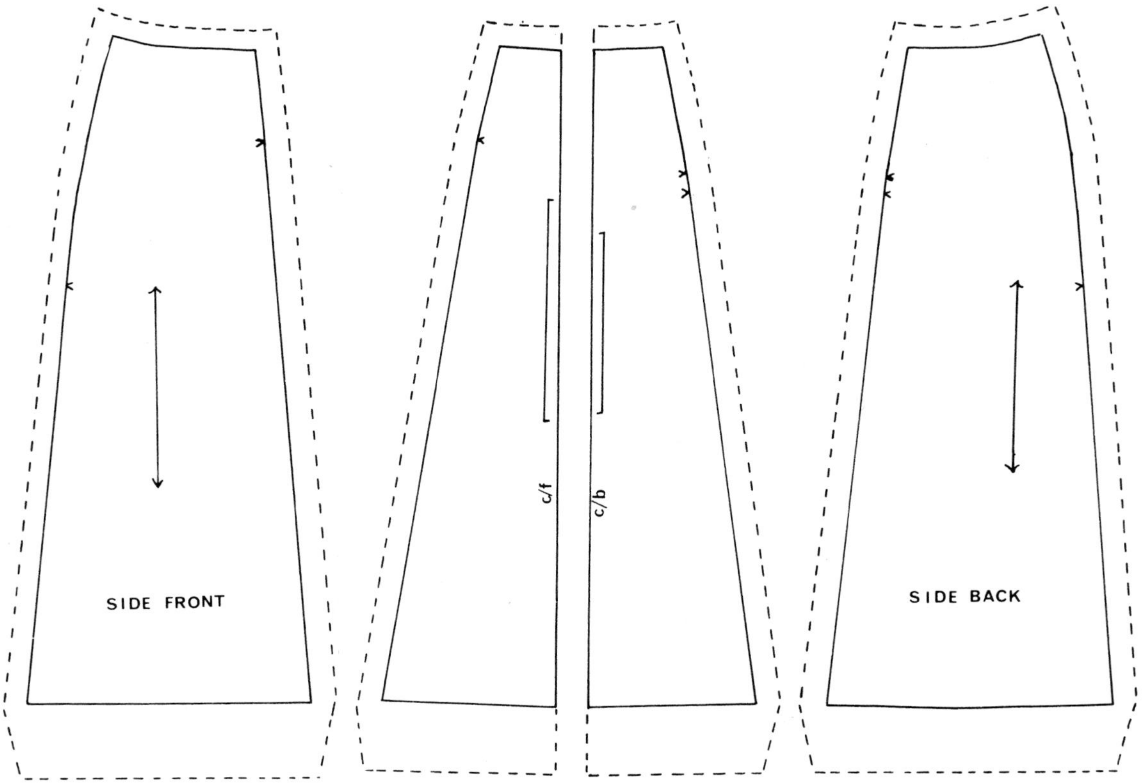

SKIRT WITH ONE GODET PLEAT IN CENTRE FRONT

This skirt has one godet pleat in the centre front.

Figure 143

Draw around the back and front skirt blocks. Add a little more fullness to the hem on the side seams. Decide upon the length and the width of the godet required, and draw this equally each side of the centre front. (This example is 16cm wide at the hem and starts 18cm from the waist down the centre front line.) Mark a notch for the top of the pleat. As this pattern has a centre front seam, the 2cm dart may be omitted, and the shaping may be transferred to the centre front seam.

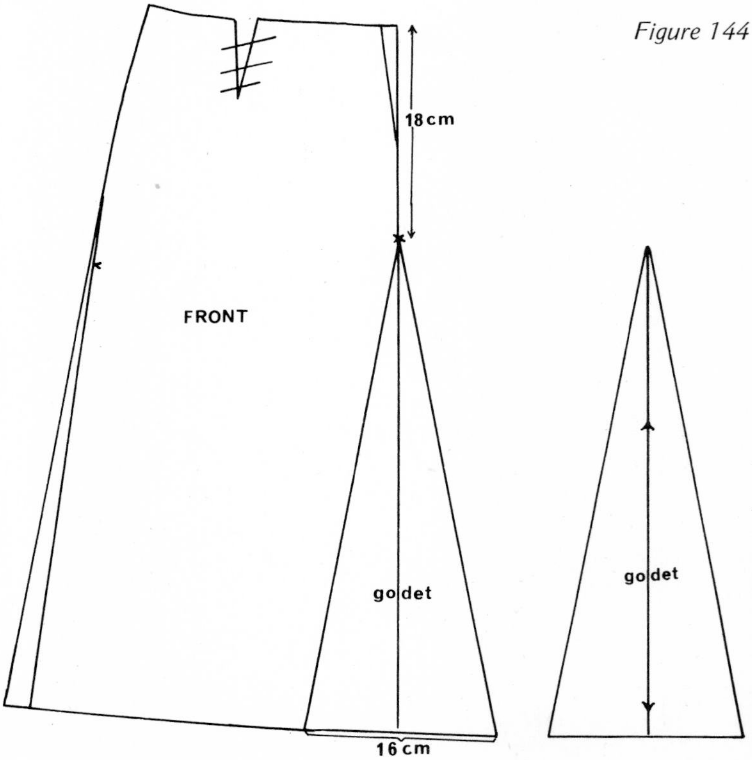

Figure 144

Trace off the godet, recording the centre front, and add seam allowances. Add seam allowances to the back skirt. The centre front has part of the pleat built onto it and will require seam allowances. Mark the crease line and the notch for the pleat position together with a grain line parallel to the original centre front. Add hem allowances to all pieces, shaping slightly as shown to ensure a flat hem.

One advantage of the godet pleat is that no bulkiness is apparent around the hip area.

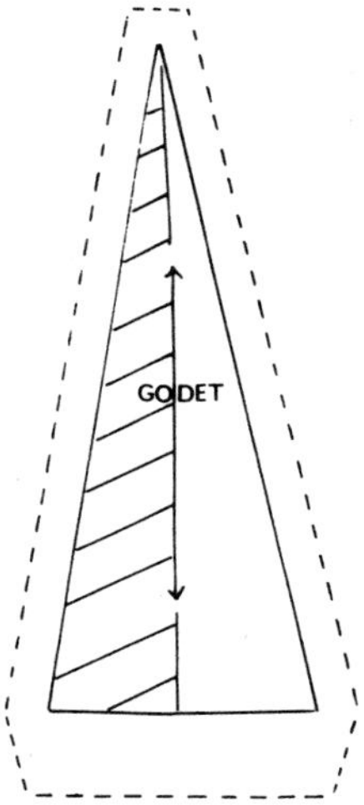

Figure 145

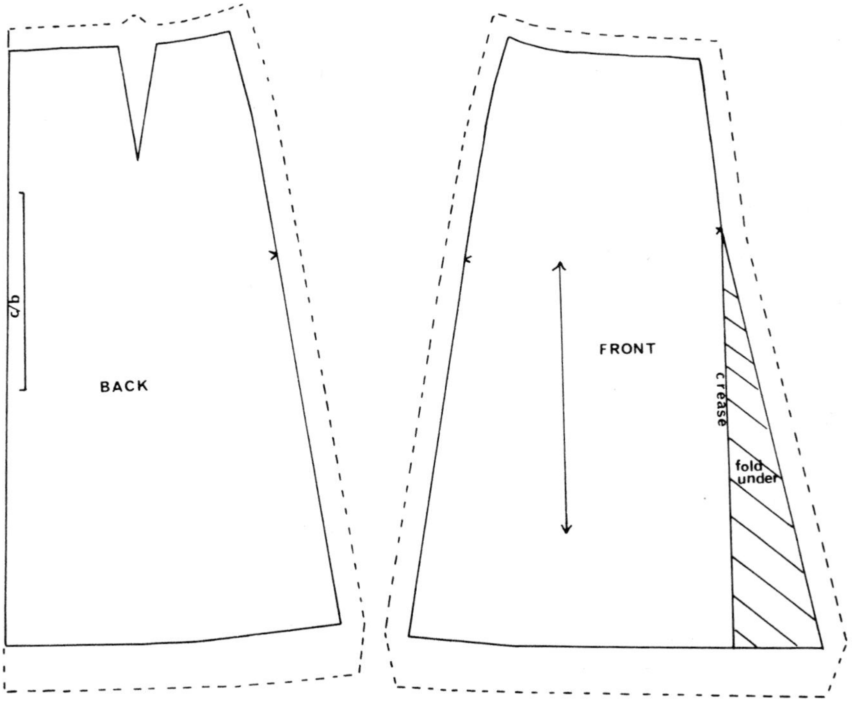

STRAIGHT SKIRT WITH KNIFE PLEAT IN CENTRE BACK

This is a straight skirt with a knife pleat in the centre back providing the stride room.

Figure 146

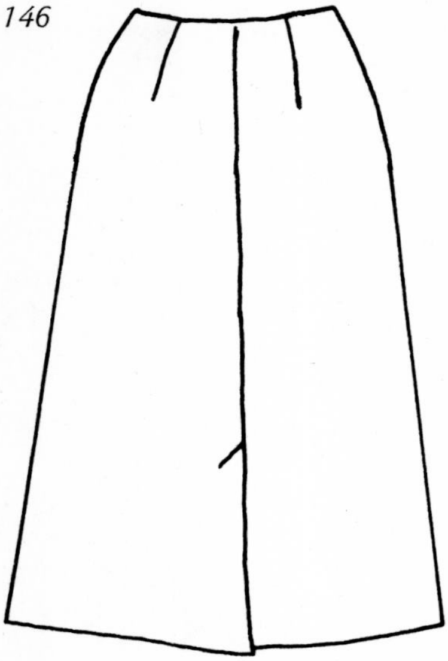

Draw around both skirt blocks. Straighten the side seams by taking off the 3cm allowed at the hem for stride room on the original block. The new side seam is illustrated by a broken line. Decide upon the length of the back pleat and the amount required for the width of the pleat. Add this to the centre back. The pleat in this example is 23cm deep and 8cm wide, *figure 147.*

Add seam and hem allowances to the new outlines in the usual way.

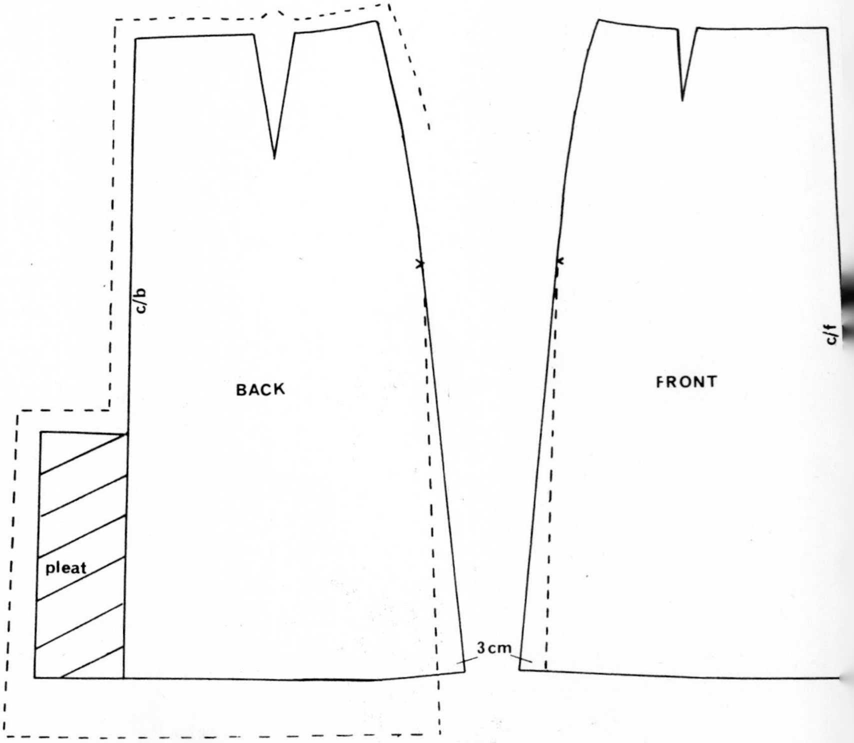

Figure 147

POCKET
A pocket is incorporated in this skirt with the side skirt and main skirt both forming part of the pocket.

Figure 148

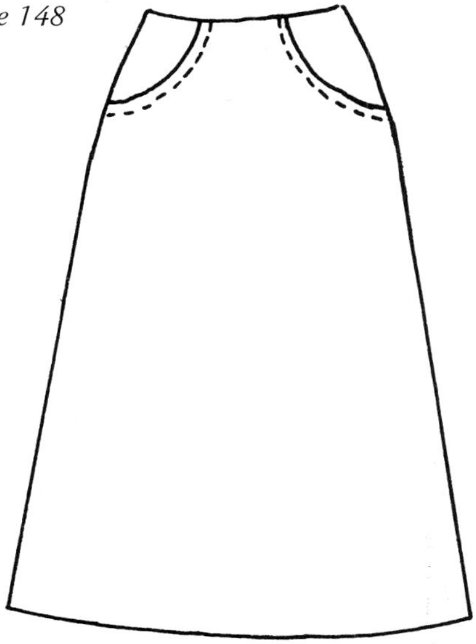

Draw around the front skirt block. Decide upon the shape of the pocket required, and draw this in. Mark notches at the side seam and pocket facing seam as shown. The broken line indicates the depth of the pocket. Mark a grain line on the side skirt piece, running parallel to the centre front.

Figure 149

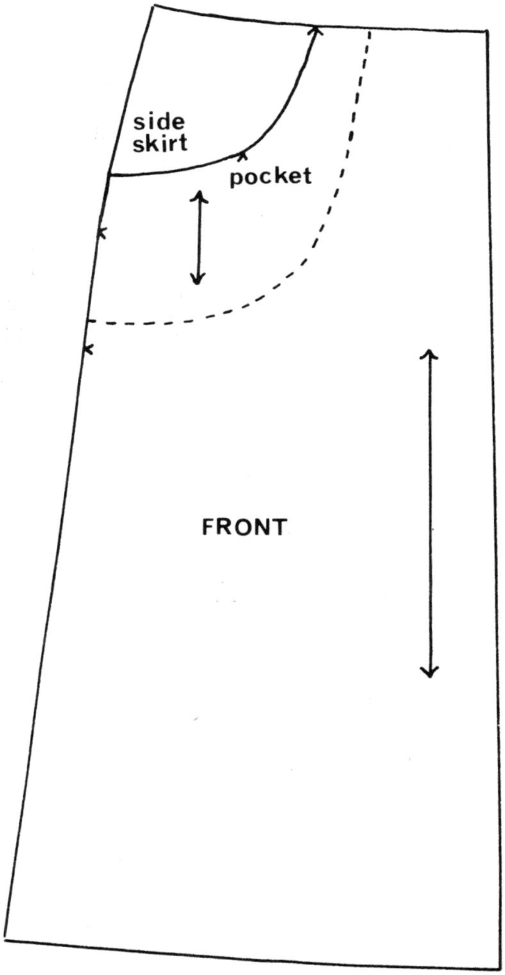

Trace off the side skirt/pocket piece, and add seam allowances. Record the grain line and notch.

Figure 150

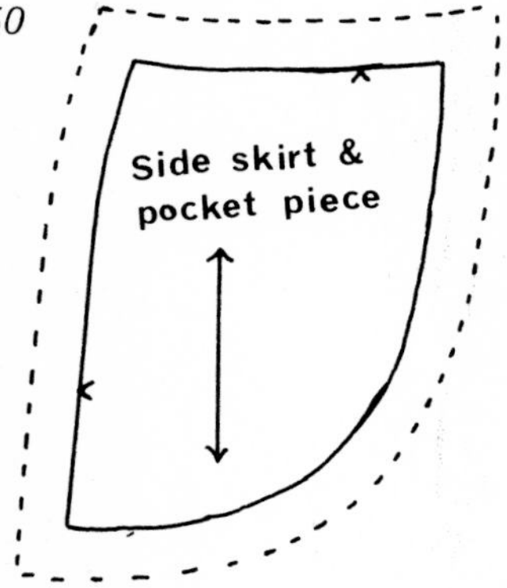

Trace off the facing/pocket, record the notches and add seam allowances.

Figure 151

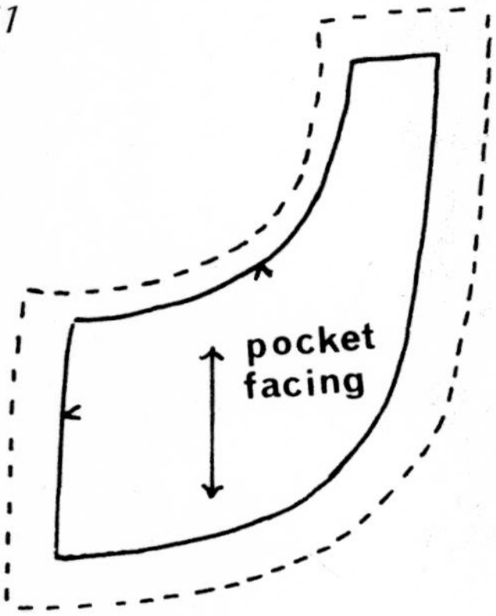

Add seam and hem allowances to the main skirt piece. Record the notches at the side seam and pocket seam.

Figure 152

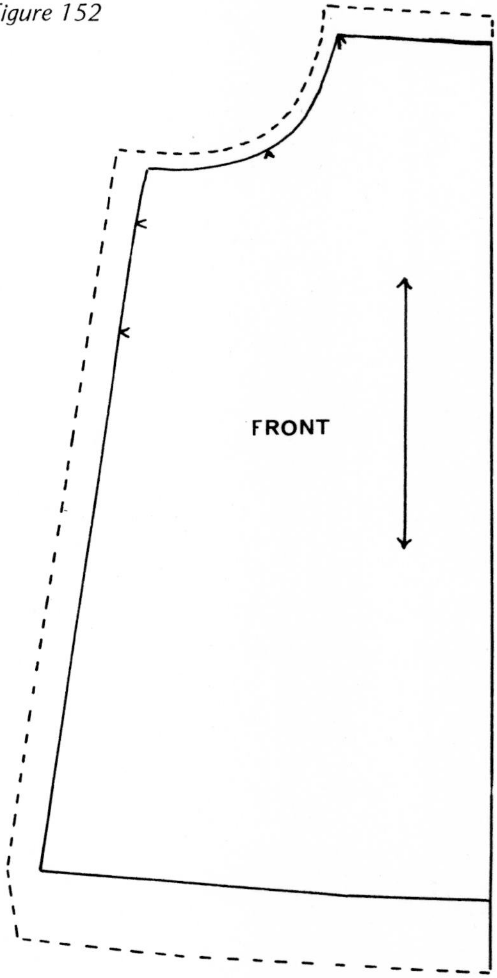

FLARED SKIRTS

The basic block may be used to construct flared skirts. A very gentle flare may be gained by simply eliminating the back and front waist darts.

Figure 153

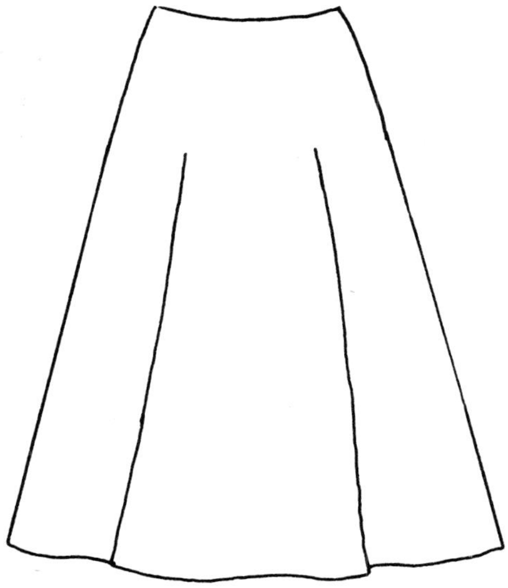

Figure 154

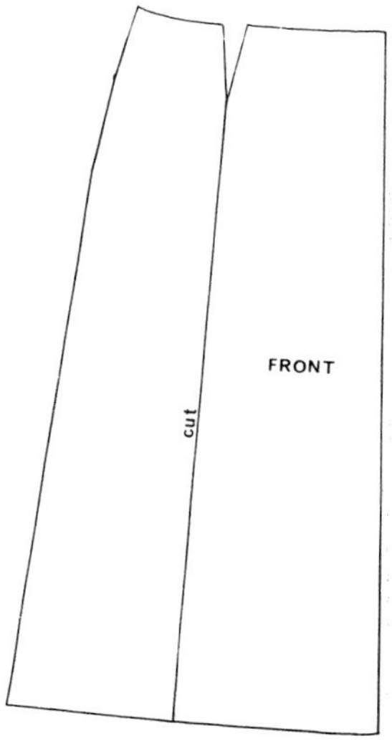

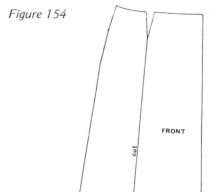

This method may be used to obtain a greater degree of flare. Although the shape at the waist is altered, the size remains the same. When this is pulled around the body, the amount of spread added to the hem will fall into flounces; therefore the greater is the spread, the fuller the flare.

To do this, draw around the skirt blocks, marking the waist darts. Draw a line form the apex of the darts to the hem line (*Figure 154*).

Cut out the patterns and cut along the line from the hem to within 0.2cm of the dart apex. Close out the darts spreading the fullness to the skirt hem. Note that the shape but not the size of the waist has changed, except for the dart suppression. Redraw the new outline, and add seam allowances. A more flared effect is achieved if the centre front and centre back lines are placed on the bias of the fabric when cutting out. If this method is adopted, it will be necessary to include a centre front and centre back seam, *figure 155*.

Figure 155

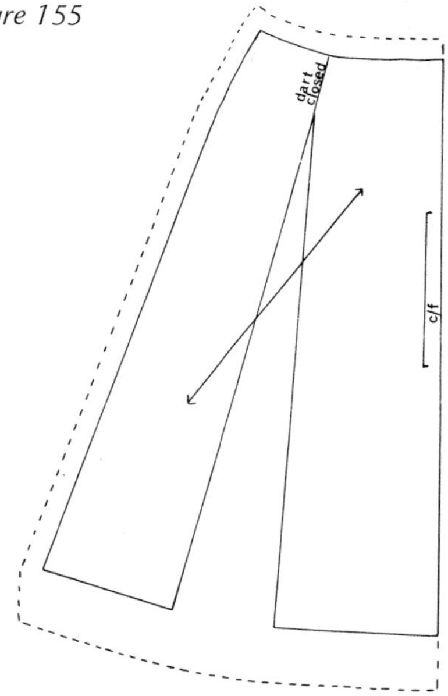

CIRCULAR SKIRT

For a full circular skirt the block must be spread out to such an extent that the side seam is at right angles to the centre front and centre back respectively.

Having closed out the darts on the back and front skirt, draw two lines from the waist to the hem as shown. Another line is drawn from a point approximately 12cm down the side seam to the hem, *figure 157.*

Cut up each line from the hem to within 0.2cm of the waist or side seam, and spread the skirt evenly. Redraw the new outline, straighten the side seam, mark the centre front and centre back and add seam allowances. A smaller hem allowances is usually added to a flared skirt to avoid excessive fullness when turning this up.

Whether the skirt is cut in two or four pieces will be dependent upon the length of the skirt and the width of the fabric chosen for this style.

Figure 156

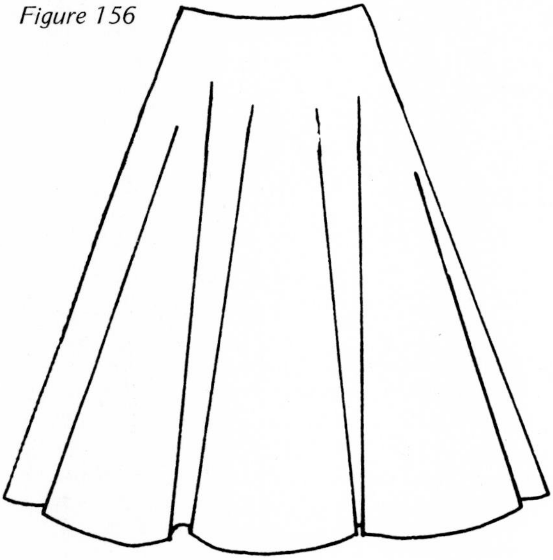

Figure 157

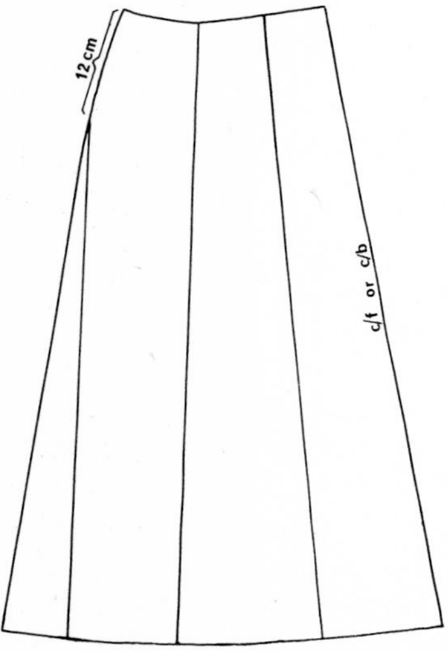

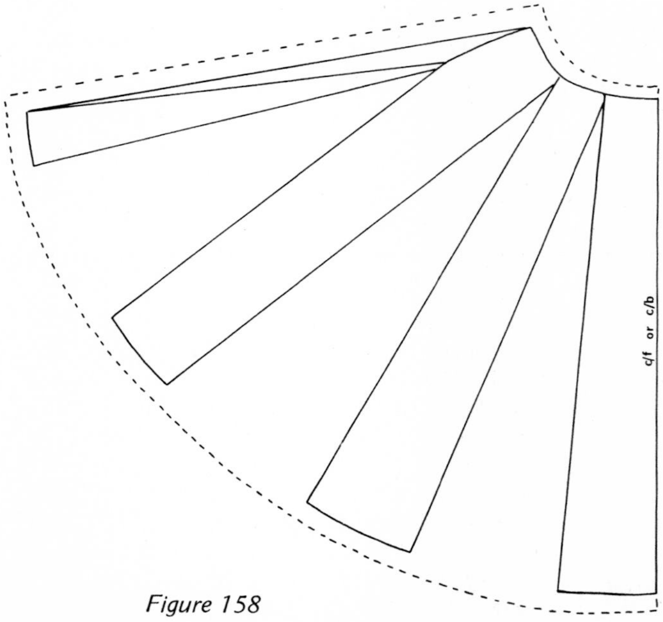

Figure 158

PLEATED SKIRTS

To construct pleated skirts, whether they be box pleats or knife pleats, it is not always necessary to use the foundation blocks. Instead the panels may be calculated using the hip and waist measurements. This requires the pleats to be evenly distributed around the body.

The following table is included for quick reference to calculations. The table gives individual panel measurements required for an eight, a ten and a twelve piece skirt to fit various waist and hip sizes.

Waist size	Eight piece one-sixteenth	Ten piece one-twentieth	Twelve piece one-twentyfourth
64	3.8	3.2	2.6
68	4.1	3.4	2.7
72	4.3	3.6	2.9
76	4.6	3.8	3.0
80	4.8	4.0	3.2
84	5.0	4.2	3.4
Hip size			
90	5.4	4.5	3.6
94	5.6	4.7	3.8
98	5.9	4.9	3.9
102	6.1	5.1	4.1
106	6.4	5.3	4.2

The above measurements are rounded up or down to the nearest tenth of a centimetre.

Knife-pleated skirts

The pleated skirt illustrated in *figure 159* is made up from ten panels. All the panels are exactly alike; therefore it is only necessary to cut one pattern piece. You will need a sheet of paper approximately 70cm x 40cm.

Fold the paper lengthwise so that you have a rectangle 70cm x 20cm. Place this on the table with the fold on the right-hand side. From the top of the sheet measure 4cm down the fold to point A (waist level).

Figure 159

A to B, the skirt length (60cm).

A to C, hip level (20cm).

A to D, one-twentieth of the waist measurement plus 0.1cm ease, i.e. 3.4cm plus 0.1cm for size 68 waist.

C to E, one-twentieth of the hip measurement plus 0.1cm ease, i.e. 4.7cm plus 0.1cm for size 94 hip.

B to F, one-twentieth of the hip measurement plus 2cm flare allowance.

(For other sizes refer to the table of measurements).

Connect D through E to F.

The underpleat allowance must now be added to this panel and in this example the pleat is 6cm at the hem.

D to G, 2cm.

Measure 12cm from D down to point H.

H to I, 3cm.

F to J, 6cm.

Connect G to I with a slight curve, and connect I to J.

Indicate the pleat by the use of slanting lines, and trace these through to the under piece of the folded paper. Line D to H is a sewing line, and the pleat is pressed on line H to F.

Add seam and hem allowances to the pattern. Note that seam allowances are not necessary on the curved line G to I, since it is line D to H that is sewn.

Figure 160

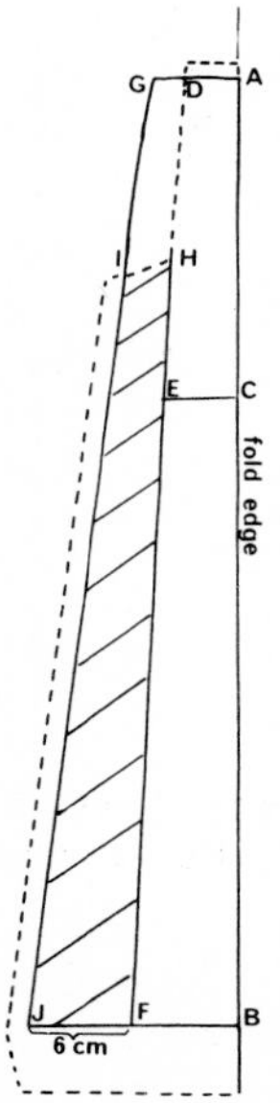

Open the pattern piece, and draw a grain line along the fold. The fact that ten pieces must be cut should be written on the pattern.

Figure 161

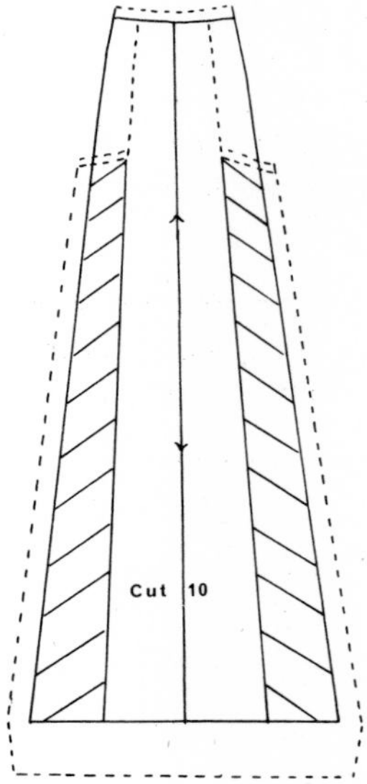

A skirt with pleats need not necessarily be made up of panels. There are several ways of looking at this. It may be found to be economical on cloth to have small panels, especially if a fabric without nap is being used, enabling the pattern to be turned. However, a manufacturer may consider it too expensive to machine so many seams and would probably choose to have less panels.

To cut a pattern for this skirt without seams, draw around the folded pattern, omitting the seam and the hem allowances. Record the pleat together with the slanting lines and the sewing line D to H.

Now open the pattern, and place this to the left of the outline matching the pleats. Draw around this, and repeat this process again to the left. Mark all the pleats and sewing lines. Note that this pattern piece now comprises two and a half panels, and, when the centre front or centre back is placed to the fold, five panels will be accounted for. Therefore it will be necessary to cut two pieces in cloth. If the width of the cloth will not allow for this, a seam must be included at a position where this seam will be hidden under the pleat.

Figure 162

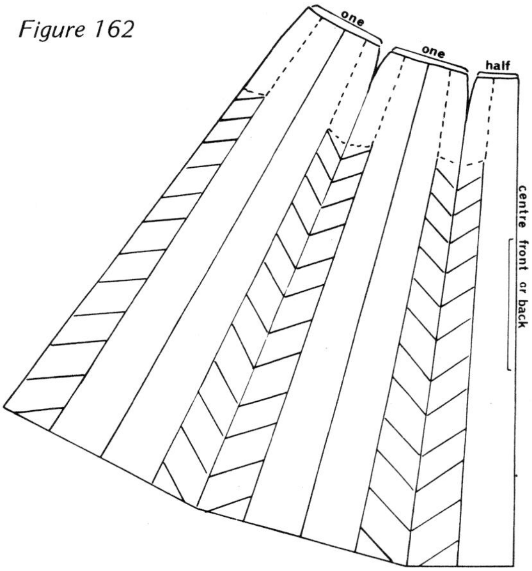

Add seam allowances and the hem allowance. One advantage that a ten-panelled skirt has over this two-piece skirt is that the centre of each panel is cut on the straight grain and therefore hangs better.

To construct a skirt with twelve or eight pleats, follow exactly the same procedure as described for the ten-pleat skirt, the only difference being the measurements A to D and C to E.

For twelve pleats A to D and C to E should be one-twentyfourth of the waist and hip respectively plus ease. For eight pleats one-sixteenth of the waist and hip plus ease is the measurement required for these points.

Refer to the table to find these proportions. Twelve pieces will be cut for the twelve-pleat skirt and eight for the eight-pleat skirt, and these instructions should be marked on the appropriate pattern.

Box-pleated skirts

This eight-panel box-pleated skirt is constructed in a similar way to the knife-pleated skirts.

Figure 163

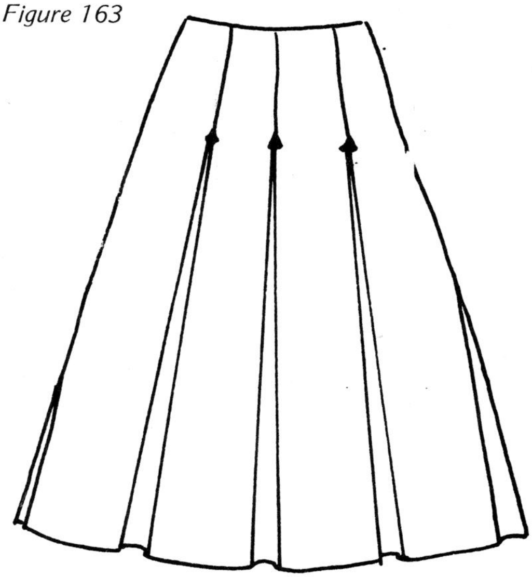

Fold a sheet of paper measuring 70cm x 60cm lengthwise, forming a rectangle 70cm x 30cm.

A is the waist level.

A to B, skirt length.

A to C, hip level (20cm).

A to D, one-sixteenth of the waist measurement plus 0.2 ease.

C to E, one-sixteenth of the hip measurement plus 0.2 ease.

B to F, one-sixteenth of the hip measurement plus 2cm flare allowance.

Refer to the table for the one-sixteenth proportions.

Connect D through E to F.

The pleat must be added now, and this is where the difference is seen between a knife pleat and a box pleat. A box pleat requires double the amount of underpleat, so that the two folded edges meet together when the skirt is made up.

D to G, 2cm.

Measure 12cm down the line from D to point H.

H to I, 3cm.

F to J, 6cm.

Connect G to I with a slight curve, and connect I to J.

The pleat area I to J and H to F must be transferred to the left-hand side to form a box pleat. To do this, fold the paper under the pleat, along line I to J, and trace through the pleat area.

Figure 165

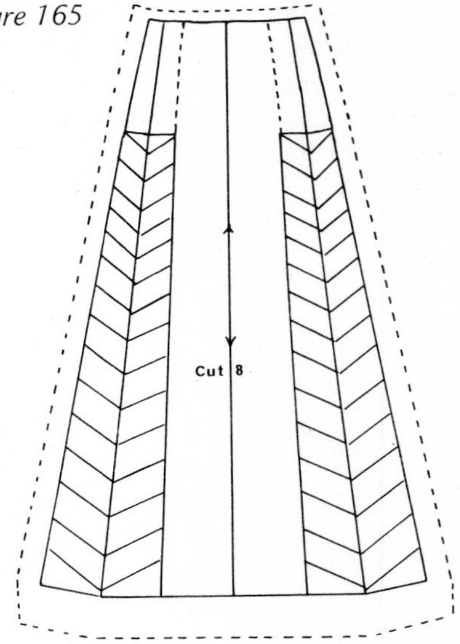

Figure 164

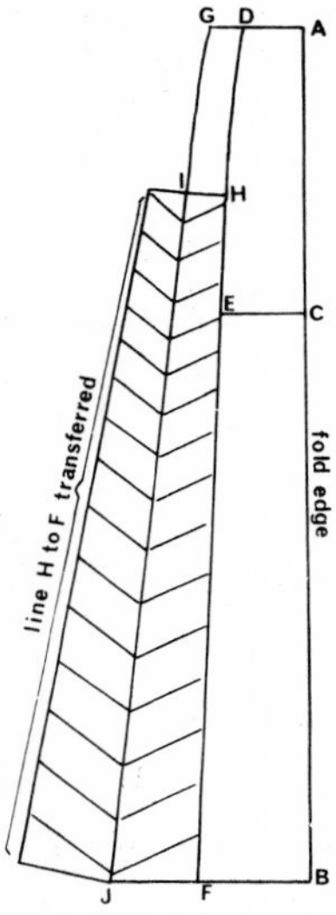

Open the pattern, and add the seam and hem allowances. Indicate on the pattern that eight panels will be needed.

To construct the eight-panel box-pleated skirt without panel seams, place the open pattern piece, without seam allowances, with the pleat along a straight line. Draw around this, and mark the pleats. Place the template pattern again to the right of this, and outline once more, matching and marking the pleats.

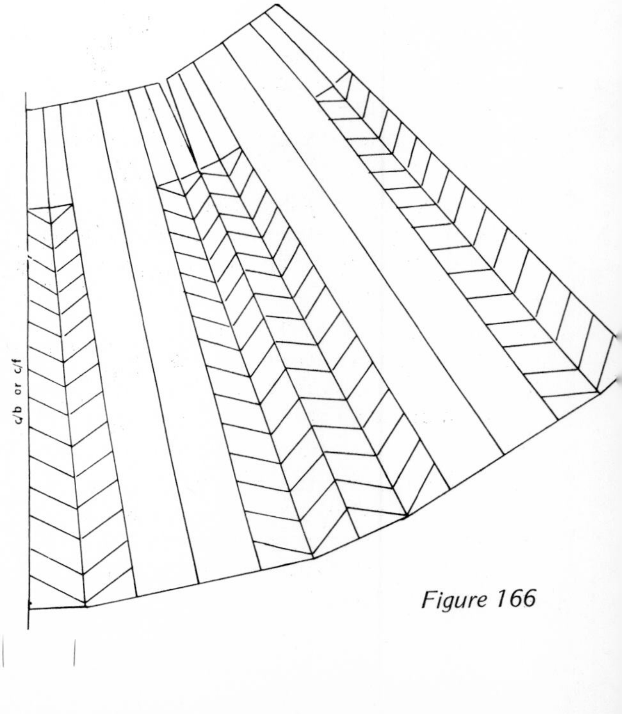

Figure 166

Add seam and hem allowances to complete the pattern.

The straight line is the centre front or centre back and should be placed to the fold of the fabric. As the back and the front are the same, two pieces will need to be cut in fabric. If the fabric chosen is not wide enough to allow the centre to be placed to a fold, a seam must be included at the centre front and centre back.

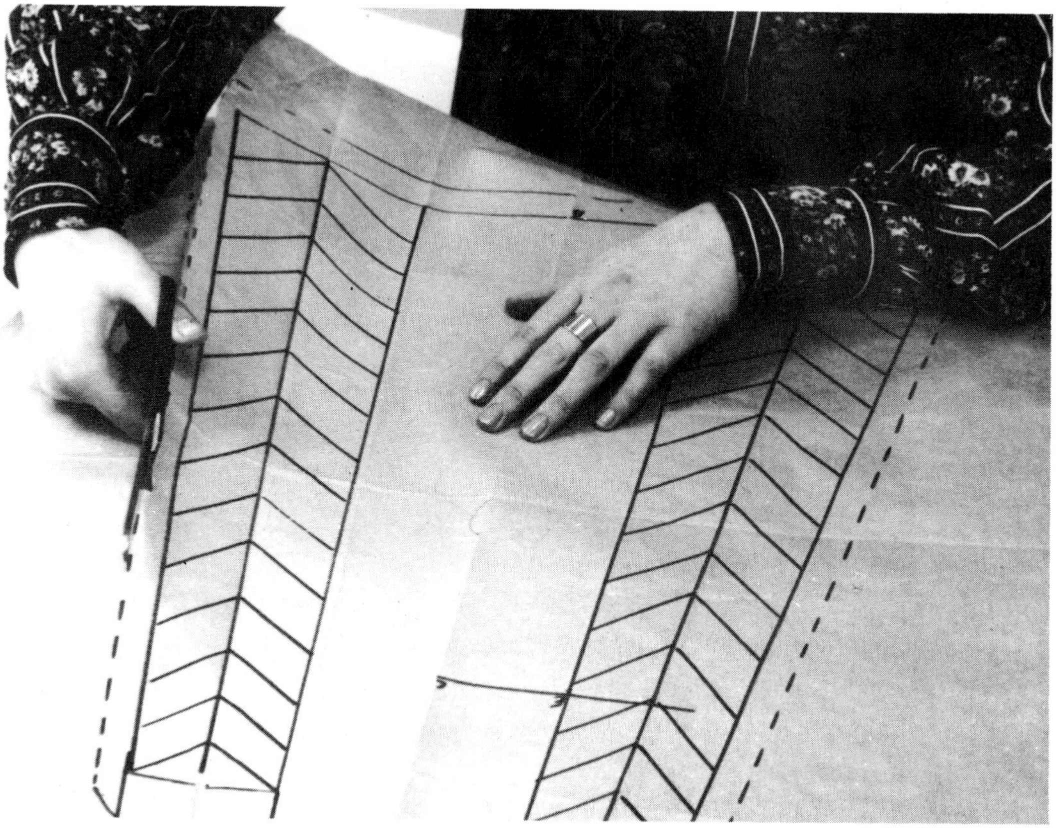

Figure 167 Cutting a pattern for a box pleated skirt

SEVEN

Trousers

CONSTRUCTING THE PATTERN BY MODIFYING THE SKIRT BLOCK

The skirt block may be used for the initial stage in constructing a trouser pattern. It will be necessary to have two additional body measurements for this pattern. These are (1) body rise or crutch and (2) the outside leg length. To take the crutch measurement, you must sit upright on a flat surface and must measure from the waist to the flat surface. This measurement, on an average figure, will be in the region of 28cm to 34cm. The outside leg is measured from the waist, down the side, to the ankle.

Place the back and front skirt blocks, matching the hip line, along a horizontal line previously drawn on a large sheet of paper. The sheet of paper must be at least the waist-to-ankle measurement plus 4cm in length and the total hip measurement in width.

Outline the skirt above the hip line. From the mark A (centre front waist), measure the depth of crutch to B (30cm in *figure 168*).

B to C is 8.5cm and at right angles to the centre front line (add 0.2cm for every 4cm hip increment above 102cm).

Draw a line across from C to the centre back line. This line is the crutch line, and it is at right angles to the centre front line. Extend this line to the left of the centre back line by 10cm (pointD); add 0.2 for every 4cm hip increment above 102cm.

From point B measure outwards at 40° by 4cm.

Measure down the centre front from A to E, a distance of 14cm. Using these points for guidance, draw in the front fork with a suitable curve.

For the back fork, measure outwards from the crutch line by 4cm in just the same manner as with the front.

Lower point D by 2cm below the crutch line. At the waist line the centre back is raised by 1cm above the original skirt outline, and 1cm is also taken out of the centre back. Draw in the back fork, crossing the centre back line of the skirt outline at approximately 12cm, down from the waist line. Since 1cm has been taken out of the back for the trouser, it will be necessary to reduce the back dart accordingly. Reshape the waist line as shown.

Point F is midway between the back and front side waist points.

F to G is the side leg length (waist-to-ankle measurement). This line is a right angles to the hip line. Draw a line at right angles to line F to G to represent the ankle line.

H is the point at which the line F to G crosses the crutch line.

I is midway between C and H.

H to J is the same measurement as H to I. Note that J is not midway between H to D. Drop a perpendicular line from J and I respectively to meet the ankle line.

The knee area is easily found by placing the skirt block over the draft and by marking the hem line position where this meets these perpendicular lines.

Figure 168

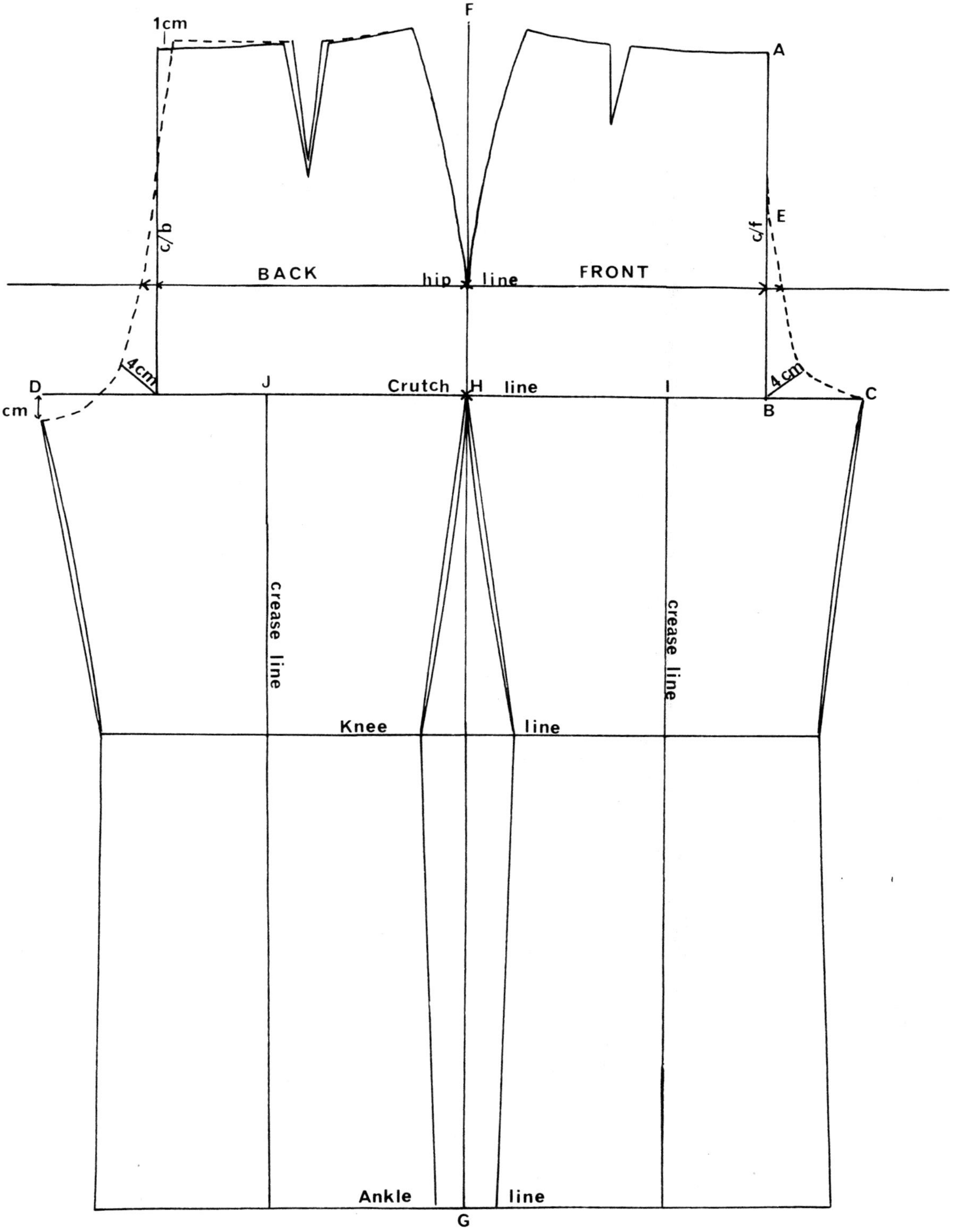
F
1cm
A
E
c/b
c/f
BACK
hip
line
FRONT
4cm
4 cm
D
J
Crutch
H
line
I
C
2 cm
B
crease line
crease line
Knee
line
Ankle
line
G

The width of the trousers at the knee and ankle varies considerably with fashion. However, for the purpose of this draft a measurement of 13cm on either side of the front crease line has been used and 13cm for the side back. 14cm is allowed for the centre back since the back fork is greater than the front. The ankle is flared out 1cm more than the knee measurement.

Connect points D, H and C respectively to the knee and ankle. Slightly curve these lines to obtain a better finished shape.

Trace off the back and front trouser patterns separately, and add seam allowances. Record the crease and grain lines, and mark the balance notches.

The front waist darts may, if desired, be repositioned to be in line with the crease line.

Figure 169

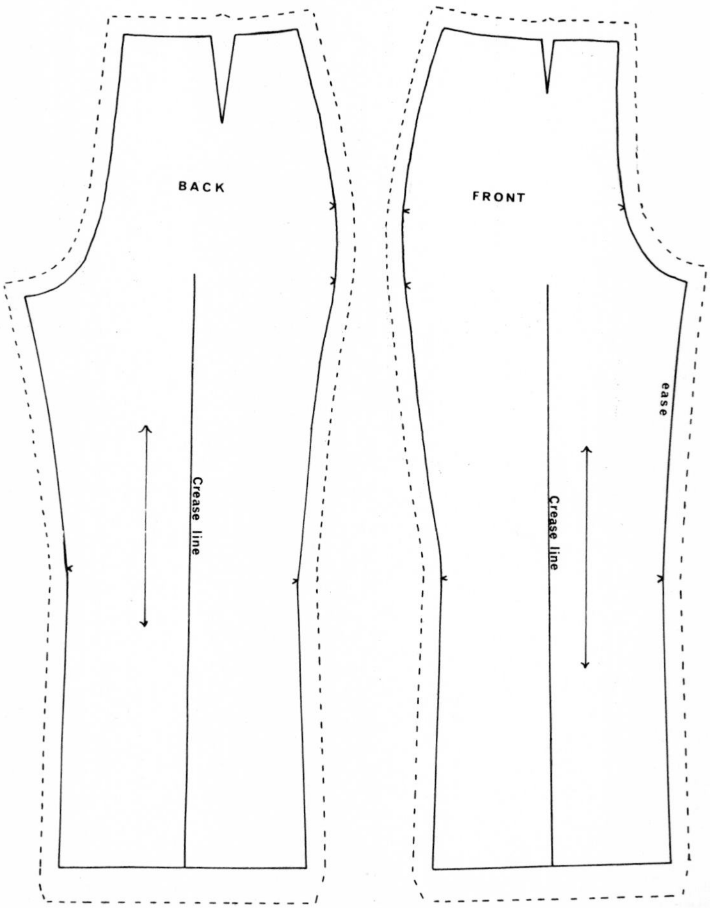

EIGHT

Style variations

Having studied and practised all the various design features and basic examples given on the previous pages, it is now possible to include these in the design of complete dresses. Watch the fashion trends, and plan accordingly. Study all garments illustrated in magazines, worn by television personalities and in fact people you meet from day to day. Look for different features, such as dart and seam arrangement, and note whether the fabric has been used to its best advantage. Observe the trimmings and fastenings (it is important to be able to get in and out of a garment comfortably). With a knowledge of pattern cutting you will find your eyes seeing features that had hitherto passed unnoticed. In fact, you may find that you have studied the cut of a garment so carefully, that its colour has not made any impression.

When deciding upon a style for yourself, be careful not to be over enthusiastic and not to use too many features on one garment, remembering that a simple but well-cut garment has much to commend it. Fashion changes so rapidly that, although some of the style features given in this book may appear to be outdated, they will undoubtedly have their usefulness restored within a few seasons. The basic principles of cutting and spreading a part of the pattern to create flare, of dart manipulation, of cutting collars and sleeves, etc., remain independent of fashion trends.

Bear all these points in mind before deciding upon the style to be created. Think about the subsequent cutting and making up of the garment. Consider the properties of the fabric, i.e. whether it will drape or whether it is too stiff and also whether it is too flimsy to give the desired effect. Study the print or weave of the fabric. It is of little value to create a style where the style lines are intended to be the main feature, if the fabric has an all-over print and the line will not be well defined. Many fabrics may 'make' the design. For example, checks and stripes can look very attractive if one part of the garment is cut on the bias with the remainder on the straight grain.

When you have decided upon the design, each stage of the cutting must be carefully planned. The initial step is usually to draw any new lines or features onto a copy of the block. Work with the back block to the left-hand side and the front to the right, as on the orignal draft. Although you are cutting a flat pattern, always bear in mind that the body is three demensional. The examples of complete garments that follow are intended to help you to understand the order and procedures that have to be adopted when combining several techniques together.

Figure 170

SLEEVELESS SUN DRESS

This sleeveless sun dress has a scalloped neck line and armhole. The bodice has soft gathers over the bust at the centre front, eliminating the use of darts. The neck line is large enough to pass over the head without a further opening. A zip fastener may be fitted into the left side seam, enabling the fitted waist to pass over the bust and shoulder when dressing and undressing. The skirt is circular.

Having noted the features, amendments must be made to your block in the order that follows

(1) Outline the back and front blocks, using the front block with a shoulder dart.

(2) Draw lines from the centre front to the apex of the shoulder dart and underbust dart as described in *figure 52.*

(3) Draw an additional line from centre front to the side seam line.

(4) Mark a grain line on the front bodice parallel to the centre front.

(5) Draw in a guide line for the shape of the neck (broken line).

(6) Decide upon the size and number of scallops and draw in these, using the broken line and scye line as a guide, *figure 171.* It is a good idea to cut a semi-circle in card to the size of the scallop required and to use this as a template.

Figure 171

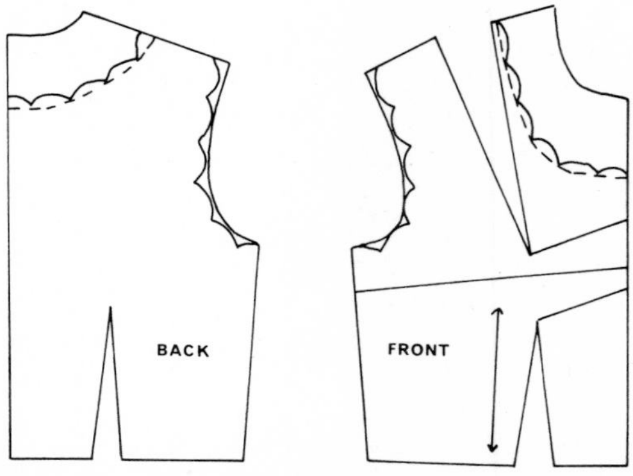

Figure 172 Tracing off a scalloped neck line

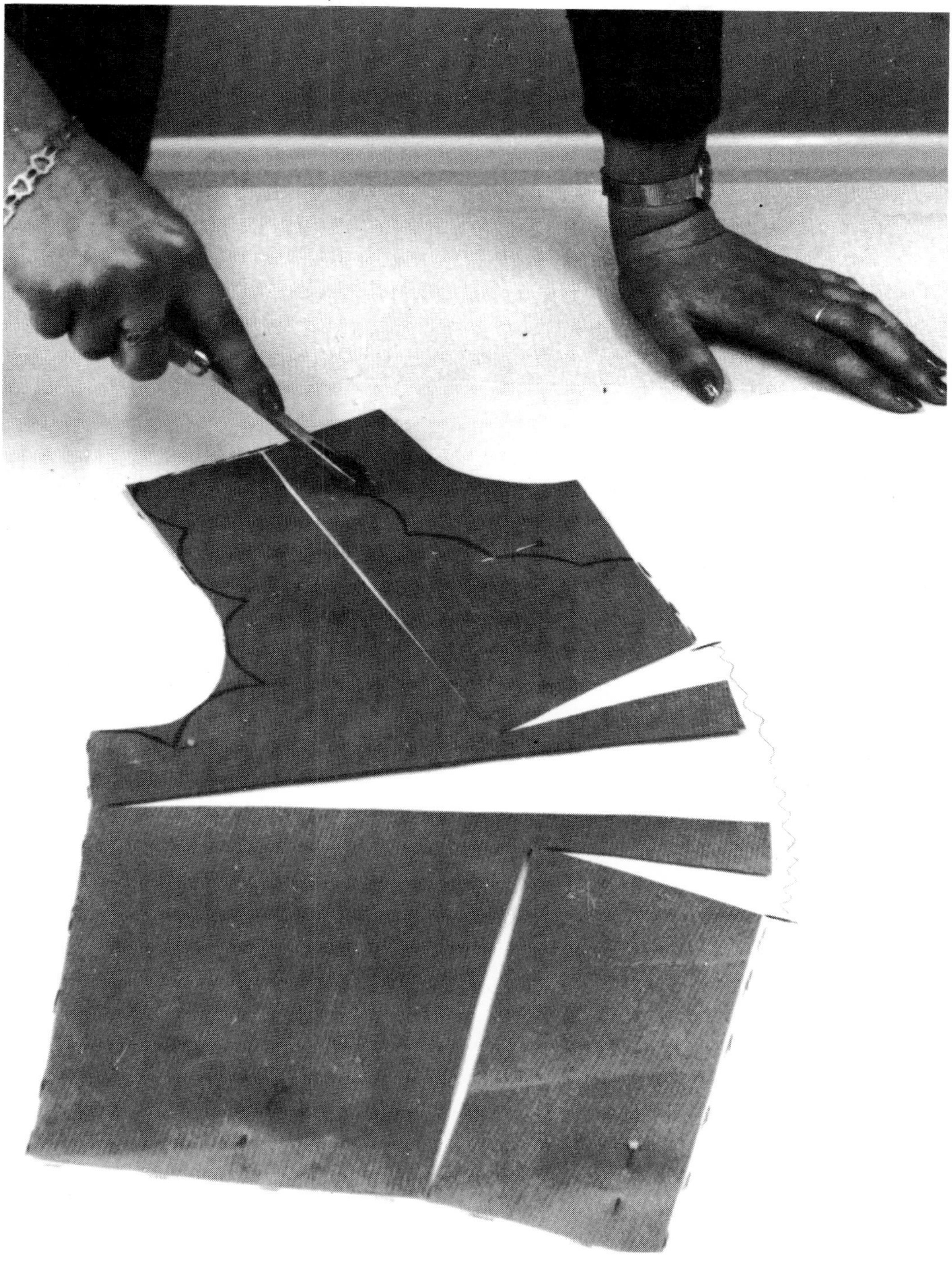

(7) Having marked all these amendments on a copy of the block, cut out the block with the new neck line.

(8) Cut along the lines from the centre front to within 0.2cm of the dart apex and side seam respectively.

(9) Close the darts, and spread the pattern as described in *figures 52* and *53.* Redraw the new shape, and record the grain line.

(10) Add seam allowances. It is advisable to add only a small seam allowance along the scallop edge to avoid bulkiness, *figure 173.*

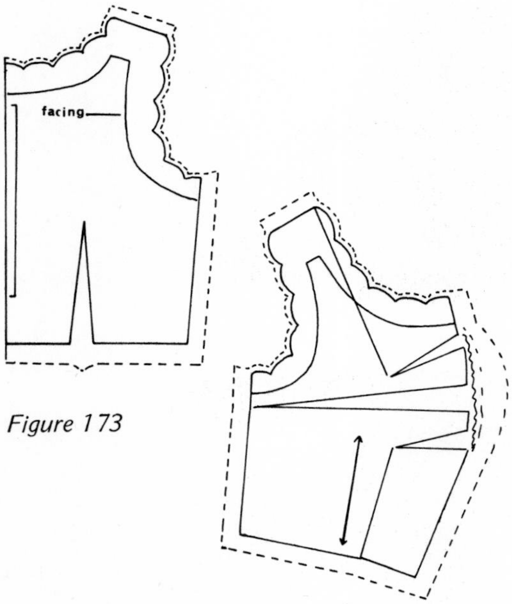

Figure 173

(11) Reshape the centre front line over the bust area to allow for gathers.

(12) Draw in the facing line on the main pattern pieces.

(13) Trace off the back and front facings and seam allowances.

Figure 174

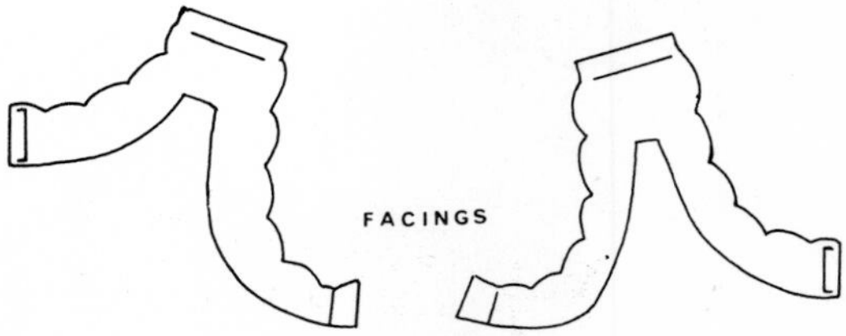

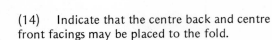

(14) Indicate that the centre back and centre front facings may be placed to the fold.

The circular skirt pattern may be cut as described in *figures 156* to *158.*

DAY DRESS WITH 'FALL-AWAY' SHIRT COLLAR

The style shown in *figure 175* has a 'fall-away' shirt collar, and the centre front is slit and faced below the yoke seam just deep enough to allow the garment to pass over the head. A zip fastener would be sewn into the left side seam to enable the fitted waist to pass comfortably over the shoulder and bust when dressing and undressing. When a collar is used in this way, it is advisable to use a side seam opening rather than a back zip to avoid a break in the back of the collar. Having decided how one gets in and out of the dress, other features must be thought about. This style has a yoke seam running from the underarm position through the front chest and cross back area respectively. The yoke and short sleeve are cut in one piece as in a Magyar style. Soft gathers are used to create fullness over the bust, and the back is slightly gathered to correspond to this. The waist is fairly well fitted with no underbust darts. The waist seam is covered by the use of a belt. The skirt has a slight flare, but the fullness is principally created by the use of godet pleats.

Having noted all these details the most convenient order of cutting must be planned as follows.

(1) Outline a copy of the back and front Magyar block, the construction of which is described in *figures 126* to *128*. Record the slash line, *figure 176*.

(2) Shorten the sleeve to the desired length.

(3) Draft in the straight shirt collar as described in *figures 75* to *78*.

(4) Draw in the yoke line and mark the balance notches, one for the back and two for the front to avoid confusion.

(5) Mark a grain line on the front yoke, this being parallel to the centre front. The centre back bodice and yoke will be placed to the fold, so a grain line is not essential. The lower part of the front bodice will also be placed to a fold.

(6) The lower centre front bodice will require a slit to enable the garment to pass over the head, therefore this point must be marked with a notch. This slit should be approximately 14cm from the centre front neck.

Figure 175

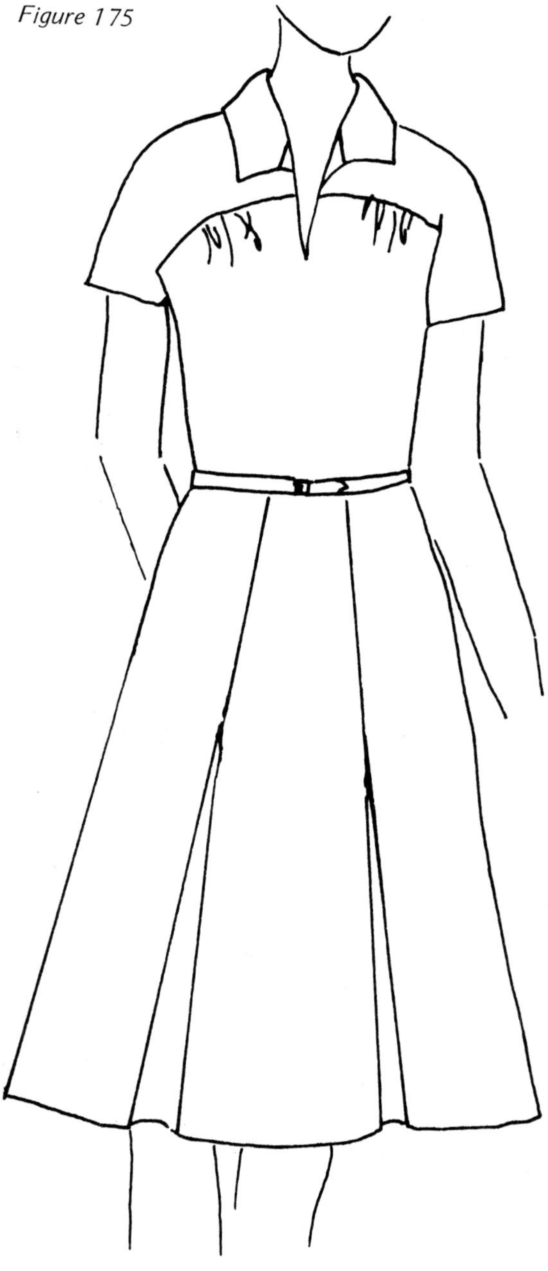

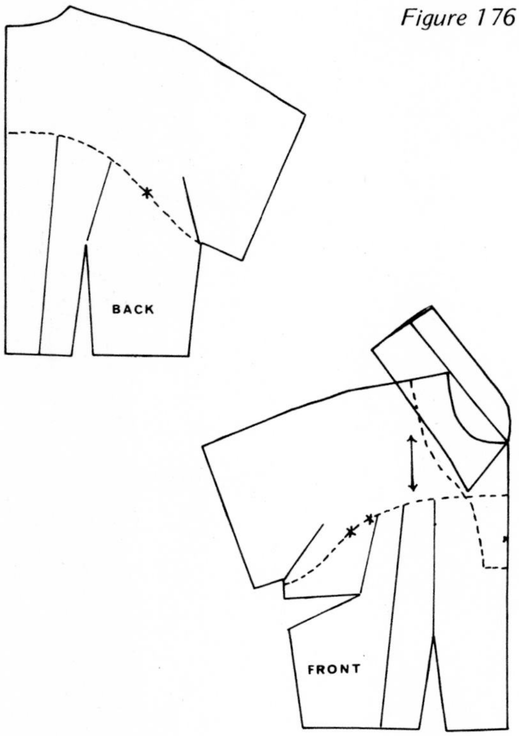

Figure 176

(7) Draw in a broken line to mark the front facing.

(8) Draw a line from the yoke seam to the apex of the underbust and underarm darts on the front block. Draw a line from the yoke seam to the back dart as shown.

(9) Draw in an additional line from the yoke seam to the waist seam as shown.

(All these details should be recorded on the block as shown in *figure 176.*)

(10) Trace off the collar, and add seam allowances to complete the pattern piece (*figure 177a*).

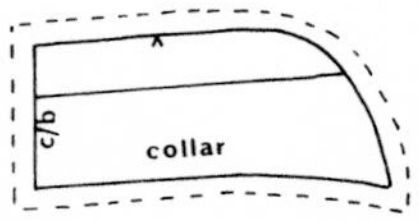

Figure 177a

(11) Trace off the facing, and add seam allowances at the neck and front. Since the centre front bodice will be placed to the fold and since only a part of it will be opened by a slit, the front seam on the facing will taper off as illustrated in *figure 177b.*

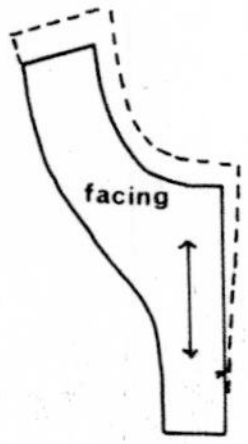

Figure 177b

(12) Cut along the yoke line, separating the shoulder area from the lower bodice.

(13) There is not an underarm gusset in this style; therefore, extra length must be allowed at the underarm position by slashing and spreading the pattern. Follow the procedure described in *figures 136* to *138.*

(14) Add seam allowances to the back and front yoke pattern pieces and record the notches, *figure 177c.*

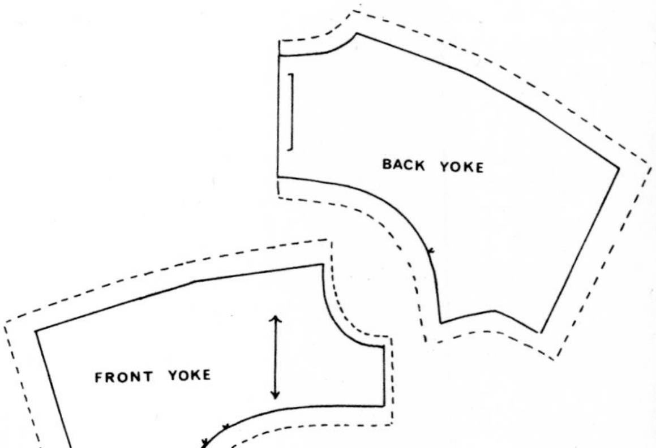

Figure 177c

(15) Turning to the lower bodice back and front pieces, slash each line from the yoke to the apex of the darts. Close out the darts, creating fullness at the yoke seam. To create extra fullness, slash from the yoke to the waist seam, and spread.

(16) Draw around the new outline, record notches, indicate the gathering line and add seam allowances, *figure 177d*.

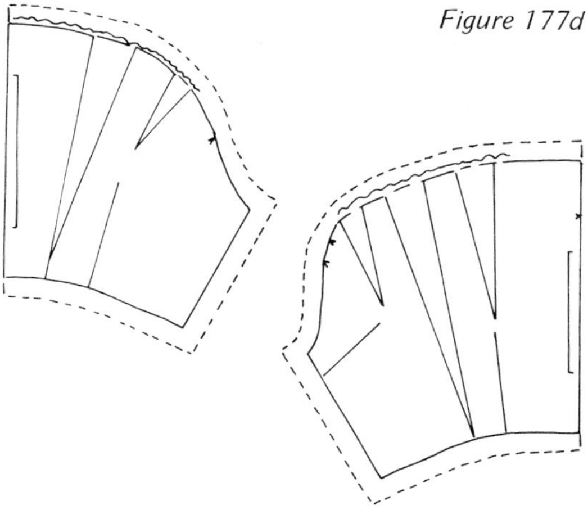

Figure 177d

(17) Outline the skirt blocks, and add a slight amount of fullness at the side seam as in *figure 178*. Mark the waist dart.

(18) Decide upon the position and length of the godet pleat. In *figure 178*, a perpendicular line is dropped from the apex of the dart to mark the centre of the godet. Mark notches on this line.

Figure 178

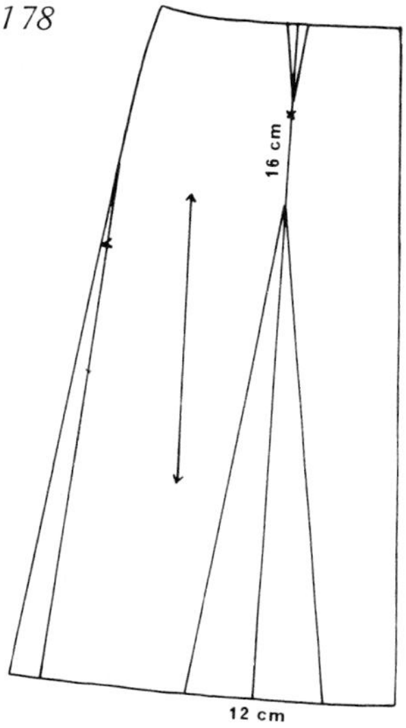

(19) Draw in the godet. This is 12cm wide at the hem, and the apex of this is approximately 16cm from the waist line.

(20) Mark a grain line on the side section parallel to the centre front.

(21) Trace off the godet pleat, and add seam allowances, *figure 179*.

(22) Trace off the centre front panel and the side front panel, and add seam allowances. Mark the pleats, and record notches and grain line, *figure 179b*.

The back skirt may be cut with godet pleats in the same way as the front, or alternatively it may be left plain with just the extra fullness added to the side seam.

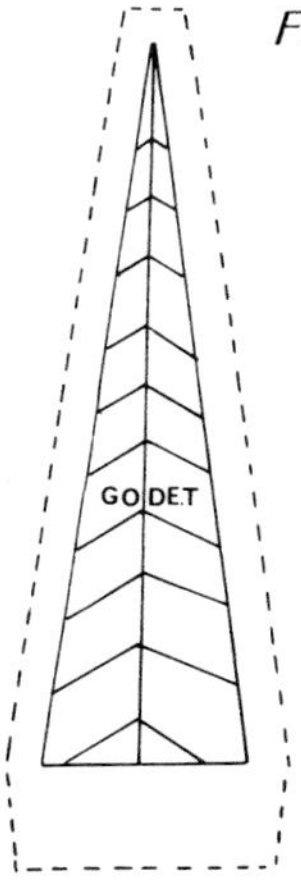

Figure 179a

Figure 179b

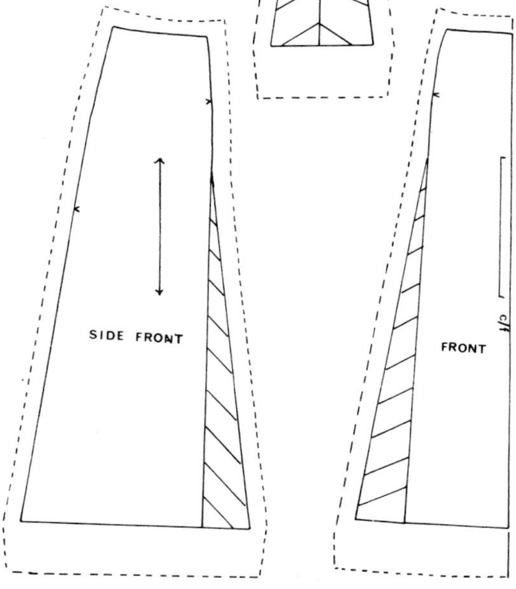

SKIRT AND OVER BLOUSE

The style shown in *figure 180* is a separate skirt and over blouse. The skirt is an eight-panel box-pleated style, and the construction instructions are described in *figures 163* to *166*.

Figure 180

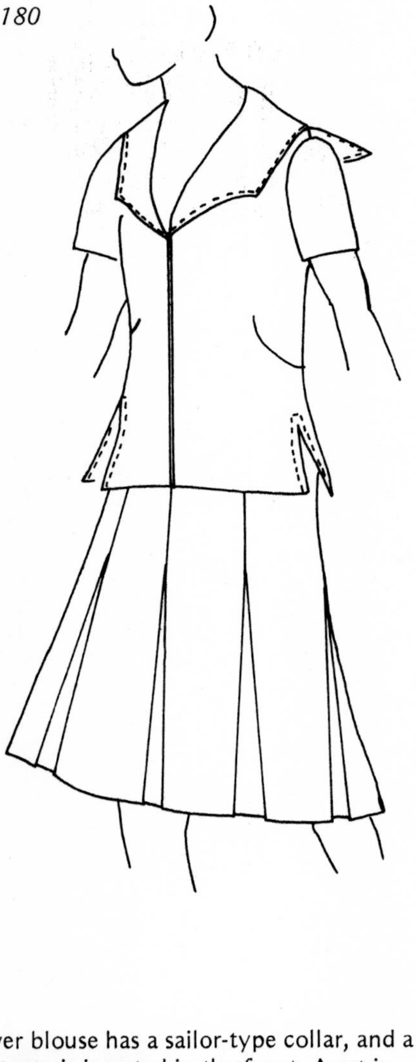

The over blouse has a sailor-type collar, and a zip fastener is inserted in the front. A set-in short sleeve is used. A curved dart is featured, and the side seam has a vent over the hip which is top stitched to match the collar.

In this case, the procedure is as follows.

(1) Transfer the shoulder dart on the front block to a new position at the side seam. The underbust dart may also be reduced slightly, transferring some of the shaping to the side, allowing a closer fit below the bust. Instructions for the dart movement are described in *figures 25* to *27*.

(2) Adjust the front neck to a V, and take out a small amount at the neck point. Adjust the back neck accordingly.

Figure 181

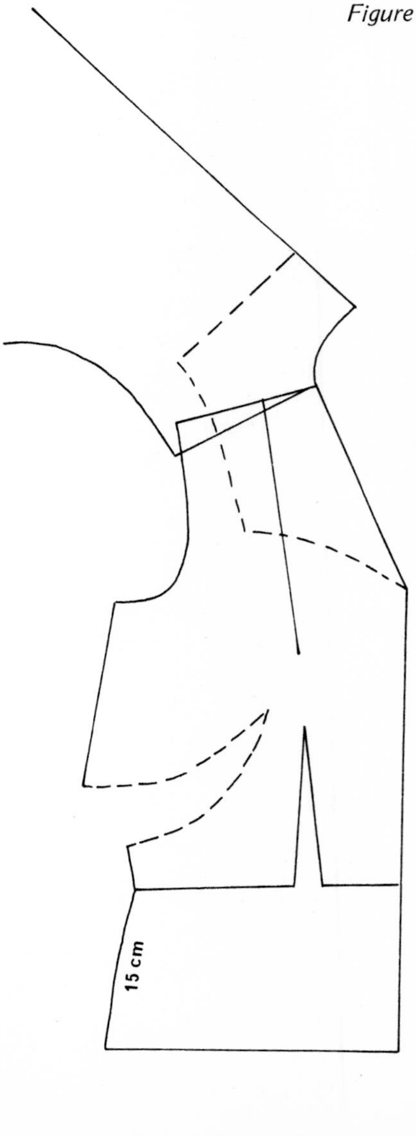

(3) Place the back block against the front, matching the neck points and overlapping the shoulder point. Draw in the collar shape. The sailor collar is cut as a flat collar as described in *figures 72* to *74.*

(4) Lengthen the back and front bodice by approximately 15cm and, using the skirt block as a template, curve the side seam to fit over the hip.

(5) Trace off the collar, and add the seam allowances to complete the pattern piece, *figure 182.*

(6) Add seam allowances to the back and front bodice pieces.

(7) The back dart should be extended by approximately 10cm below the waist as shown in *figure 183a.*

(8) The vent may be faced, or a simpler method would be to add a little extra to the seam allowance to enable this to be neatened and top stitched, see *figure 183a* and *b.*

(9) The sleeve is the shortened version of the straight sleeve, *figure 96.*

Note that the centre back is placed to the fold and that the zip fastener is sewn into the front seam.

Figure 182

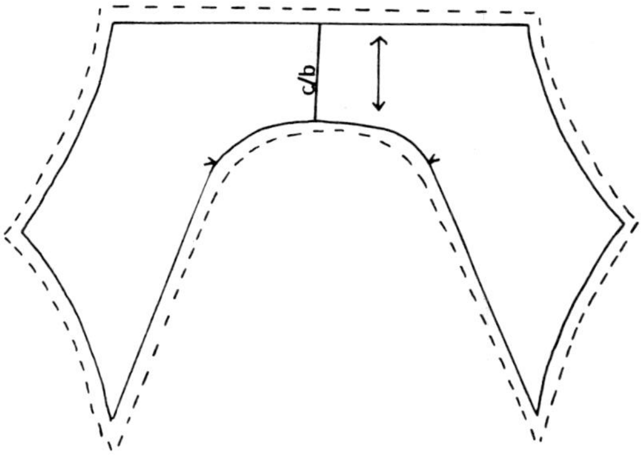

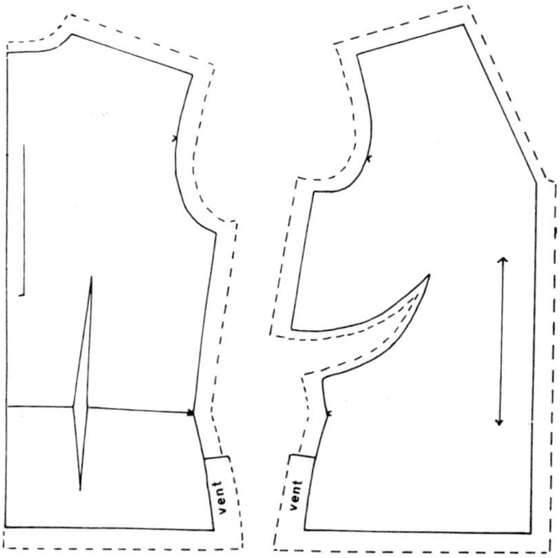

Figure 183a *Figure 183b*

ANKLE-LENGTH DRESS WITH TIERED SKIRT

This ankle-length dress has a tiered skirt. A band fits the waist and is shaped to fit under the bust. The bodice has a V neck and soft gathers under the bust. The short sleeves are flared in keeping with the flared skirt. A zip fastener would be inserted into the centre back seam.

Figure 184

(1) Outline the back and front bodice, using the block with a shoulder dart.

(2) Adjust the neckline to a V shape at the front, and reshape the line at the neck point and back.

(3) Draw in the style seam line (broken line in *figure 185*).

(4) Mark balance notches across these lines, one for the back and two for the front.

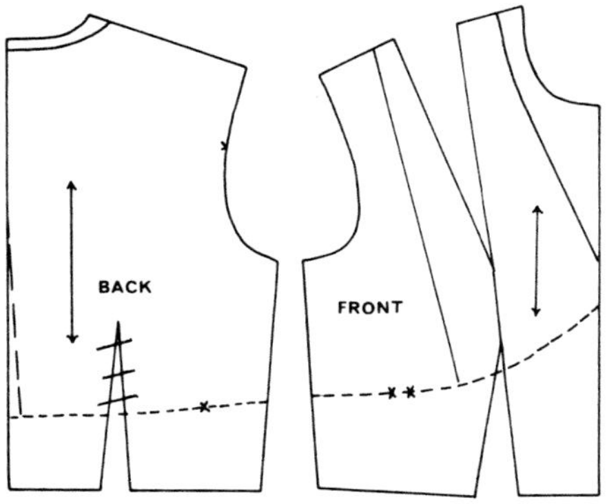

Figure 185

(11) Trace off the front bodice. Cut along the line from the style line to the shoulder and from the underbust dart to the shoulder dart, and spread the pattern to obtain fullness at the underbust position. Redraw this new outline, add seam allowances and record notches and grain line, *figure 186c.*

(12) Cut out the front waist band, and close out the dart. Redraw the new outline, and add seam allowances and notches. Indicate that the centre front is placed to the fold, *figure 186d.*

(5) The lower part of the back dart will be closed out when cutting the waist band. However, an amount must be taken out of the back seam of the bodice to correspond with this. This shaping is shown by a broken line on the centre back. This method of centre back seam shaping rather than the use of a dart gives a better overall appearance.

(6) Connect the apex of the shoulder dart to the apex of the underbust dart with a straight line.

(7) Draw in a line running from the shoulder to the style line.

(8) Draw in grain lines on the bodice pieces, being parallel to the centre front and centre back.

(9) Trace off the bodice piece above the style line, shaping the centre back by tracing the broken line. Record the grain line and notches, and add seam allowances, *figure 186a.*

(10) Cut out the back waist band, and close out the dart. Redraw the new shape, and add seam allowances, notch and grain line, *figure 186b.*

Figure 186a

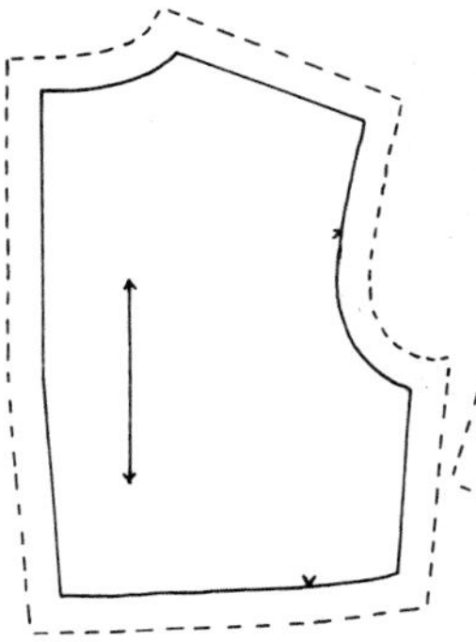

Figure 186c

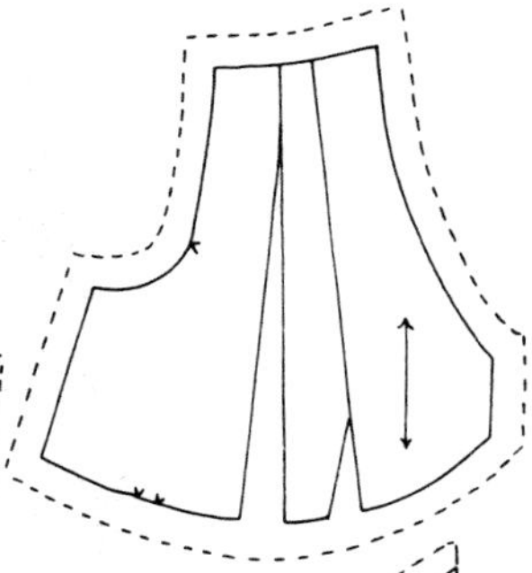

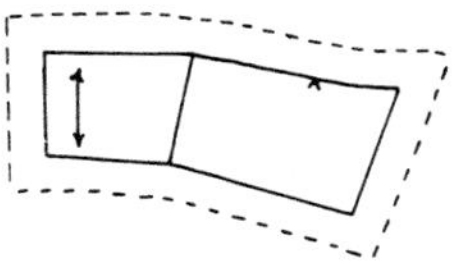

Figure 186b

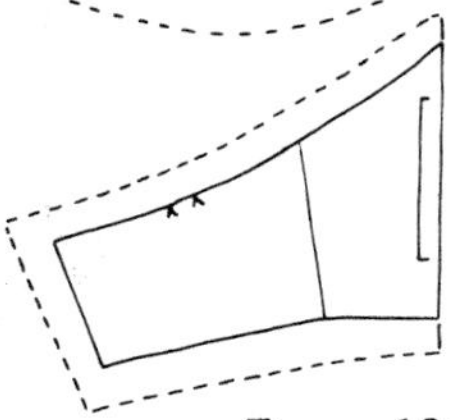

Figure 186d

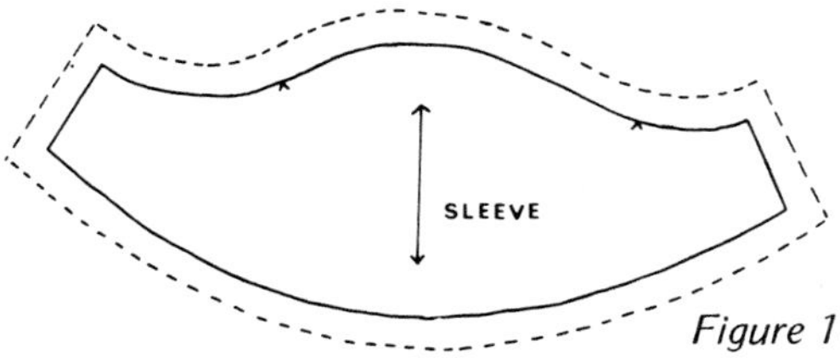

Figure 186e

(13) The sleeve is cut and spread to obtain flare as described in *figures 101* to *103.* Cut facings for the neck line in the usual way.

(14) Close the waist darts, and spread the hem of the skirt to obtain a gentle flare as described in *figures 153* to *155.*

(15) Extend the skirt from knee length to ankle length by adding the appropriate amount to the centre front and side seams, *figure 187.*

(16) Decide upon the depth of the tier seam. The example used in *figure 187* is 36cm from the waist line. Draw in the tier seam as shown with a broken line.

(17) From the tier line draw three equally spaced lines to the ankle line. Mark a balance notch on the tier line.

Figure 187

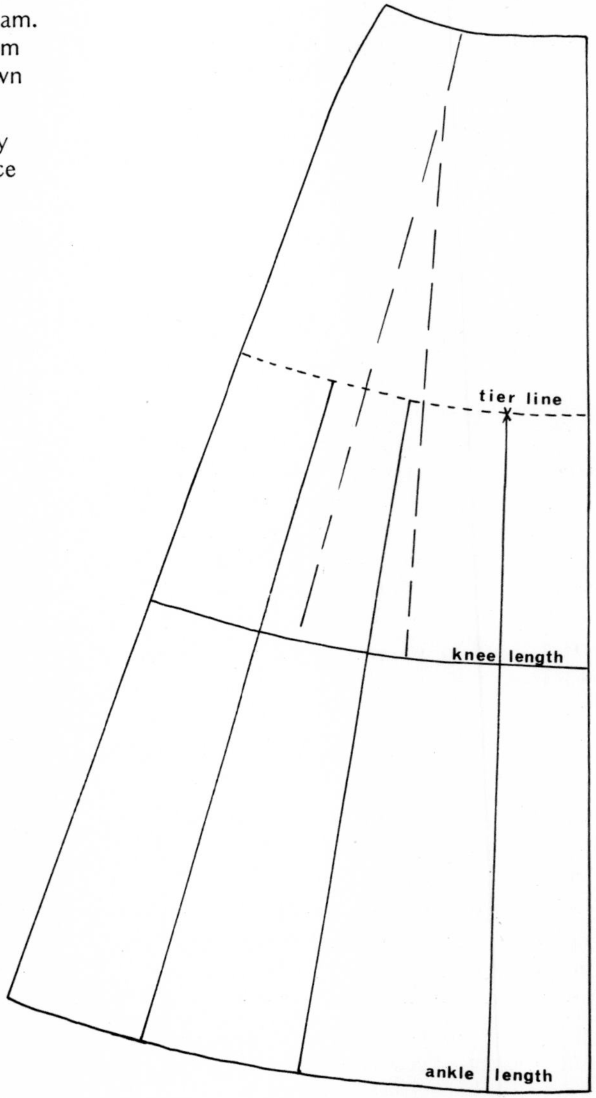

(18) Trace off the skirt above the tier line add seam allowances, *figure 188a.* Record the balance notch.

(19) Cut along the tier line and up each line from the ankle line to the tier line.

(20) Spread this pattern, allowing approximately 12cm flare at each cut. Redraw the new outline, record the notch and add seam allowances, *figure 188b.*

Whether or not the centre front is placed to the fold will be dependent upon the width of fabric to be used. A greater amount of spread will give a fuller flare, and this may be advisable when a soft fabric is to be used. It is also advisable to make an under skirt from the same pattern to obtain the best effect.

Figure 188a

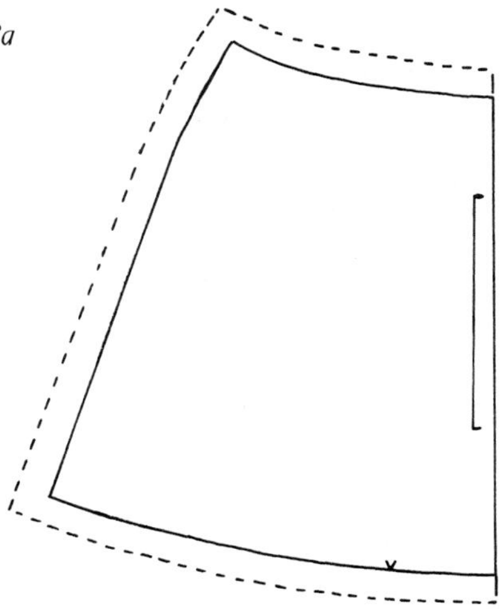

Figure 188b

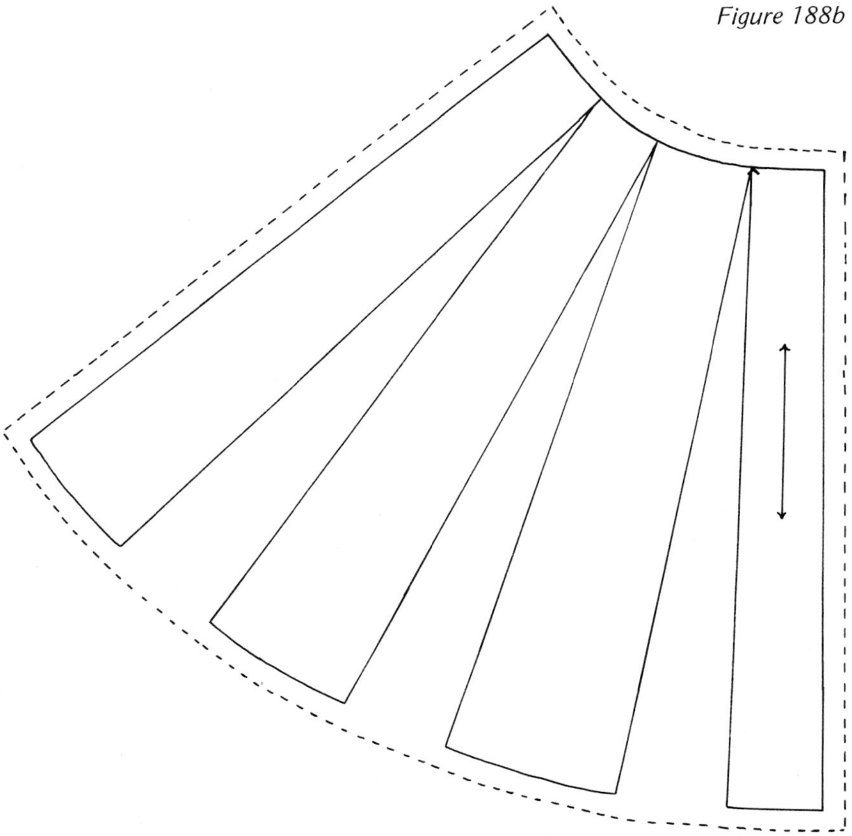

ONE-PIECE OR STRAIGHT-THROUGH DRESS

All the previous styles have had a waist seam, but a one-piece or straight-through dress block may be made by simple adaptation of the bodice and skirt blocks.

To construct this block, draw a horizontal line across a large sheet of paper. Place the back and front blocks onto the paper, with the bust line along the horizontal line. Outline the bodice blocks, and extend the centre front and centre back lines below the waist. Place the centre back and centre front skirt blocks against these extended lines. Note from the illustration, *figure 189,* that the waist lines of the bodice and skirts do not match and that the centre front and centre back gain a little length. The side of the bodice and skirt overlap slightly.

The back skirt is usually wider at the waist than the bodice, and this must be adjusted to correspond to the bodice. Therefore, reshape the side seam of the hip slightly as shown by a broken line. The back dart in the skirt must be repositioned to line up with the bodice dart, and, since the bodice dart is generally less in width than the skirt, this will compensate for the loss on the side seam.

The front bodice block is larger than the skirt at the waist, and this time you must 'give and take' a little, as illustrated by the broken lines. In *figure 189a,* approximately 1cm has been taken from the side bodice, but approximately 1.5cm has been added to the skirt. To compensate for the loss at the side bodice, reduce the width of the underbust dart by 1cm. Adjust the skirt dart to line up with the bodice dart.

Trace off the new outline, and add seam allowances. It is advisable to make this pattern up in test cloth for a fitting. It may be necessary to make adjustments to the darts and side seam shaping. When satisfied with the fit, copy onto card, and keep this with the other blocks.

Figure 189a *Figure 189b*

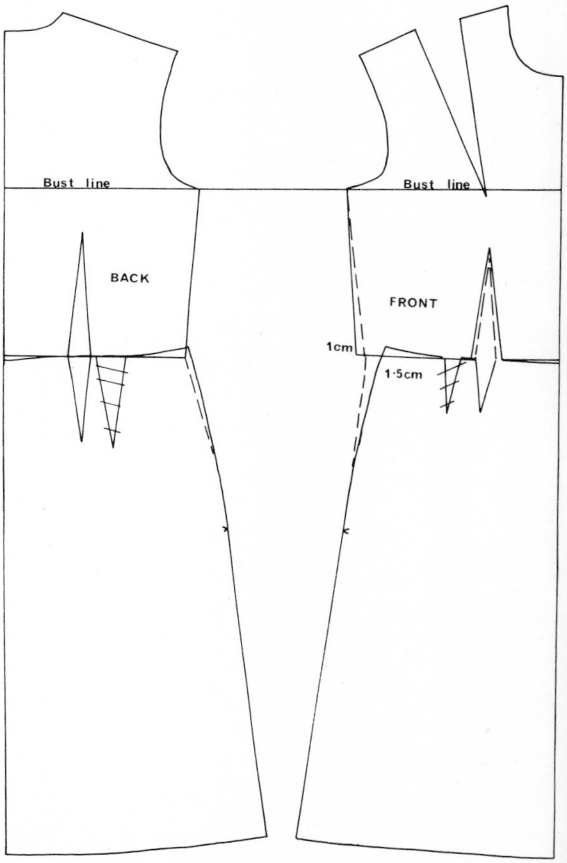

PRINCESS-STYLE DRESS

It is desirable to use your straight-through dress block for this princess-style dress. This style is ever popular and suits so many figure types. A good fit can usually be achieved because of the vertical seams running through the waist area.

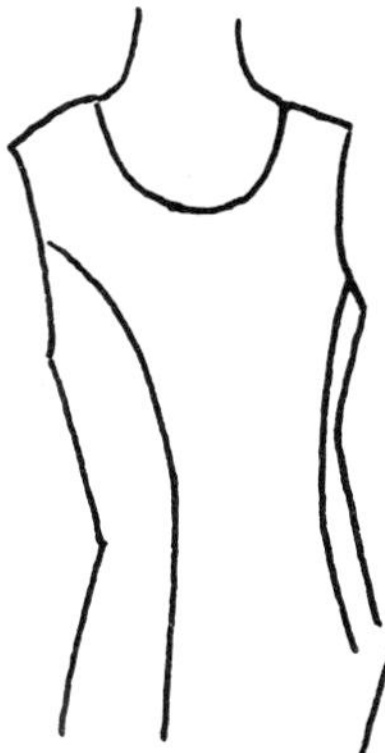

Figure 190a

Figure 190b

(1) Draw around the back and front straight-through dress blocks. The front block must initially have the dart transferred from the shoulder to the mid scye position as described in *figures 19* to *21*. This new dart should be slightly curved.

(2) Draw a curved line from the apex of the back bodice dart to the mid scye position as shown by the broken line.

(3) The apex of the curved dart on the front block must be joined to the underbust dart with a line.

(4) Drop a perpendicular line from the apex of the back and front skirt darts to the hem line.

(5) Decide upon the amount of flare required, and add this to either side of the perpendicular line at the hem; connect to the dart apex. This procedure is similar to that indicated in *figure 141*.

(6) Draw in the grain lines on the side front and side back panels parallel to the centre front and centre back respectively.

(7) Mark balance notches at the waist and on the curved lines, as shown.

(8) To add extra interest the style shown in *figure 190b* has a yoke, with the suggestion that

Figure 191

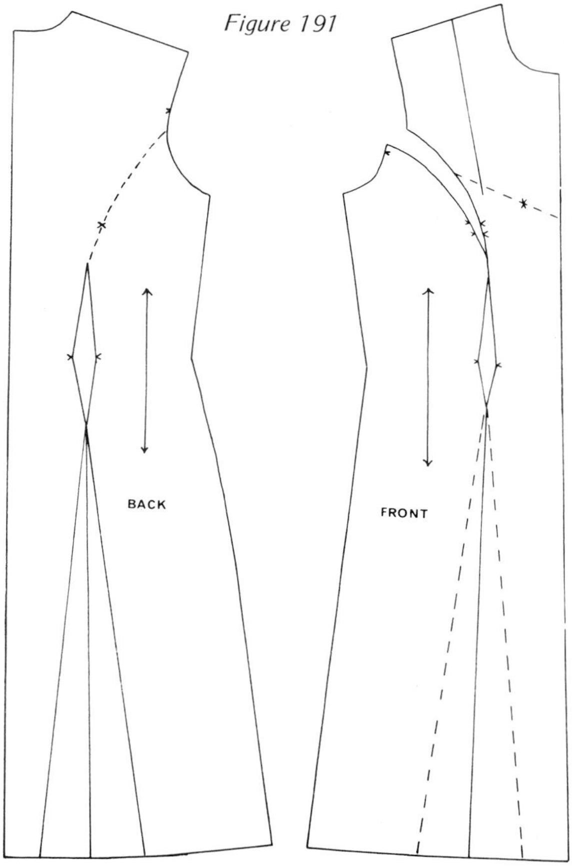

a contrast material may be used for this. In *figure 191,* the broken line from the curved seam to the centre front is this yoke style line.

(9) Each panel may now be traced off, remembering that the flare allowance on the draft overlaps. *Figures 32* and *141* will remind you of the procedure to adopt.

(10) Draw each outline, and add seam allowances to each panel. Record the grain lines and notches. The sleeve pattern is the shortened straight sleeve.

This style is very useful for a pinafore dress as illustrated in *figure 190a.* This of course is cut in the same way, but the centre front panel is cut all in one, omitting the yoke seam. The neck line is cut deeper and facings are cut as described in *figures 55* to *57.*

Figure 192

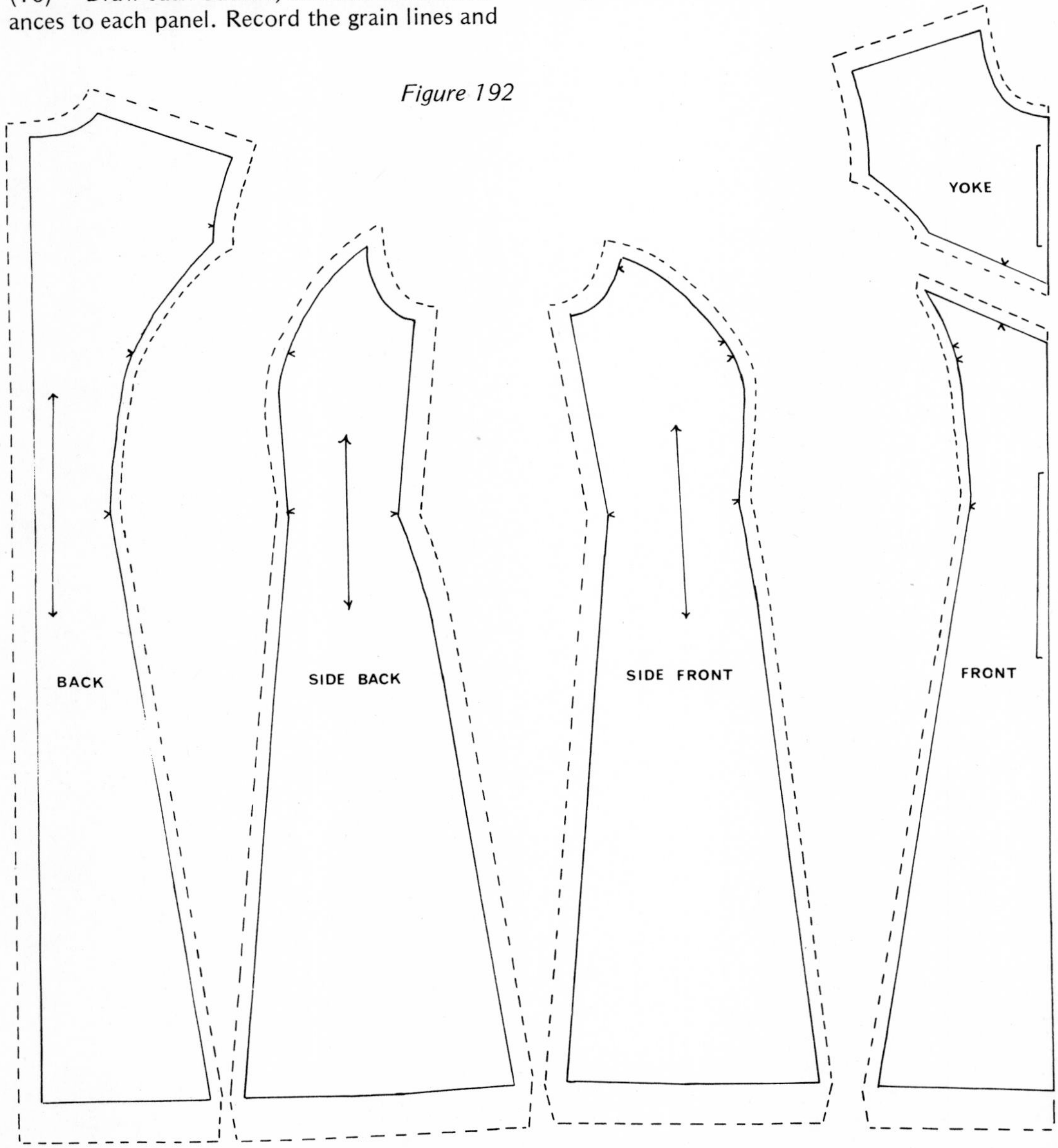

SMOCK DRESS

This simple smock dress is cut from the straight-through block. It has a flat collar with the front yoke opening to enable the dress to pass over the head comfortably. A short straight sleeve is used.

(1) Draw around the front block, and place the back block so that the neck points meet and so that the shoulder points overlap. Draw the collar outline as described in *figures 67* and *68*.

Figure 193

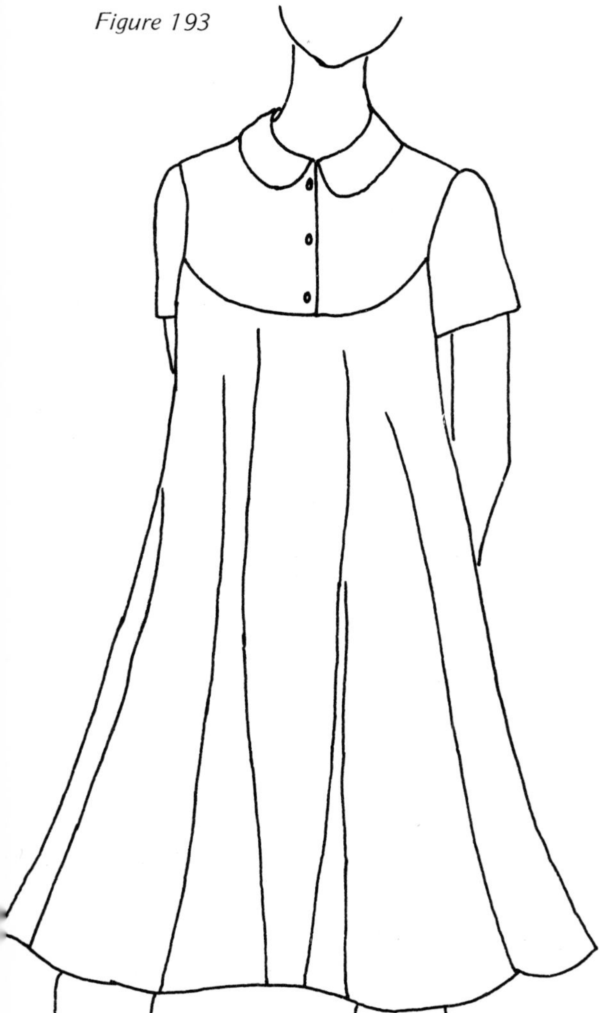

Figure 194

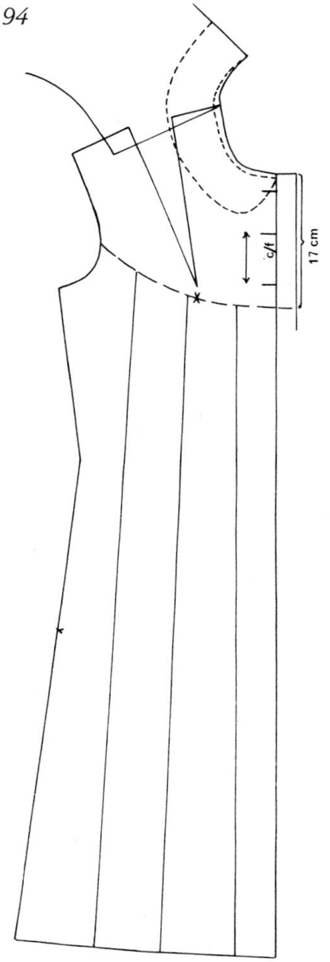

(2) Draw in the yoke seam from the scye to the centre front. This style seam should meet the centre front at a point approximately 17cm from the centre front neck to allow an opening deep enough to pass over the head.

(3) Add the button clearance to the yoke piece, and mark the position of the button holes.

(4) Mark a grain line on the yoke piece.

(5) Mark a balance notch on the yoke seam.

(6) Draw three lines from the yoke seam to the hem, dividing the block into four sections.

(7) Trace off the collar, and add seam allowances. If a roll is required for the collar, follow the instructions described in *figure 69*.

(11) Cut along the yoke seam on the draft, and cut up each of the three lines from the hem to within 0.2cm of the yoke seam.

(12) Spread the pattern to create flare in the usual way. Redraw the new outline and record notches. Add seam allowances to complete the pattern.

It may be necessary to include a centre front seam, but this is entirely dependent upon the width of the fabric to be used.

Figure 195

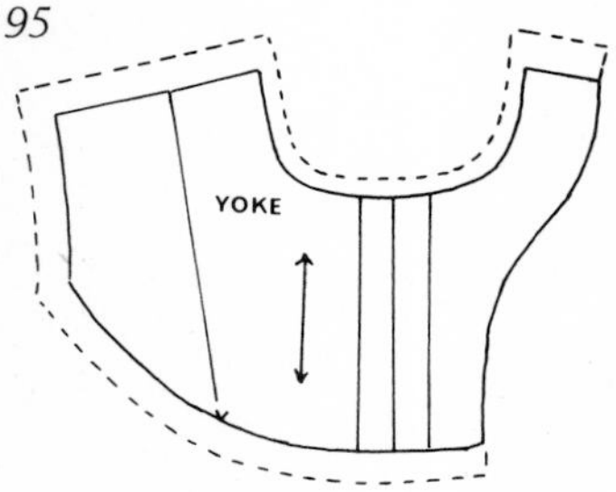

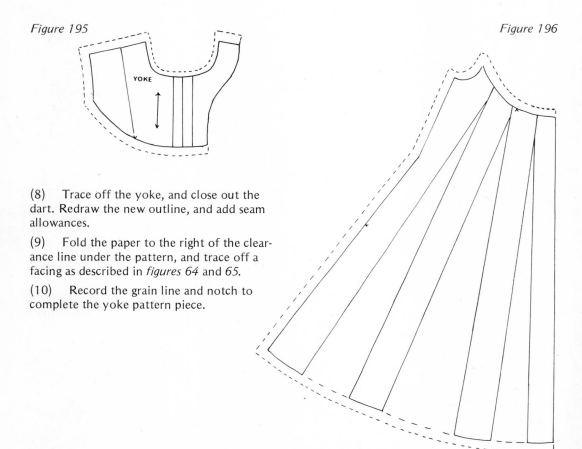

(8) Trace off the yoke, and close out the dart. Redraw the new outline, and add seam allowances.

(9) Fold the paper to the right of the clearance line under the pattern, and trace off a facing as described in *figures 64* and *65*.

(10) Record the grain line and notch to complete the yoke pattern piece.

Figure 196

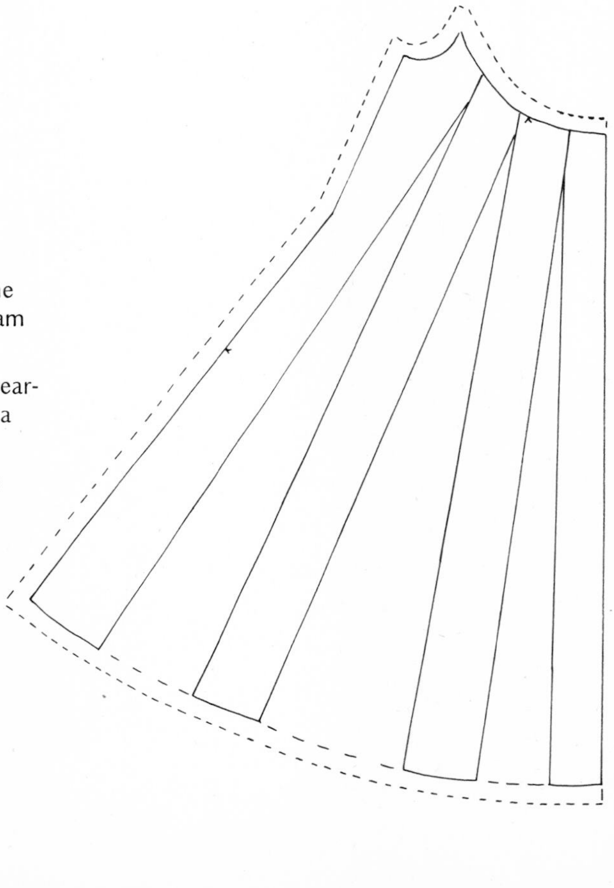

STRAIGHT-THROUGH DRESS WITH REVERS AND FRONT OPENING

The straight-through block is used for this dress. The features to be noted are the revers and the front opening to just below the waist. The side pockets are incorporated in the panel seams. The sleeve is set into the scye without excess fullness, but fullness is gathered into the cuff at the wrist.

Figure 197

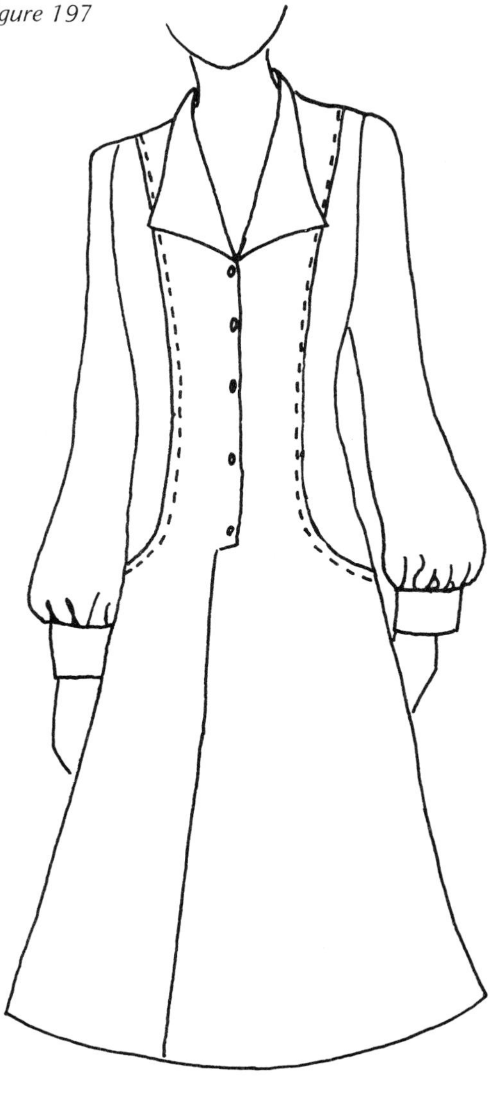

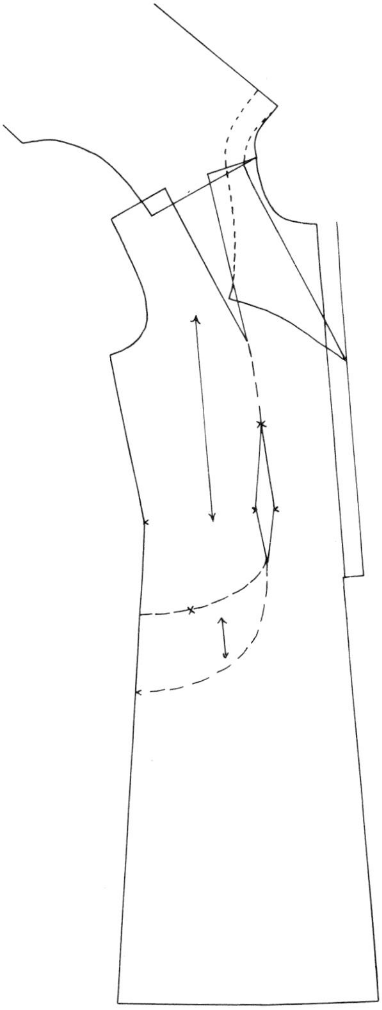

Figure 198

As with all the other examples of style variations the main planning is carried out on a copy of the block.

(1) Outline the front block, and position the back block along the shoulder, matching at the neck point and over lapping at the shoulder point.

(2) Add button clearance to the centre front bodice, bringing this below the waist, far enough to make dressing and undressing simple. This should be at least 9cm below the waist line.

(3) Draw the rever shape on to the front bodice, and continue the outline through to the centre back as shown by a broken line. (This is only a narrow band designed to form a small stand at the back neck.)

(4) Connect the apex of the shoulder dart to the apex of the underbust dart as shown by a broken line.

(5) Mark balance notches at the waist and apex of the underbust dart.

(6) Mark a grain line on the side panel.

(7) Draw in the style line and pocket from the apex of the skirt dart as shown by a broken line.

(8) Mark a balance notch on the pocket style line and at the hip level. Draw in a grain line.

(9) Trace off the side panel, and slightly reshape the bust area if necessary (refer to *figures 29* and *30* for guidance). Record the grain line, and mark the position for the pocket as shown in *figure 199a.* Add seam allowances.

(10) Trace off the pocket facing, and add seam allowances in a similar way to that described in *figure 151.*

(11) Trace off the centre front panel, marking all the notches.

(12) Trace off the rever and back neck band, and transfer this to the right of the V neck line as described in *figures 84* to *87.*

(13) Draw in the new outline on the front panel, and add seam allowances. Mark a grain line parallel to the centre front, *figure 199c.*

(14) Cut a facing for the rever and front opening as described in *figures 86* and *87.*

The straight-through back block may be used for this dress, without a centre back seam, since the dress has a front opening.

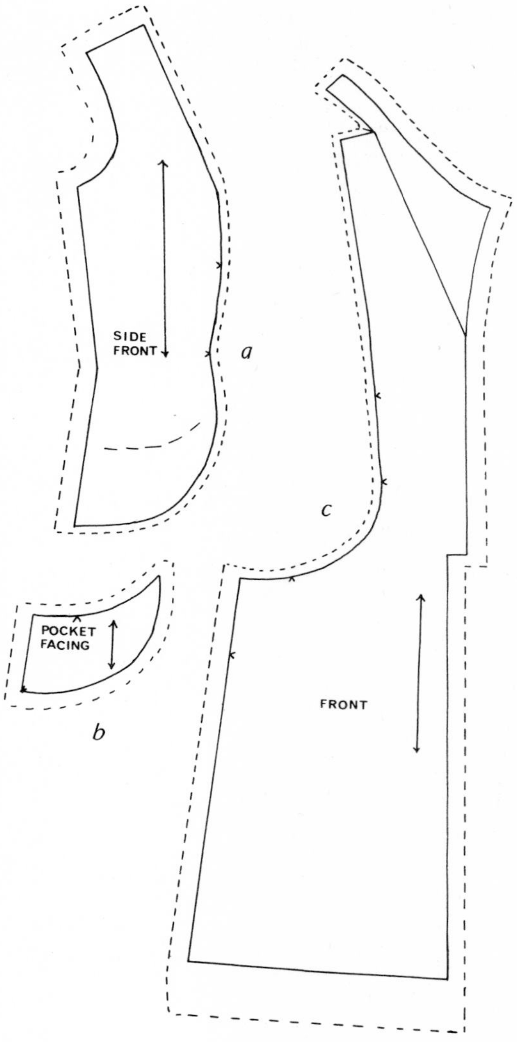

Figure 199

(15) Take a copy of the straight sleeve with the dart transferred to the wrist position, and shorten this by approximately 8cm (cuff line).

(16) Divide the sleeve into four sections as shown in *figure 200.*

Figure 200

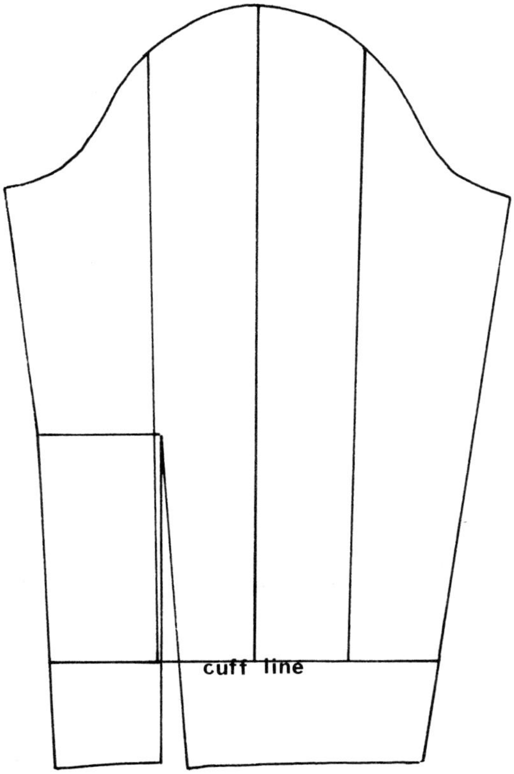

(17) Cut out the sleeve, and cut from the cuff line to the sleevehead, spreading in the usual way to achieve the desired amount of fullness, *figure 201a.*

(18) Reshape the cuff line, and mark the position of the slit as described in *figure 115.*

(19) To make the pattern for the cuff, draw a rectangle.

This should measure twice the depth of the cuff, i.e. 16cm by 28cm for the average width for a cuff plus overwrap. Add seam allowances, and mark the fold line as shown in *figure 201b.*

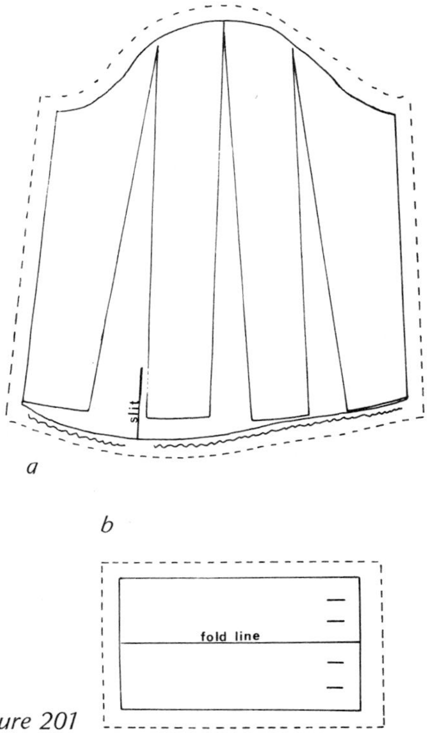

Figure 201

Figure 202

DRESS WITH FLARED OVER SKIRT AND DIPPING HANDKERCHIEF POINTS

This dress has a flared over skirt with dipping handkerchief points. The bodice is bloused slightly with a flared collar forming a short cap sleeve, and a zip fastener is inserted in the centre back seam. To give an enhanced effect, the over skirt and over bodice are made up in a soft flimsy fabric such as chiffon. The neck line is bound with a bias strip of the under skirt facric, and there is a further suggestion of this fabric at the waist where a piping strip may be used. It is advisable to plan and cut the under dress first.

(1) Draw around the bodice blocks and adjust the neck line to the desired shape, *figure 203.* Add seam allowances to the scye, shoulder, side, centre back and waist. Since the neck line is to be bound, a seam allowance is not necessary here. Mark these pattern pieces as being the under bodice.

(2) Using the pattern as a template, cut armhole facings, omitting a shoulder seam as shown in *figure 204.*

(3) Using the skirt block, close out the waist dart, and spread to obtain flare as described in *figure 155.*

(4) Add seam allowances, and mark these as being the under skirts, *figure 205.*

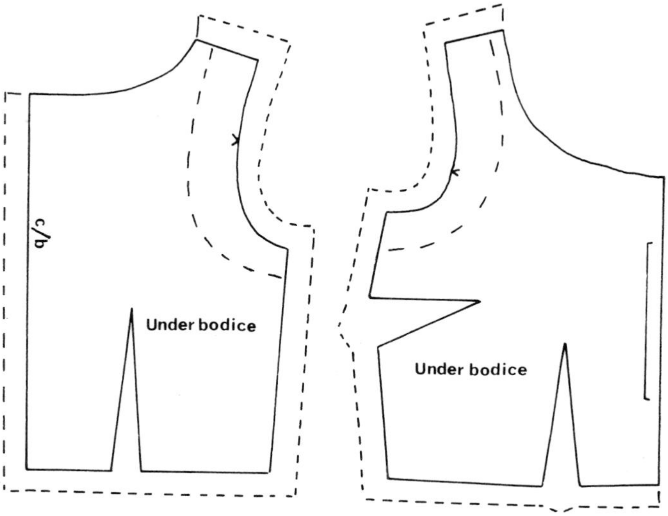

Figure 203

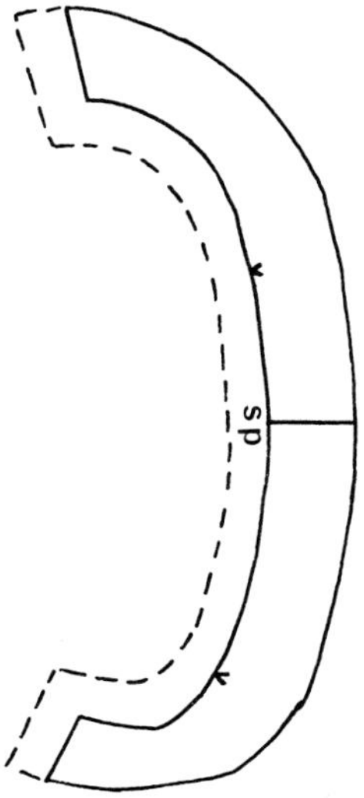

Figure 204

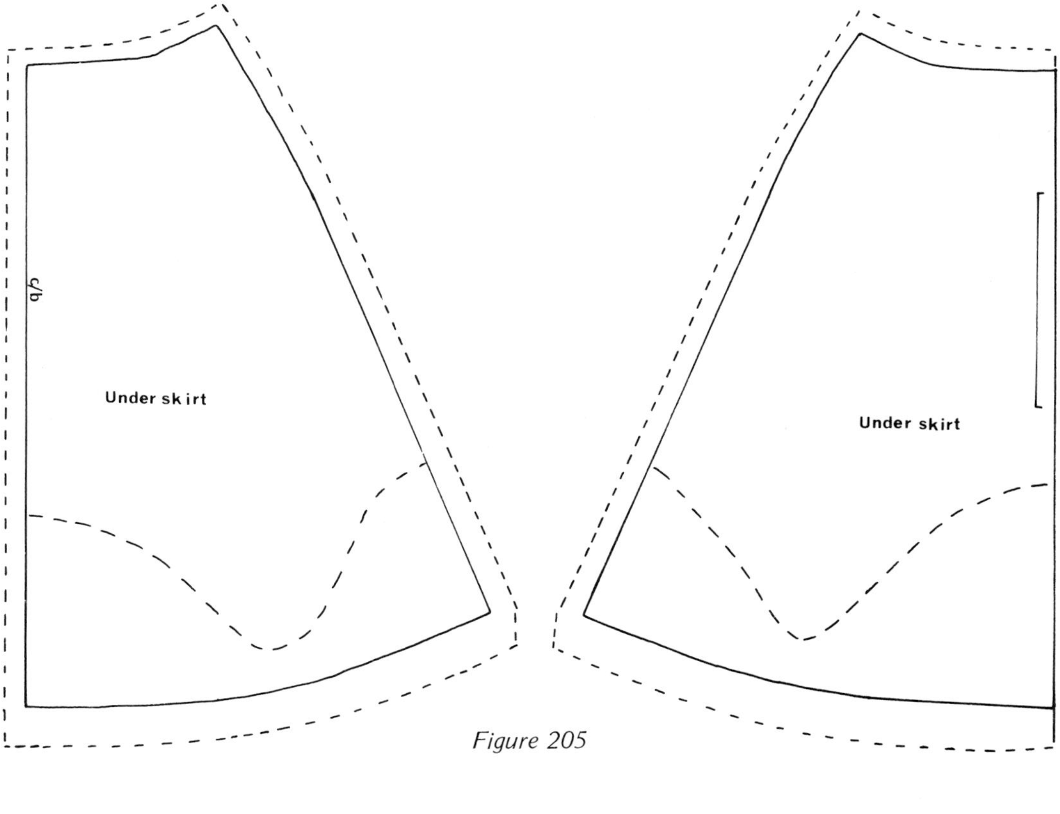

Figure 205

(5) To construct the over bodice, take a copy of the under bodice without seam allowances, and draw two lines from the waist to the neck on the back and one line from the waist to the neck on the front. Draw a further line on the front block from the waist to the apex of the underarm dart.

(6) Cut along these lines from the waist to within 0.2cm of the neck, and dart and spread as illustrated in *figure 206.*

(7) Because this bodice is intended to blouse over the waist slightly, add approximately 4cm to the length of the bodice.

(8) Add seam allowances, and indicate that the waist is to be gathered, *figure 206.*

Figure 206

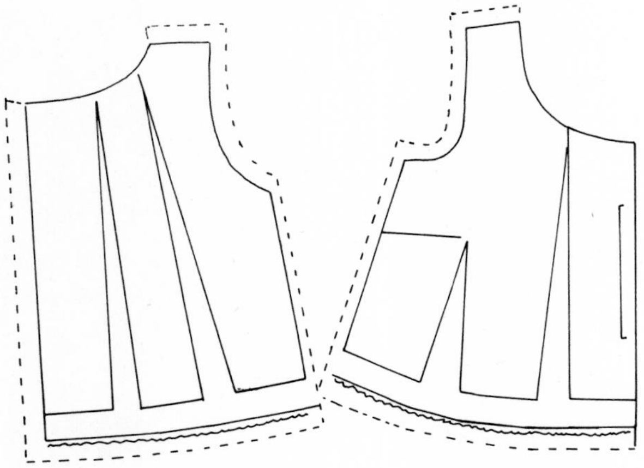

(9) To cut the collar, use the under bodice. Fold away the shoulder seam and arrange the patterns as shown in *figure 207.* Draw in the collar shape (broken line). Note that the collar extends beyond the shoulder point to incorporate the cap sleeve.

Figure 207

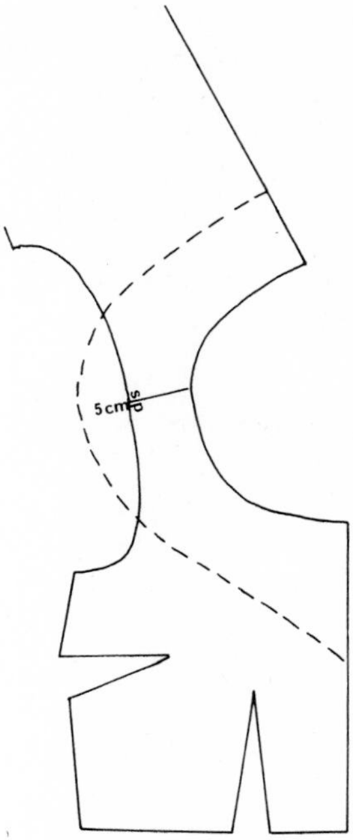

(10) Trace off the collar, and cut from the fall edge to the neck edge at regular intervals.

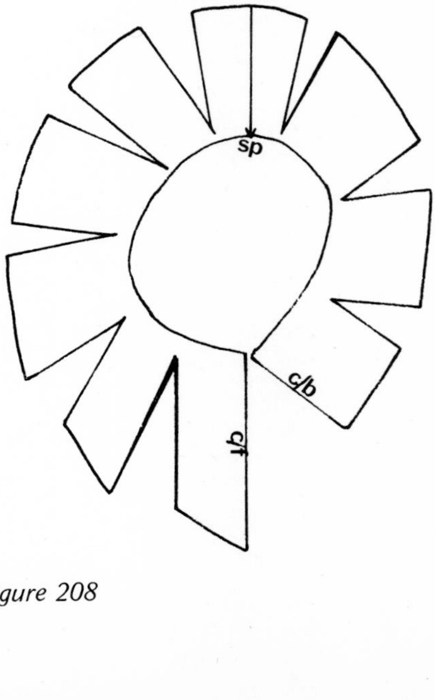

Figure 208

(11) Spread the pattern to achieve a flounced collar and cap sleeve, *figure 208.* If a collar were to be cut from the pattern as in *figure 208,* it would necessitate a centre front seam which would look out of place if cut in a flimsy fabric. It would be better therefore to have a seam in the shoulder position, enabling the centre front to be placed to a fold. This is illustrated in *figure 209*.

Figure 209

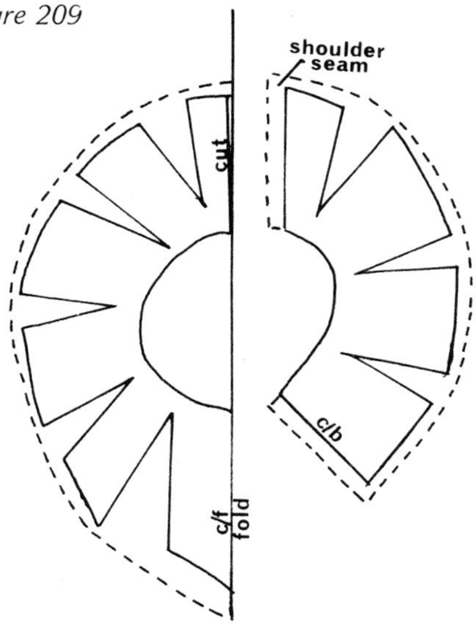

(12) Returning to the skirt, mark the outline of the over skirt on the under skirt pattern as shown by a broken line in *figure 205.* Note that a curved line is used rather than a point. This is to avoid difficulty when hemming.

(13) Trace off the over skirt, and draw four lines from the waist to the hem, *figure 210.*

(14) Cut along these lines from the hem to within 0.2cm of the waist, and spread to obtain the amount of flare required, *figure 211.*

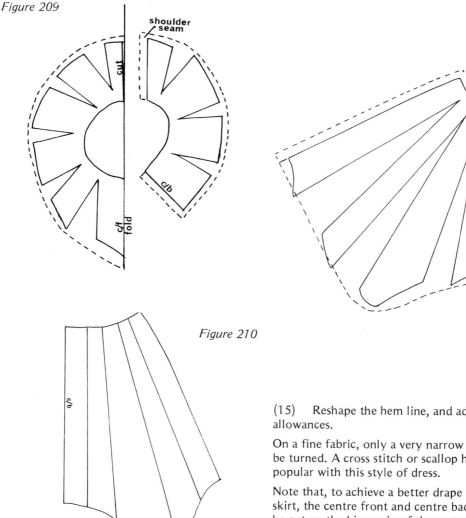

Figure 211

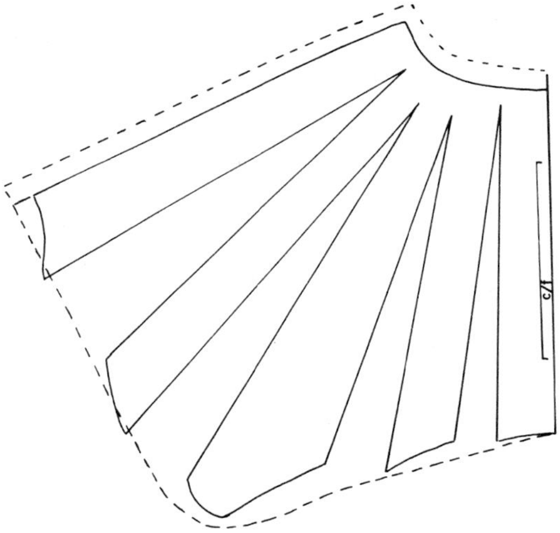

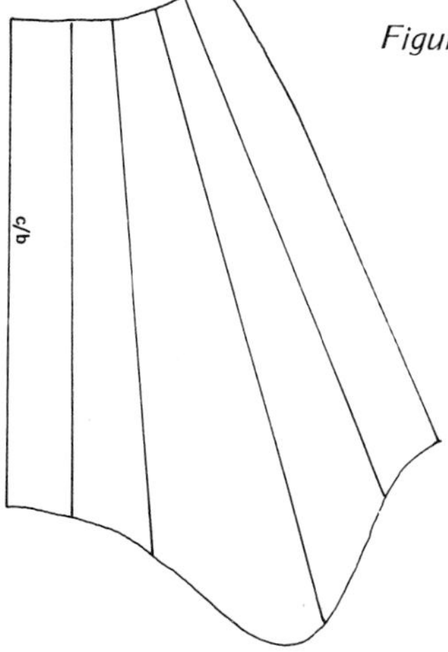

Figure 210

(15) Reshape the hem line, and add seam allowances.

On a fine fabric, only a very narrow hem would be turned. A cross stitch or scallop hem is popular with this style of dress.

Note that, to achieve a better drape of the over skirt, the centre front and centre back should be cut on the bias grain of the material ('on the cross'). Refer to *figure 217* for further cutting details.

NINE

Calculating the fabric requirement

When the complete pattern is cut and when you are sure all details such as grain lines, balance notches and fold placings are recorded, the amount of fabric required may then be calculated. Fabric widths vary—for example, cloths produced on a knitting loom are generally wider than those produced on a weaving loom. Although fabric is now sold in most stores by the metre, the widths are often given as approximations only in metric, i.e. a 36in. fabric will be given as 90cm approximately, a 45in. as 114cm, a 54in. as 138cm and a 60in. as 150cm. It is a good plan to calculate the requirement for several different widths before you go shopping. You should of course have an idea in your own mind of the type of fabric suitable for the design you have created and also an understanding of the properties of that fabric.

The simplest way to calculate your requirement is to use the straight table edge to represent the fold edge of the material, and a metre stick or tape measure to represent the position of the selvedge, or vice versa. The distance between the table edge and the tape should be half the width of the proposed material.

Start by first placing the larger pieces on the table; fit these in as economically as possible, noting which pieces are laid to the fold and which are laid to the selvedge. Then fit in the smaller pattern pieces. Sometimes it is more practical to allow for the fold to be opened in parts (as illustrated with the sleeve in *figure 213* where the material is approximately 90cm wide). Having laid all the pattern pieces on the table, take the overall length measurement. This is the amount of fabric that will be required. It is advisable in most cases to place all the pattern pieces to run the same way as the fabric. This is because, although a pattern repeat may be reversible, an upside-down piece may shine a slightly different shade to the rest of the garment. This is particularly apparent with some knitted fabrics. Of course, there are exceptions to this rule, and, if you are absolutely sure a fabric is exactly the same either way, skirt panels, etc., may be dovetailed.

Many materials have quite distinctive repeat patterns, and this is something that requires extra thought when calculating the cloth requirement. Extra fabric will be needed to match patterned cloth, and therefore it is advisable to buy at least two extra pattern repeats to the cloth length. Depending upon the design of the cloth a pattern repeat may vary considerably, and this is a point to bear in mind when deciding on the original dress design.

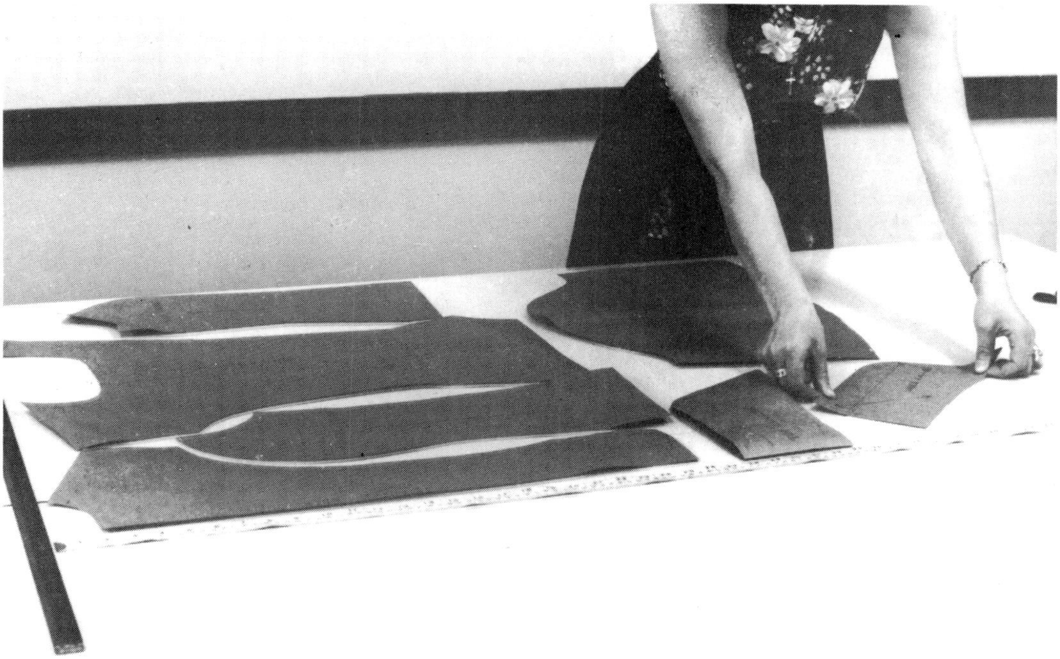

Figure 212 Calculating the fabric requirement

Figure 213

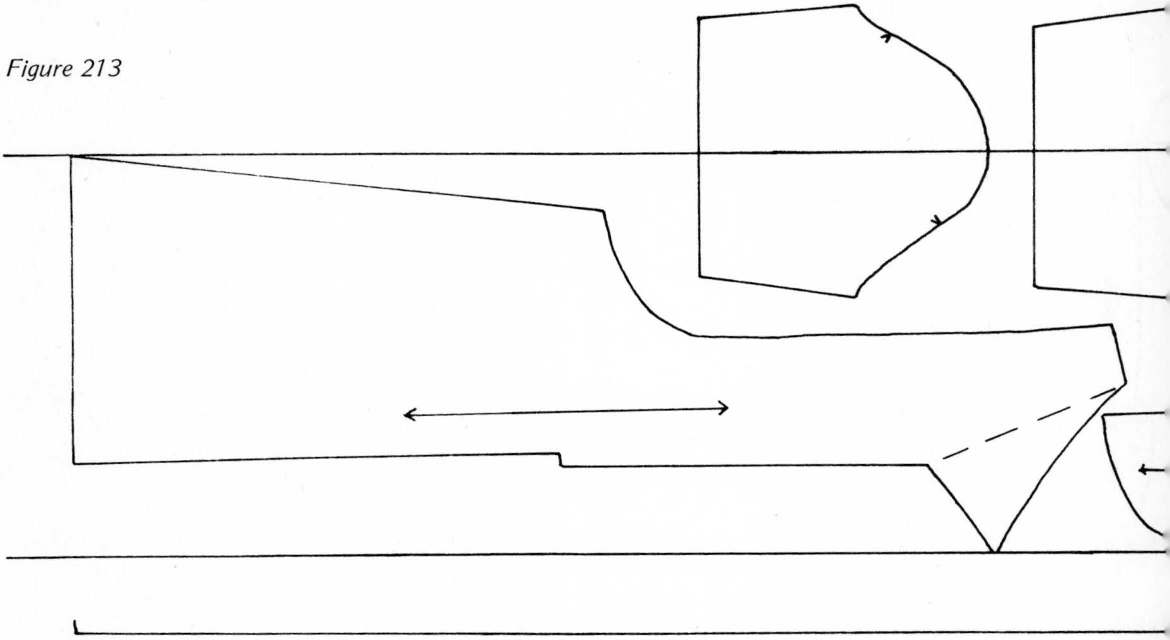

The home dressmaker would usually lay up and cut on double fabric (with a fold), and *figure 213* shows a dress calculated for a 90cm wide fabric. The sleeves are intended to be cut singly, and you will note that these have been turned to make a left and right sleeve. As a general rule gingham, dress linen, brushed rayon, needlecord, etc., are woven on 90cm looms.

Figure 214 shows the same dress calculated for a 150cm wide fabric. Double jersey wool, knitted crimplene and courtelle are usually this width or sometimes wider. Note that the neck facing has been opened out on the double cloth, although only one will be needed. It is of course more economic to place the facing there rather than to increase the overall length by placing it to the fold.

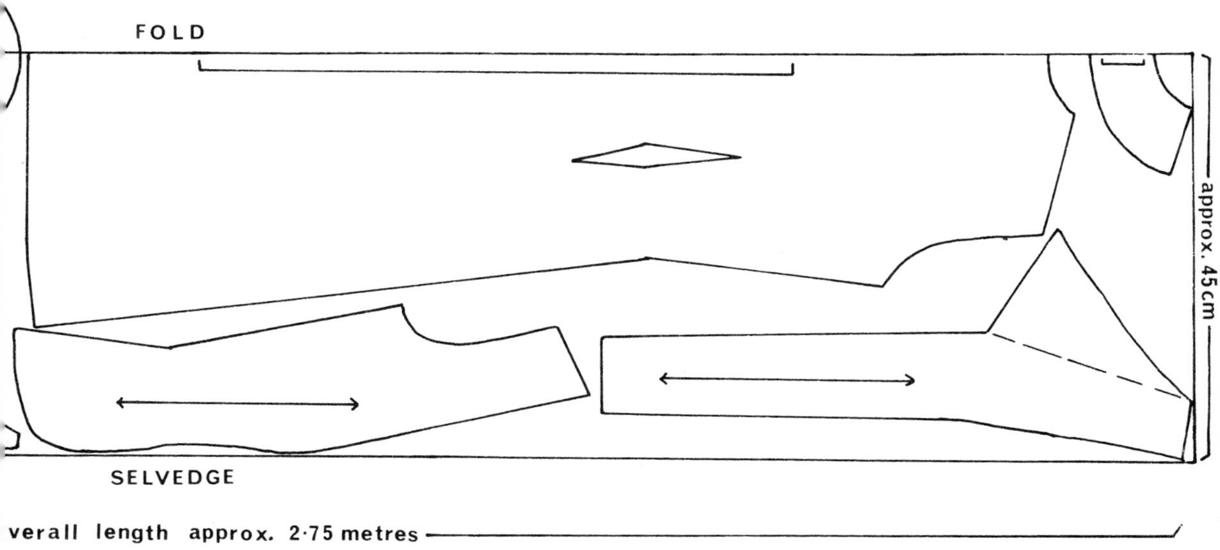
FOLD
SELVEDGE
approx. 45cm
verall length approx. 2·75 metres

Figure 214

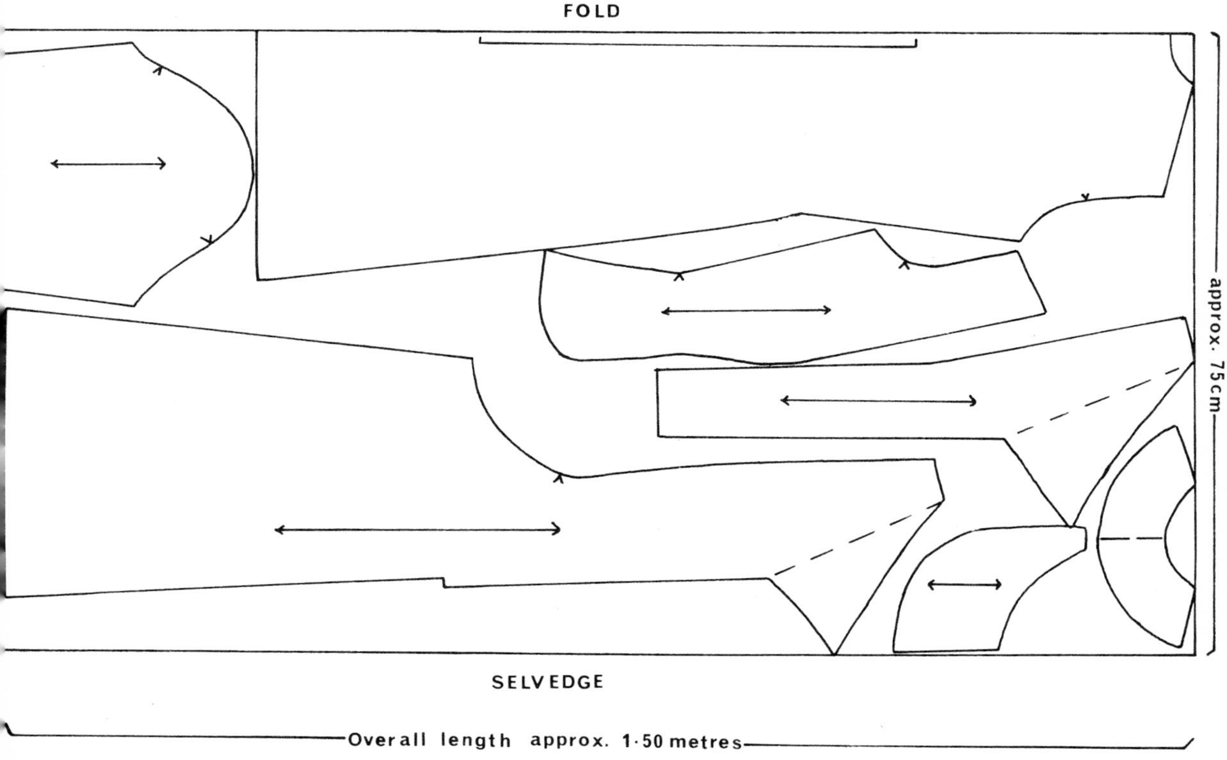
FOLD
SELVEDGE
approx. 75cm
Overall length approx. 1·50 metres

Figure 215 is an example of the dress calculated for 114cm wide fabric. The pattern pieces have been turned and dovetailed here to shorten the overall length. It is most important that this dovetailing should only be considered when there is no doubt that the fabric is exactly the same either way. Light-weight polyester/cottons, chiffon and georgette are often 114cm wide, while heavy woven fabrics like velour, tweeds and tartans are usually 138cm wide.

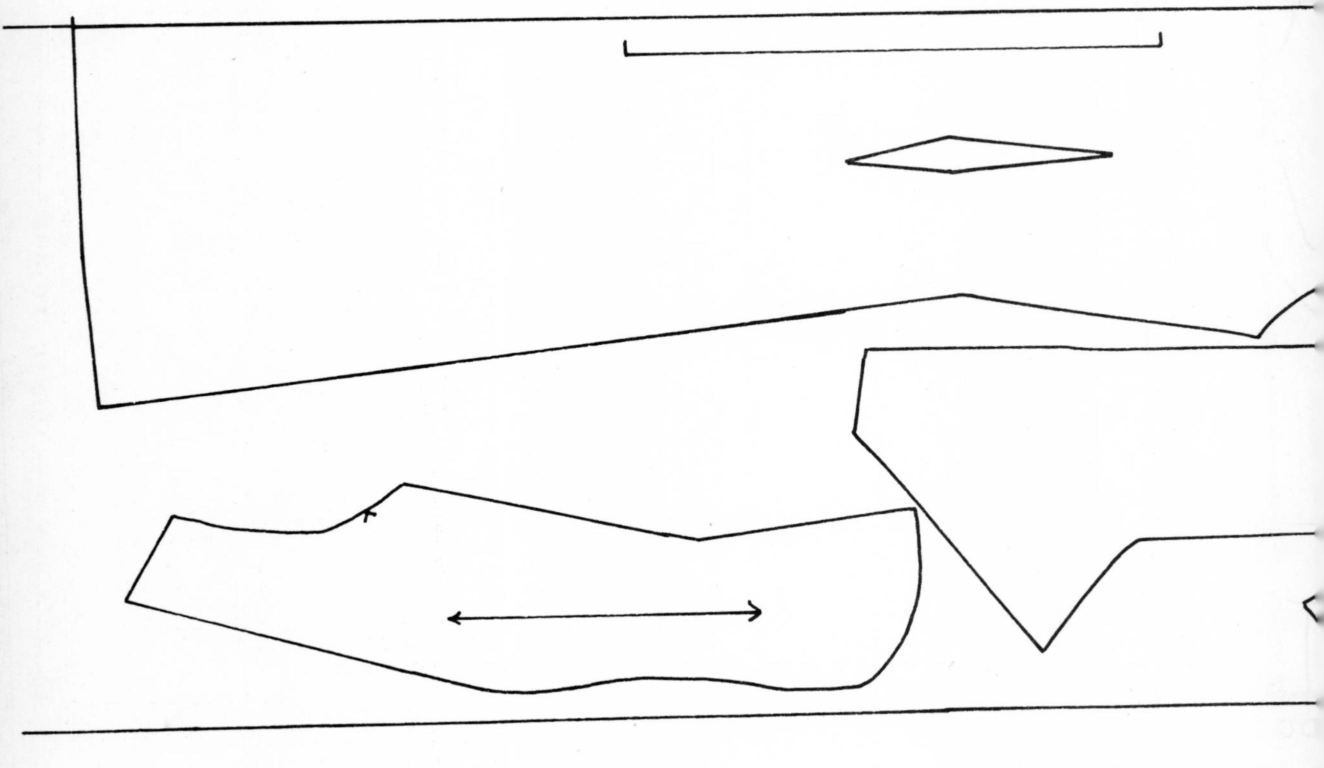

Figure 215

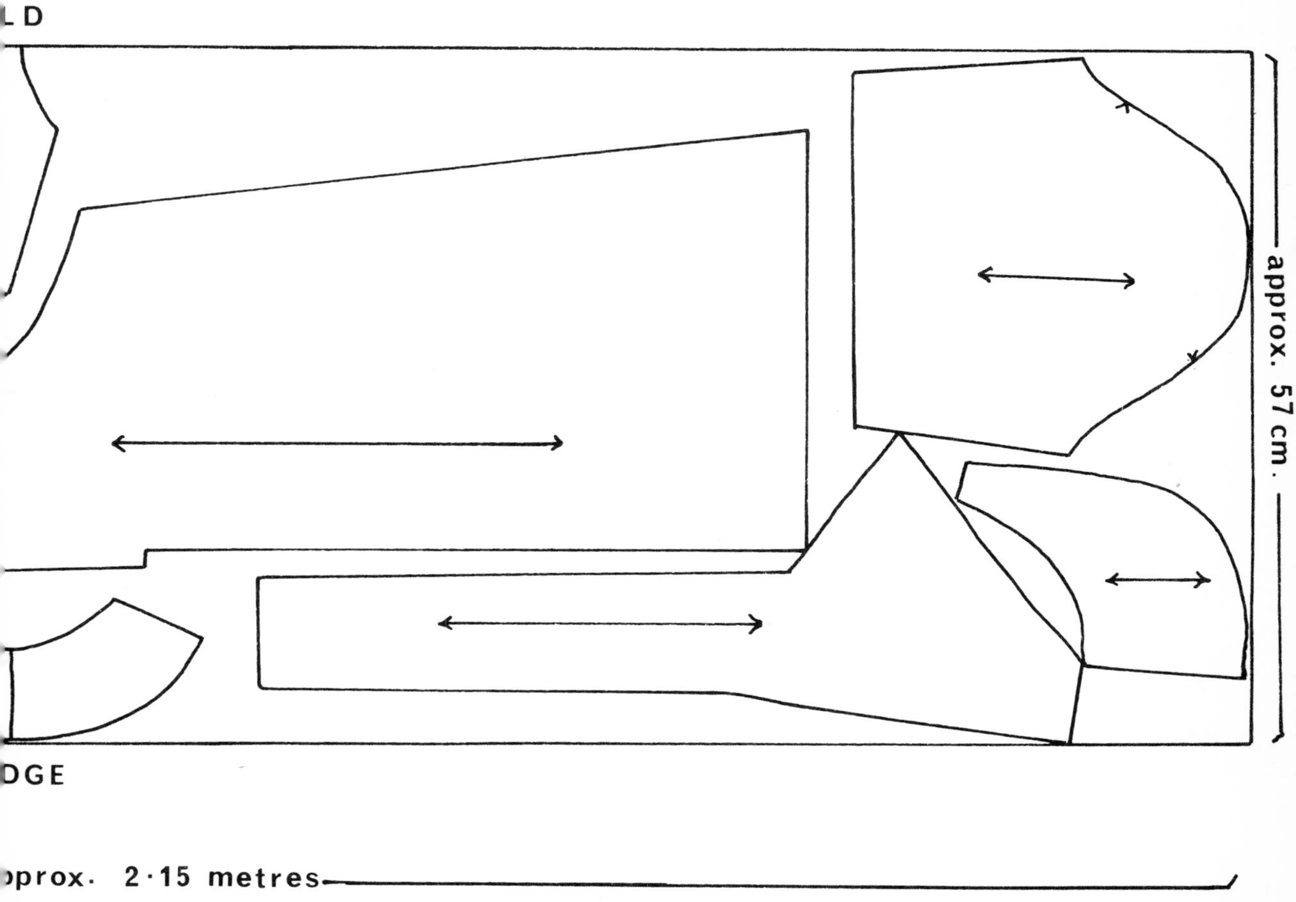

Figure 216

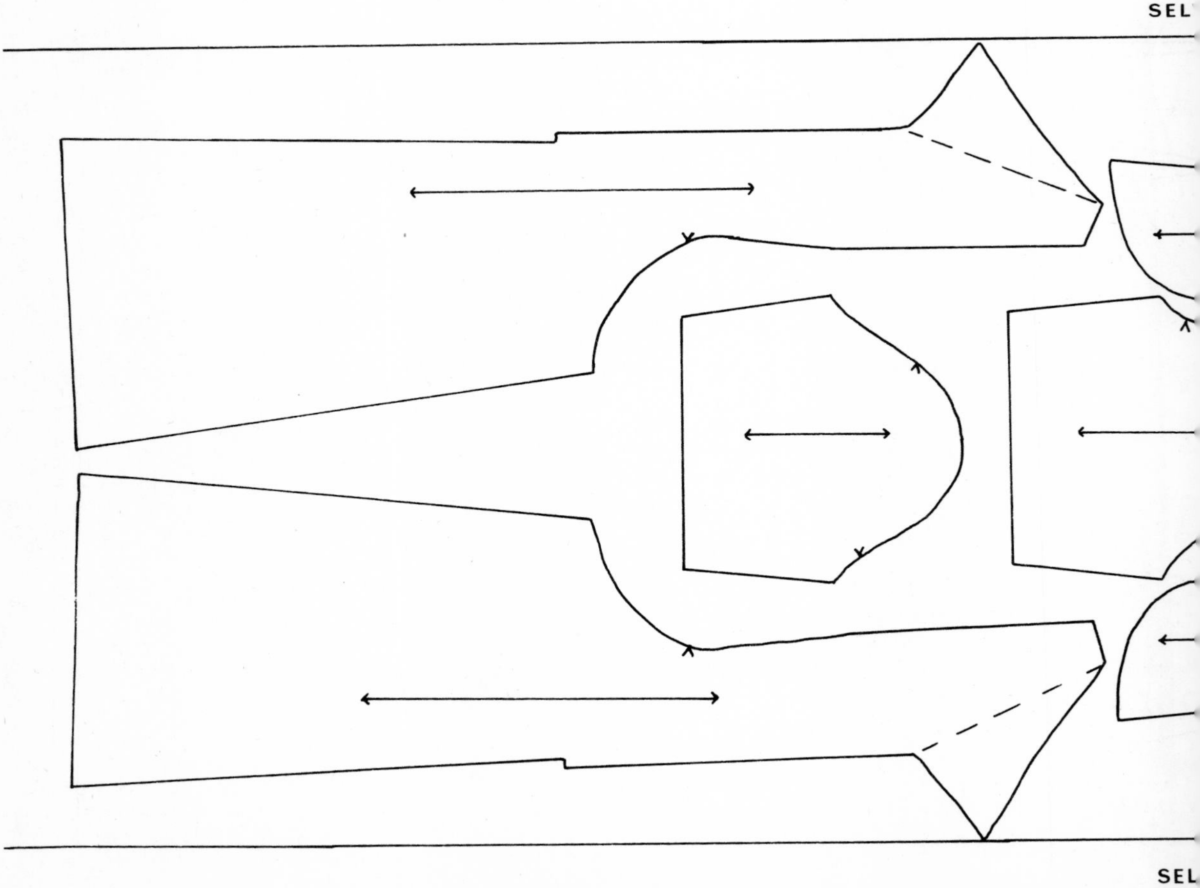

Large floral or figured motifs printed on a fabric should be arranged symmetrically on the garment, and stripes or plaids must match on seams. It is an advantage in this case to plan the lay for calculation on a single fabric, since in this way the complete design can be seen. Each pattern piece must be cut as a single item, remembering that side panels, sleeves, etc., of which two for each garment are required, must have a pattern piece for each side. *Figure 216* illustrates the dress calculated for single 90cm cloth.

It is worthwhile to note that, if you were calculating the amount of fabric required for several copies of a dress, such as would be produced in a factory, then you would usually work out a single lay (e.g. *figure 216*) and you would multiply this by the number of garments required. This is because it is difficult to lay up and cut accurately against a folded edge through several layers of cloth.

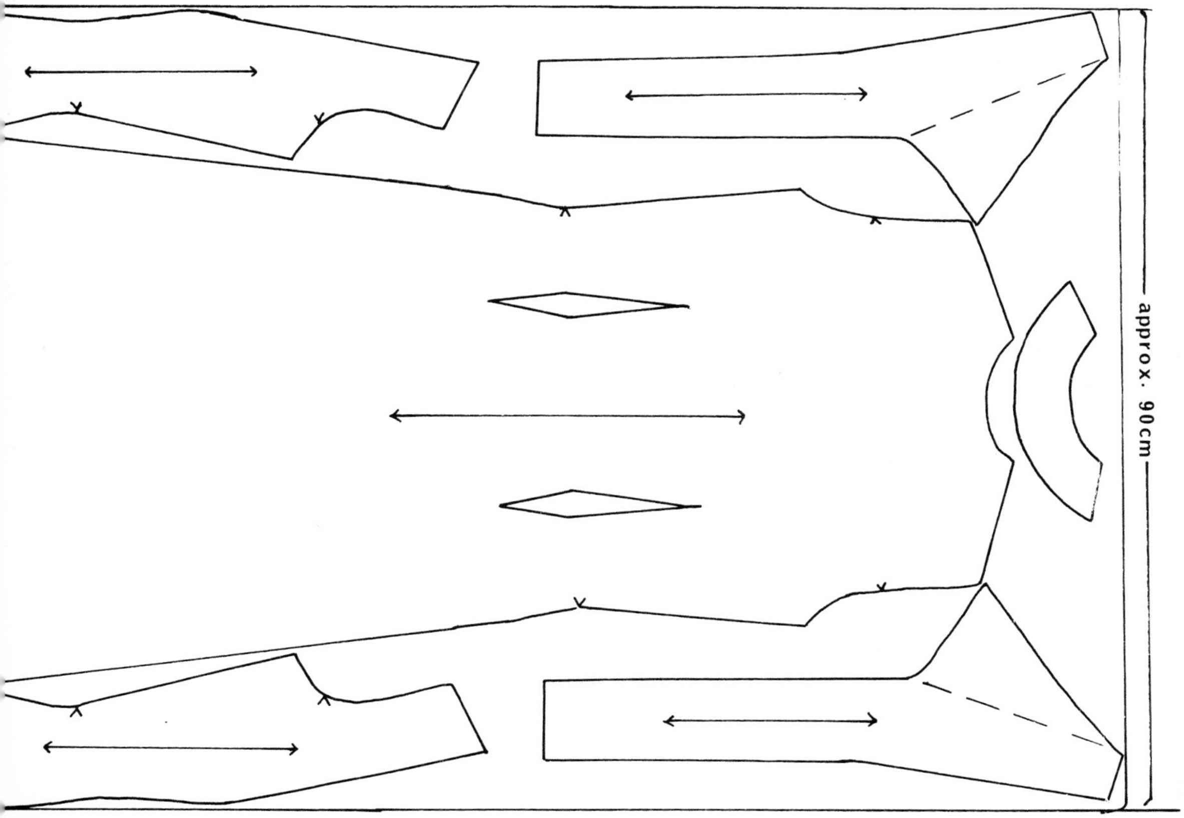

Figure 217

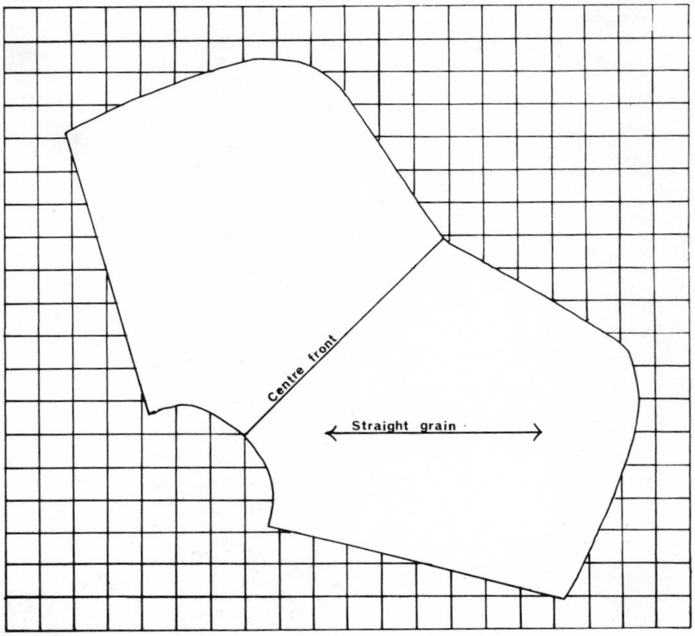

Usually the centre back and centre front of a garment are placed along the straight grain of the fabric, i.e. running parallel to the selvedge. However, to achieve a better drape, say on a flared skirt, it is sometimes better to place the centre back and front on the bias of the cloth. This may be done by including a centre front seam in a skirt as suggested in *figure 155.* If a pattern similar in style to the over skirt in *figure 202* is to be cut, a seam in the centre front would be inappropriate. Therefore, a full front skirt pattern should be made to be laid on single fabric. *Figure 217* illustrates the over skirt pattern piece with the centre front on the bias and with the grain line in the appropriate position. Special attention should be paid to details similar to this when calculating the cloth requirement.

Lastly, make a list of all other haberdashery required to complete the garment, i.e. number and size of buttons, length of zip, interfacing, thread, etc. These are all part of the garment and should be considered in totalling the cost.

Figure 218 *Preparing to cut several copies of a dress (courtesy of* Ladies Pride)

INDEX